PLAYS

PREFACES

&

POSTSCRIPTS

OF

TAWFIQ AL-HAKIM

Volume One

Theater of the Mind

Translated From The Arabic
By
William M. Hutchins

PLAYS

PREFACES
&
POSTSCRIPTS
OF
TAWFIQ AL-HAKIM

Volume One

Theater of the Mind

Translated From The Arabic
By
William M. Hutchins

UNESCO Collection of Representative Works

This volume has been accepted in the Contemporary Arab Authors Series of the UNESCO Collection of Representative Works.

First Edition/Three Continents Press, Inc. Washington, D. C.

Plays, Prefaces & Postscripts of Tawfiq al-Hakim, in two volumes
Volume One: *Theater of the Mind*
ISBN: 0-89410-148-X
ISBN: 0-89410-134-X (Paperback)
LC No: 80-80887

For information, inquire of the publisher:

Three Continents Press, Inc.
1346 Connecticut Avenue, N. W., Suite 1131
Washington, D. C. 20036

Cover Design by Tom Gladden

The photograph of the earth was supplied by the National Aeronautics and Space Administration from the flight of Apollo 17 [AS17-148-22725(H)].

Photographs of Tawfiq al-Hakim were supplied by the Office of Public Information, UNESCO.

Angel: How beautiful the Earth would be if man here were able to see, to love, to let compassion flow from his soul like the water of this brook.

Angels' Prayer

First Moon Creature: We also gaze at your beautiful planet . . .
Second Creature: There it is: a large sapphire in a handkerchief.
Third Creature: A blue sapphire in the palm of the clouds.
Fourth Creature: It fills us with fear . . . and admiration.

Poet on the Moon

CONTENTS

Volume One

Theater of the Mind

Introduction

A One-Man Egyptian Theater Tradition

Tawfiq al-Hakim's prolific literary career has already lasted more than half a century. Today he is considered the leading dramatist of Egypt and the rest of the Arab world. In his comments about his work he has described himself as an Easterner and therefore a spiritual playwright, a social critic and therefore a reformist playwright, and a pioneer and therefore a diverse playwright. This introduction attempts to test these points with reference to the eleven plays selected for presentation here in English translation. It is hoped to identify in this way some of the themes and characteristics which give the plays of Tawfiq al-Hakim their diverse unity.

Al-Hakim has written in the preface to his play "King Oedipus" that since he is an Easterner he still retains some measure of his religious sense. He has given man's spiritual and material aspects equal attention. He has rejected mere superstition. In short, he is a modern Muslim who is a playwright. This fact reveals itself in a number of ways. Some of his plays are of Islamic inspiration. His work "Muhammad" (1936) is a documentary pageant recounting the Prophet's life. It is almost a Muslim passion play. *Ahl al-Kahf*[1] ("The Sleepers of Ephesus," 1933) is based on a Qur'anic sura. The heroes are Christians who awake in a cave after three centuries of miraculous sleep to find themselves transformed into saints. When their attempts to re-establish their emotional ties to the world fail, they return to the cave to die. A central portion of the play is a tragic romance between one of the saints and the look-alike great great grandniece of the saint's long deceased true love. From Qur'anic material al-Hakim has created a love story. Whether consciously or not, he has followed Gibbon's suggestion that the legend of the Seven Sleepers "would furnish the pleasing subject of a philosophical romance."[2]

"The Wisdom of Solomon" is also a philosophical love story based on the Qur'an. In the preface he says he used the Qur'an, the Bible and the *Thousand and One Nights* "to create a picture in my mind . . . Nothing more and nothing less." With the exception then of his "Muhammad," he has used Qur'anic stories as a starting point, not an end.

Some of Tawfiq al-Hakim's plays have distinctly Islamic features, cultural or religious. *As-Sultan al-Ha'ir* (1960, "The Sultan's Dilemma," translated by Denys Johnson-Davies)[3] has a medieval Islamic setting. Its plot hinges on the medieval Mamluk system of government by a military slave elite. His "Shahrazad" takes up where the *Thousand and One Nights* left off and examines the prospects for wedded bliss of Shahrazad and King Shahriyar. The play is full of images from the literature of the Islamic mystics: the beloved who represents the Beloved, God; the suppliant lover ignored by the beloved and the destruction caused by the love; the lover as a moth and the beloved a candle; the executioner; the tavern and its patrons and flight from the material body; the mirror of the soul;[4] water which is a colorless clarity but the source of a hundred thousand colors.[5]

When Shahrazad is seen by a pool of water in a marble basin, the young vizier asks what secrets her eyes, "clear as this water" conceal. Shahriyar also exclaims, "How much this clear water frightens me! Woe to anyone who plunges into clear water . . . " Shahriyar compares Shahrazad to Nature and complains that both are veiled by clarity. It is reported that Muhammad said that everything or that all creation is made from water.[6] If water is the substance of everything and Shahrazad is like water, she is identifiable with Nature. She compares herself at times to a mirror in which others see themselves. In this respect she is a perfect mystic saint and so in turn a reflection or manifestation of God.[7]

It is arguable that "Shahrazad" is more an outgrowth of these Islamic mystic images than of the *Thousand and One Nights*. The latter work may have a mystical character, of course. In either case, al-Hakim begins his own explanation of the play with a quotation not from a Muslim mystic but from the Belgian author Maurice Maeterlinck (1862-1949). [8]

Among other parallels in al-Hakim's play with the literature and tradition of Islamic mysticism is the Queen of Sheba's attempt in the "Wisdom of Solomon" to revive her beloved with her tears like a true Sufi lover. Oedipus weeps tears of blood for his beloved Jocasta. In "Princess Sunshine," the dervish-like Moonlight provides the princess with a short course in Sufi ethics. The play also includes the mystical concept of the perfect man.[9]

Some of Tawfiq al-Hakim's plays are Islamic by omission rather than by inspiration or imagery. He cites the example of the great philosopher al-Farabi who was inspired by the difficulty of Greek philosophy to rethink it and thereby create an Islamic philosophy. Al-Hakim asks why an earlier Arab author did not take "Oedipus" and remove the difficult aspects of Greek mythology and pagan belief to present it either stripped to its naked human element or cloaked with "a diaphanous gown of Islamic belief." In his own adaptation of the play he has, he says, divested "the story of some of the superstitious beliefs that the Arab or Islamic mentality would scorn." The sphinx, for example, has been demoted to a lion made the subject of a fiction by Teiresias. The Greek gods are united in a single supreme being. Oedipus is provided with a character flaw—curiosity—and Teiresias made a villain to keep the play from conflicting with modern Islamic notions of God's justice. The tragedy could not have been caused by divine malice. The formula is that man acts out his free will but does that, unknown to himself, within the framework of the divine will.

Oedipus' doubt of the accuracy of a particular oracle has been changed to a general questioning of divine revelation. The Priest accuses Oedipus of making divine revelation "a subject for scrutiny and exploration." Thus al-Hakim has introduced to the play the perennial Islamic controversy between reason and revelation, between philosophy and theology. In the process he has made Oedipus a philosopher king. Teiresias borrows a question from medieval theology when he asks about God's knowledge of particulars: What did God know and when did he know it? In this way, in a relatively subtle manner, al-Hakim has transformed the Greek play into an Islamic one.

Thornton Wilder wrote of his plays in *The Angel that Troubled the Waters* that almost all of them "are religious, but religious in that dilute fashion that is a believer's concession to a contemporary standard of good manners . . . "[10] This statement seems to capture the sincere yet tasteful religious character of Tawfiq al-Hakim's plays. The whimsically devout tone of al-Hakim's "Angels' Prayer" has much in common with that of Wilder's "Now the Servant's Name was Malchus," in which Jesus commiserates in Heaven with Malchus over the problems of being mentioned in the Bible, or of "Hast Thou considered my Servant Job?" which is a conversation between Satan, Christ and Judas as Christ ascends followed by Judas.

Al-Hakim's religious interests have extended to the Bible. Bible quotations are found in "The Wisdom of Solomon" and "Angels' Prayer." He has gone beyond the Bible, which is within bounds acceptable to Islam, to the Egyptian goddess Isis, who is clearly not one of the approved Muslim sources of divine guidance. If he has written a "Muhammad," he has also written an "Isis" (1955). He referred to the goddess in his novel *'Awdat ar-Ruh* ("Return of the Spirit," 1933)[11] and in "Shahrazad." The heroines of both these works are Isis figures as is Prisca in the "Sleepers of Ephesus."[12]

It is arguable that in "Isis" the ancient legend is used as a vehicle for al-Hakim's ideas about the role of women in society. Osiris too is more a hero-scientist than a god-king. "Return of the Spirit" is a novel that attempts to portray the rebirth of the essential Egyptian personality, and so reference to Isis on its title page is logical. Al-Hakim's Shahrazad resembles Isis more convincingly than the young girl in "Return of the Spirit," and the play centers on Shahriyar's futile quest to learn Shahrazad's true identity. It has been said of Isis that some of her worshippers "were wholly unable to satisfy their minds as to her true identity."[13] In the *Golden Ass* of Apuleius the hero addresses a prayer to the goddess: "I beseech you, by whatever name, in whatever aspect, with whatever ceremonies you deign to be invoked . . . "[14] How relieved Shahriyar would have been had Shahrazad answered him: "I am Nature, the universal Mother, mistress of all the elements, primordial child of time, sovereign of all things spiritual, queen of the dead."[15] What seems an Islamic play then has a strong undertow going another way. Shahriyar, the moth, is consumed not only by his love for the candle-like beloved but by a need to know who she is. This desire to know the ultimate truth was also the undoing of Oedipus.

In short, the spiritual dimension of al-Hakim's plays transcends sectarian divisions. He speaks rather of a religious feeling by which he understands, "man's sense that he is not alone in existence." Man perceives that he has free will but that it is free within the framework of an external, Heavenly will.[16] Man's efforts are a struggle with forces beyond his grasp. For man's power and knowledge there are limits which man must test, even though he knows his efforts will be met by Heaven's mockery. Life then is a kind of prison. Al-Hakim in fact called his autobiography *Sijn al-'Umr* ("The Prison of Life," [17]1964). Shahriyar in "Shahrazad" compares himself to a liquid which even though poured from container to container is always confined. The Treasury Inspector and his aide in "Princess Sunshine" turn themselves in for punishment. They say that their guilt has become a mobile prison for them. In "Voyage to Tomorrow" the convicts are released from a prison of stone only to be launched into the even more confining prison of space. In the "Sleepers of Ephesus" the saints struggle against their fate of being three hundred years too late. In "Fate of a Cockroach" the valiant struggle of an Ubu-Roi style king of the cockroaches to climb out of a slippery bathtub inspires the submissive husband to rebel against the demands of his educated and pushy wife by delaying her bath. He loses. In "King Oedipus," Teiresias has struggled to impose his will on Thebes: to have the people choose their own king on the grounds of service not descent. He acts but finds he has exposed himself to divine mockery. The fisherman in the "Wisdom of Solomon" comments after Solomon's death: "Whenever we go too far in deceiving ourselves about our capacities, Heaven makes us an object of ridicule and mockery." Al-Hakim points out that neither Mishilinia in the "Sleepers of Ephesus" or Shahriyar, Solomon, Oedipus, or Pygmalion submitted to their destiny without a challenge and a struggle. They lose of course, but the struggle must continue. It is a human necessity.[18]

This struggle, "manifest or hidden, between man and the divine forces dominating existence" is the authentic substance of tragedy for al-Hakim. He says that a play which lacks the religious feeling is not a tragedy. Tragedy then is not primarily a question of structure, style, or of psychological effect. Although Corneille and Racine still "had a remnant of the religious feeling," a glowing ember, they were headed away from true tragedy. Tragedy had become a struggle between one will and another or between two emotions.

Al-Hakim goes farther out on the same limb and declares that since "no thinker in the Western world today truly believes in the existence of a god other than himself," no Western poet is able to write a tragedy of lasting worth. As an Easterner, however, Tawfiq al-Hakim has been able to preserve some measure of his "original religious sense." He can, therefore, understand the true essence of tragedy. Al-Hakim must have been prepared for European disagreement. He was upset, however, when one European critic agreed with him too readily, saying that the harsh, blind, inevitable destiny in Sophocles' "Oedipus" is alien to Christianity. The critic thought al-Hakim correct in supposing that a Muslim author would believe in such a destiny and so have a better chance for success with the play than a Christian European.[19] Al-Hakim felt obliged to add a postscript stating Islam's balanced view of free will and predestination.[20]

In al-Hakim's plays the struggle is not necessarily between man and destiny or man and God. The "sublime, unseen forces" are abstractions like "time, reality, space, etc." In the "Sleepers of Ephesus," for example, there is a conflict between man and time. The saints cannot reconcile themselves to the miraculous lapse of three centuries. Al-Hakim points out that there is another conflict in the play too, one between fact and truth. It is a fact that the saint and the princess love each other, but the truth is that he is her great great grandaunt's fiancé. This conflict is their tragedy. Al-Hakim says he chose to adapt "Oedipus" rather than another play by Sophocles, because he saw in it this same conflict between the reality of the love between Oedipus and Jocasta and the truth of their twice knotted relationship. In al-Hakim's "Pygmalion" (1942) when Galatea comes to life she feels she is awakening from a long sleep. She recognizes the fact that Pygmalion is her husband, but he finds he cannot tell her the the truth of his double relationship to her as sculptor and husband, lest he alarm her.

In his "Oedipus" al-Hakim clearly attempted to provide human motivations and natural explanations for events that Sophocles could ascribe to divine will. Teiresias is changed from a spokesman for the god Apollo to a doubter and a plotter. It was his idea that the infant Oedipus should be destroyed. Oedipus denounces Teiresias as the true criminal. Teiresias is thus the villain of the play and the origin of all the fortunes and misfortunes of Oedipus. Oedipus, however, is also at fault. Just as Shahrazad chides Shahriyar for his deceptive love of discovery, Jocasta reproaches Oedipus his pursuit of truth which has shattered their happiness. He has played too freely with the veil of truth. Since al-Hakim has made the Theban predicament a fiction created by Teiresias, Oedipus is said to have left Corinth simply because he learned he was an adopted son. He leaves to cease living what he thinks a falsehood and to learn the truth about his birth. In al-Hakim's modern tragedy "Incrimination," a professor of criminal psychology allows his love of science to drug his conscience while he becomes criminally implicated in an event he is observing for his research. It seems in these several cases that in spite of his wish to distance himself from modern, Western concepts of tragedy al-Hakim has, with the possible exception of his "Shahrazad," not wandered too far.[21]

The spiritual conflict which al-Hakim has most persistently examined in his plays is that between the subjective reality of the heart and the objective truth of the intellect. (The Arabic terms can also be translated the other way round: the truth of the heart opposed to the reality of the intellect.) Oedipus trys to comfort Jocasta by mentioning the reality of their loving hearts. Jocasta replies: "The actuality is as you described it, but the truth, Oedipus . . . What shall we do with the screaming voice of truth?" Solomon's love for the Queen of Sheba and his might and magic are also facts, but the truth is that her heart belongs to another. Even the wisdom of Solomon could find no stratagem to unlock that heart. In "Food for the Millions" Nadia refuses to offer any evidence besides her emotions. Her brother accepts their validity. In La'bat al-Mawt ("Death Game," 1957) an historian dying of exposure to atomic radiation falls in love with a cabaret dancer who performs under the name of his historical heroine Cleopatra. The dancer scolds him for his fear that the fact of his terminal illness makes their true love impossible. "Your mistake," she explains, "is in giving weight to expressions of age and time in questions concerning the heart and love."[22]

The future foreseen in "Voyage to Tomorrow" features a struggle between the ruling party advocating technological advance whatever the emotional price and an opposition party favoring outmoded concepts like holy and romantic love. The doctor who was released from prison to become a spaceman voices his support for love with its flower and its thorn. He is forthwith marched back to prison, by a robot. Al-Hakim's short story, "In the Year One Million" ends with a successful revolt by a religious group against the rule of science which had imposed the power of the intellect and robbed people of the heart. Death then reappears in the world followed by fear but also by love which gives rise to art and poetry.[23]

In this way, the conflict between the fact of the heart and the truth of the intellect has been extended to include conflicts between science and religion and science and art. Al-Hakim has also turned it into a competition between power and wisdom in the "Wisdom of Solomon." The great powers that Solomon possesses are his downfall when the jinni tempts the prophet to use them in an unwise and dishonorable way. In al-Hakim's novel ar-Ribat al-Muqaddas ("The Sacred Bond," 1944) his hero is bound to the spirit and the heroine who conducts a flirtation with him is bound to the body. Here is the same conflict in a different form.

Not surprisingly this spiritual conflict also extends to include oppositions between dream and reality, sleep and consciousness, and between art and life. The princess in the "Sleepers of Ephesus" says that if she listens to her intellect it reminds her of the material body and of the terror that awaits them. The heart tells her of a bright future, for three centuries to the heart are only a dream. The saints reassembled in their cave ask each other whether their experiences have been dream or reality, sleep or waking. The simple shepherd dies testifying to his belief in God and the Messiah, but his last words are "I die not knowing whether my life was dream or reality."[24] The sophisticated vizier saints enlarge the question to include art, for "Dreams at times like art do not convey reality as it is but by their genius lend to it a beauty or hideousness it never had."[25] In "Food for the Millions," after the mysterious images appearing on the wall have transformed her life and vanished, Samira asks her husband why, if the characters in the images were imaginary, she and her husband might not prove imaginary too.

In his story "Before the Marble Basin," al-Hakim chats with his character Shahrazad. He finds that she thinks him a ghost or fiction of her creation. If he is remembered over the years, it will be because of his characters, not vice versa.[26] Shahrazad in the play that bears her name is a representative artist and art itself. Shahriyar with all his hard-earned wisdom is unable to learn whether art is a question of a beautiful body, a great heart, or a great intellect. Shahrazad protests she is none of these. Rather, men see in her their own souls. Oedipus protests similarly that he has never been a hero, for the people have simply projected their fantasies on him. Teiresias has acted as editor of those naive imaginings. It was Teiresias who taught Oedipus the riddle and its answer so his commonplace daring in killing an ordinary lion could be transformed into a fictive heroism. When Oedipus complains that his life is a lie, Teiresias calmly suggests that the lie may be his natural ambiance. The first person narrator-hero of *Raqisa al-Ma'bad* ("The Temple Dancer," 1939) is a self-confessed worshipper of the god of art who is temporarily distracted from his devotions by a beautiful Italian dancer. The narrator jokes with the dancer that he is one of those who "fill the world with lies and misrepresentation." She replies with a dancer's wisdom, "A well ordered lie is more truthful than the truth . . . What is art if not a beautiful, well ordered lie."[27]

Al-Hakim's answer or solution to these problem conflicts is quite simple. It is to balance the two opposing forces. He has written a book on this subject. Sanity, for example, consists of a healthy balance between emotion and reason.[28] In "Angels' Prayer," the angel who fails to mediate World War II does succeed in mediating a quarrel between a monk and a scientist. The angel reasons, "What is religion save the belief of the heart, and what is science but the belief of the intellect?" The heart and the intellect, "the two lofty and luminous principles in man," should unite forces. The philologist in "Tender Hands" becomes a new person, he says, when his heart is awakened by emotion. The hero who awakens and balances these principles is the artist, whether the novice author in "Return of the Spirit," the poet in "Poet on the Moon," or Shahrazad. Shahrazad is said to have resurrected Shahriyar. She asks the vizier, "Was he dead?" He replies, "Worse than dead . . . He was a body without a heart, matter without spirit." In the alternate ending for "Princess Sunshine," Moonlight explains that although he may have formed the reformer, she has formed him too by forming his heart. At the end of the "Sacred Bond," it is observed that the force which is woman has been released from seclusion like an afreet from a jug. Who will refine this force so it can serve lofty and not base or trivial aims? Who better than the hero, the ascetic author.

The spiritual concerns of Tawfiq al-Hakim's plays are then related to social and reformist concerns. If he is a spiritual or religious playwright he has also written plays of social reform. These themes meet in the character of the poet hero. The artist's function is to form the reformer, not the masses.[29] In his postscript to "Food for the Millions," he uses the image of the modern artist having to leave the gilded castle of tradition to explore in the desert. This same image is a basic part of "Princess Sunshine." Moonlight calls the princess to leave her palace for the desert. Moonlight is the artist busy forming the reformer. Since he is an artist, it is not right for Moonlight to marry the reformer he has created. If he did that he would cease to be a man of thought and become a man of action. He would lose his freedom of thought.

In al-Hakim's works, confidence is expressed in the social importance of the poet's role. In "Return of the Spirit," the schoolboy hero announces his intention to enroll in the arts section so that he can become an author. He wants to be the voice of the nation, to express what is in the souls and hearts of the people. His first expression is a class speech, which to his teacher's dismay is on love.[30] In "Poet on the Moon," the poet hero insists that he be included on the next space flight on the grounds that a poet, a man guided by a feeling heart, should represent mankind. He will bring back a report from the moon totally different from that of intelligent machines or mechanically minded humans.[31]

If al-Hakim thinks the artist has an important social function it is in part because he thinks art is elevating and educational. The vizier says of Shahrazad that she has raised the king from the level of a child who plays with toys to that of a man who toys with ideas. Hamdi in "Food for the Millions" makes the same progression, thanks to the mysterious theater on his wall. He deserts backgammon for a microscope and starts to write a book about ending hunger throughout the world.

The social reform themes of al-Hakim's works have quite naturally been suggested by changes in Egyptian society or in international conditions. One of the most direct and specific of his responses to conditions in Egypt was his short novel *Yawmiyat Na'ib fi al-Aryaf* (1937, *Maze of Justice*, translated by A. S. Eban[32]). It was based on his own frustrating experiences attempting to administer justice in a rural district.

There is at least a sketchy chronology for the relationship between the changes in society and the responses of his literature. He has said that at the end of World War I he felt a need to manifest the true Egyptian personality to counter British propaganda casting doubt on Egypt's inherent unity. The aim of his "Return of the Spirit" then was to "shake the dust from the Egyptian personality."[33] Following that, in the late thirties, he felt the need to define and defend an Eastern, Arab personality at a time Arab culture confronted European culture. He has said, "It was natural and necessary that there should originate in literature and the art of the novel at that time a work like *'Usfur min ash-Sharq.'*"[34] (1938, *Bird of the East,* translated by R. Bayly Winder[35]). This thought is not totally absent from his "Oedipus," for the villain Teiresias is given the line expressing what al-Hakim thinks is the modern European credo: "I see no god in existence save our volition."

Ever since the World War I period, al-Hakim has been responding to changes in the status of women in Egypt. Much has been said over the years about his attitude to women. He has been called their enemy and their friend. Al-Hakim says that he wrote his first woman's play, on the effect of discarding the veil, as early as 1923 or 1924.[36] In the "Sleepers of Ephesus," the saintly deceased Prisca is contrasted with the new improved Prisca. The fiancé of the former woman is at first disturbed by the liberties the new Prisca allows herself but at last decides he loves the modern woman just as dearly as the other. Following World War II al-Hakim noticed new tremors. Women were no longer content to discard the veil. They strove to exercise their will and liberty in a prominent way in the public arena. Meanwhile, the men were no better. They concentrated on amassing personal wealth and power. Here was the inspiration for a collection of plays called "The Theater of Society."[37] Consider for example the play satirically entitled " 'Udhri Love." ('Udhri in this context is the equivalent of

Platonic.) The heroine has promised the wealthy miser hero that she has no ulterior motives. Yet she arrives one day with a lawyer uncle to announce that she is pregnant. The miser sums up his disgust with the situation when he swears that Layla's Majnun, one of the great examples of 'Udhri love, "stole the kohl from her eyes by night to sell by day at the 'Ukaz market!"[38]

Al-Hakim as woman's friend has portrayed the bright young Prisca, the fresh maiden of "Angels' Prayer," her hip sister in "Moon Report," and Princess Sunshine. As woman's enemy he has portrayed Nihad the pregnant girl friend with ulterior motives in " 'Udhri Love" and Diplomacy, a married woman with a taste for young idealists in "Between War and Peace." Diplomacy is ready to trick both her husband War and her lover Peace at the same time. The young wife in the "Sacred Bond" appears to the ascetic thinker to be of the first type. At last he realizes she is a woman of the second variety: a mechanical broadcasting device in a woman's dress beaming her disruptive messages at the face of every passerby.[39] In "Voyage to Tomorrow," the Brunette and the Blonde represent these two types. This virgin or courtesan stereotyping, which is hardly unique to the Middle East, is found in much of al-Hakim's work.

The single most dominant characteristic of al-Hakim's portrayal of women, however, has been a liberal male chauvinism which in the context of Middle Eastern society has a reformist character. Al-Hakim has emphasized his contention that women have a special role to fill in the family and in that family writ large which is society. His "Praxagora" shows some of the problems of having women, but also men, rule society. The husband in "Fate of a Cockroach" shows his strength by pretending to let his wife dominate him. Al-Hakim has allowed heroines to be successful rulers. Bilqis, the Queen of Sheba, is a great ruler. Her country has achieved a summit of perfection under her guidance, and her secret is the quality of her soul. She subdues Solomon in all his wisdom with her heart. Princess Sunshine is prepared by Moonlight to rule and reform her land. She in turn forms his heart. Thus, for al-Hakim, woman is society's heart, man the intellect.

In *Himar al-Hakim* (Al-Hakim's Ass," 1940) the author recounts his experiences in an Egyptian village with a European film crew. One point made in the book is that Egyptian rural areas with neo-feudal economic conditions have lacked the beneficent, European neo-feudal institution of the lady of the manor who would promote the caring society in Egypt.[40] Isis in the play that bears her name is among other things the ancient Egyptian answer: the concerned Egyptian wife. Al-Hakim, that is, feels that society needs, in addition to the poet-scientist, a woman's touch. Shushu, the criminal's common-law wife in "Incrimination" is unlike the men. She has a sense of guilt. She appreciates the professor and his kindness and does not simply use him. She is genuinely upset when a policeman is killed. Here, even in the life of crime, there is a woman's touch. Similarly, Shahrazad has an elevating, spiritual influence on Shahriyar. The woman in the "Sultan's Dilemma" is an artiste. Although this play is primarily concerned with man's respect for law in a man's world, it is also interested in the influence of an artistic, spiritual woman on the man who rules that world. Al-Hakim feels that women have a natural appreciation for beauty and so can have an elevating influence like that of an artist.

Walter Kerr in a review of a "family" play reminded his readers that Sophocles' "Oedipus" is itself a family play. In this sense, a family play is "drama at it most ferocious," for families are "chained and ready to bite."[41] Al-Hakim's "Oedipus" is a family play, but it is a happy family play.[42] He regrets having had to tamper slightly with the convention of the unity of place by adding scenes inside the palace. He says he had no choice, since "the family atmosphere in the life of Oedipus" is the pivot of the idea for the sake of which he selected this tragedy. Jocasta is a model mother and wife. The play begins with Oedipus, the model husband, recounting to Jocasta and their model children his adventure with the sphinx. The author thus draws attention to their happy family life while setting the scene. When al-Hakim follows Sophocles and has Oedipus blind himself, the act seems motivated by the grief of a loving husband, not by an avenging fury.

"Tender Hands" is another of Tawfiq al-Hakim's happy family plays. Egyptian class consciousness is forgotten as the prince seeks the hand of the railway clerk's daughter and allows the scholarly son of a peasant farmer to ask for his daughter's hand. All of Egypt is to become one productive family, working together. The play ends with advice to brides: feel free to ask your husband to chop the onions but avoid interfering with his work at the office. In "Food for the Millions," after their lives have been transformed, Samira stops nagging Hamdi and encourages him to write his book. Samira imitates her role model, the mysterious maiden, by playing the piano. It is Hamdi who has the microscope.

Al-Hakim has said that some people misunderstood his goal in "Return of the Spirit" and thought he wished to encourage a return to an authentic past.[43] Some Egyptians, in fact, he says, have sought to reimpose obsolete practices on Egypt in the name of the nation's former glories. Al-Hakim responded with his "Sleepers of Ephesus." The play's message is that the three hundred year-old saints, however noble and respected, are not cut out to cope with modern society. Pay respect to the dead tradition, but do not try to marry it.

After the turmoil of World War I, when Egypt seemed at last to have set foot on the quiet path of progress, al-Hakim has said he tried to define and defend some of mankind's ideas which hold true in every age.[44] The "Sleepers of Ephesus" can be included in this category too. It is adapted from a Qur'anic story with a Christian parallel. In the play the author inserts a Japanese version even at the risk of disrupted continuity and incongruity.[45] "Shahrazad" also falls in this category as do his Greek plays "Praxagora," "Pygmalion," and "Oedipus." One might include his Faust stories as well. The question is the adaptation of the classic of whatever origin.

Following World War II, al-Hakim has said that he was concerned by a new turmoil in Egyptian society involving the selfish and aggressive quest for personal wealth and influence.[46] This concern led to his social satire in "Theater of Society." His response has also meant renewed emphasis on the need for a just, classless Egyptian society. "Tender Hands" contrasts the ridiculous old-style capitalist with the dynamic new technocrat and points to Egypt's future as a happy, classless family.[47] This image had already been central to his novel "Return of the Spirit." The male relatives sleep together in one room in Cairo like peasant farmers who sleep with their livestock. Solidarity, self-restraint, participation, simplicity are all virtues extolled in "Return of the Spirit" and then years later in "Princess Sunshine" where the princess learns the joys of manual labor. The play's first ending teaches that self-restraint and renunciation in love are better than a compromise in the ideals of love and womanhood. For, as al-Hakim teaches in the "Sacred Bond," "There is a pleasure to sacrifice in the line of duty and to self-denial in the course of honor." What is mere sensual pleasure compared to spiritual pleasure?[48]

During the last quarter century, al-Hakim has been concerned with the need to reassess values as society changes in the atomic age. "In the past," he says, "traditional art was based on making manifest what is enduring in man, like love, jealousy, hatred, envy and greed . . . " These were man's unchanging characteristics in an unchanging society. "At the beginning of the century we had clear causes. Not only for Egypt alone, the Arab East alone, but for the whole world . . . After World War II, however, the earth was shaken under the feet of the whole world." The advance of science symbolized by the splitting of the atom has led to a splitting of "human, social, and political values."[49] Art must today see what has become of the values and qualities once thought unchanging.

"Food for the Millions" takes on blood revenge. Should the behavior of Orestes or Hamlet guide our action today? Here al-Hakim has defused an explosive question by clothing it in non-Egyptian garb. The same question is central to "Song of Death" as a youth educated in the city tries to free himself from the chain of blood revenge. "Food for the Millions" is clearly concerned with the food question, as is "Moon Report." Both plays are, in addition, concerned with the injustice of the international status quo. "It has become clear," al-Hakim says, "that the political independence that peoples have won is not economic independence."[50]

In these more recent plays old values are reexamined and global, political solutions are advocated. The hero is now often a scientist. As a social hero the true scientist is potentially a poet or prophet. There is then a kind of progression from classic to modern in al-Hakim's plays.[51] With some exceptions the heroes who were philosophers, kings, prophets, or saints give way to heroes who are scientists, engineers, engineer-capitalists, diplomats, or lawyers. In "Praxagora" (1939), the hero was a philosopher who abandoned his philosophic detachment at the end to incite a people's revolt. In *Ashwak as-Salam* ("The Thorns of Peace," 1957), the hero is a young diplomat trying to reconcile two superpowers at an international peace conference in Geneva and his father and his fiancée's father back home. He laments that the sound hearts of the people are guided by the defective intellects of world leaders.[52] Osiris in "Isis" is god, king, and scientist. He combines the different forms of heroism.

Perhaps it is part of his modern realism that many of al-Hakim's heroes, even the kings, are at their most heroic when they are most humiliated. The sultan solves his dilemma by consenting to his own humiliation before the law. Oedipus at the end confesses to his daughter Antigone that he has never been a hero. She replies of course, "You have never been the hero you are today!" The lawyer hero of "Incrimination" surrenders to the authorities and thus shows his inner heroism through his outer humiliation. The doctor hero of "Voyage to Tomorrow" elects to enter prison once more rather than betray his ideals and the woman he loves.

Throughout these various responses by Tawfiq al-Hakim to the social concerns of the passing years a pervasive concern for the law has been evident. He was educated in the law both in Egypt and France and began a career in Egypt in the administration of justice. The most celebrated fruit of this experience was his *Maze of Justice*. In "The Sultan's Dilemma," the sultan hesitates over the question, "The sword or the law? The law or the sword?"[53] It is his choice of the law which makes him a true hero. The whole play is about the rule of law. In other plays there are specific legal elements including the lawyer hero and the final interrogation of "Incrimination," the former law students who found the Anxiety Bank in a recent play of that name, Mrs. Atiyat's court case and the waivers signed in "Food for the Millions," the people's court in "Oedipus," the contract in *as-Safqa* ("The Deal," 1956), and the court scene in *Hayat Tahattamat* ("A Shattered Life," 1930).

The theatrical aspect of courtroom procedures has not escaped al-Hakim. In an account of a discussion with an actor who doubts that a legal officer can retain the heart of an artist, he has compared the role of a public prosecutor to that of a director or producer of drama for the public. He compares the courtroom itself to a theater— with the onlookers fixing their eyes on the judges. He compares the use and excellence of dialogue in court and on stage. He suggests that in the defense attorney's stratagems to reveal his client's inner goodness there is a talent comparable to that of the artist who brings out a character's hidden sentiments.[54] One should not be surprised then by the frequency of legal references or of interrogative dialogue in his plays.

In addition to an abstract concern for the law a number of al-Hakim's plays feature conflicts between private and public justice. "Song of Death" asks whether revenge is an individual or a public responsibility. Oedipus and Jocasta fear most the enemy within them. The Treasury Inspector and his aide in "Princess Sunshine" find they cannot escape their guilt since it is within them. The criminal mother in "Food for the Millions" is left to her conscience. The law professor in "Incrimination" exaggerates his social guilt to settle his inner guilt. The murderers in "Voyage to Tomorrow" find themselves lost in space with their guilt.

For a period during which loyal dedication to and active participation in political and social revolutions have been good form in the Middle East and elsewhere, Tawfiq al-Hakim may seem to have been a curiously detached figure. Much of his work, however, has been devoted to providing reasoned responses to contemporary problems. His answer to his critics has been that his role is to reform the reformer not the masses. He has explained that an artist must retain the freedom of thought which distinguishes him from a party man, the man of action. Although he has spoken of seeking refuge in an ivory tower, he has not meant a withdrawal from society.[55]

Al-Hakim, finally, has written that he is a pioneer who has therefore been forced to become a diverse playwright. For him, 'diverse' or 'assorted' is itself a type of theater which may be distinguished from mental theater or theater of society respectively. Mental theater or theater of the mind is itself contrasted with material theater. The subject matter of a play determines which it is. Man's deeds are represented in the material or physical theater, man's thoughts in the mental theater. Al-Hakim has said that although his "Oedipus" is really concerned with man's thoughts, he tried to adapt the play to the material theater by hiding the thought inside the action. He tried to keep the discussion of ideas out of the dialogue. In the "Sleepers of Ephesus," the characters do devote too much time to the discussion of significant ideas. The theater of society, represented by the plays of his collection of that name, is directly inspired by the observed phenomena of society.[56] It is perhaps often satiric. Yet "diverse" plays can also be societal, rural, political, or psychological. "Tender Hands," "Between War and Peace," "Angels' Prayer," and "Not a Thing Out of Place," were all included in his "Diverse Theater" collection. The idea seems clear whether the diverse genre is or not.

Although he considers himself a pioneer in Arabic literary drama, al-Hakim is heir to the masters of Arabic literature. He has said that his works and the rest of modern

Arabic literature constitute a continuation of the innovations of al-Jahiz in the ninth century AD. Western influence on modern Arabic literature is unavoidable but limited to superficial characteristics. Outer forms may be the common property of world culture, but the spirit of Arabic literature is intact. Perhaps because it is a question of spirit rather than superficial characteristics, it is difficult to go beyond formulation of a few questions with regard to al-Hakim's relationship to al-Jahiz and other masters of classical Arabic literature. Al-Jahiz, for example, often uses coupled synonyms with great effect. Al-Hakim repeats the same expression within a sentence and repeats sentences within a dialogue. Is this use of parallel expressions an actual point in common for the two authors? Al-Hakim delights in cross-purpose and role-reversal dialogue. In " 'Udhri Love," the egotistical miser finds the lawyer uncle of his pregnant girlfriend alone in the sitting room and mistakes him for the new cook from the employment agency. Their dialogue is consequently at comic cross purposes. The prince and the doctor in "Tender Hands" reverse roles while repeating the same dialogue about which should come first: employment or marriage? Is this delight in verbal cleverness of one spirit with the tongue in cheek quality of the essays of al-Jahiz? Are the ethical emphasis and the intellectual dialogue of al-Hakim's plays related in any way to the spirit of classical Arabic prose literature which often took the form of anthologies of amusing and instructive anecdotes and quotable maxims? Has the goal of both been to provide secretarial or white-collar workers with ethical training and maxims? The *qasida,* a special form of ode, and the *maqama,* a tale of cunning fraud told with an extraordinary display of linguistic mastery, are two characteristic forms of classical Arabic literature. These two forms were defined by a relatively small number of examples with the result that for each of these genres the definition has included elements of both form and content. Does the importance al-Hakim attributes in his "Oedipus" preface to his attempt to create an original Arabic play which will be completely faithful to Sophocles' play come from an attempt to create an "Oedipus" genre in Arabic literature? If he does not think it a genre for others to continue, does he at least think he is continuing a genre based on a single work? Is it proper to speak of an "Oedipus" genre in European literatures?

Since the Qur'an, unlike the Bible, has no historical sections but is a collection of the words of God revealed to Muhammad, the sayings and acts of the Prophet are to be found in other works. One major test for these reports from the Prophet has been whether they come from an unbroken chain of pious Muslims. Does the idea of the need for a proper marriage between Greek and Arabic literatures rest on the assumption that, without an authenticating chain of writers, Arabic drama will be illegitimate? If al-Hakim thinks literature a chain that must proceed link by link, is this idea from the Islamic tradition rather than from Hugo?

However much al-Hakim has felt himself a recent bud on the deep-rooted tree of Arabic literature, he has equally felt himself a pioneer of Arabic theater considered as literature. He has written that there is a natural development for literatures. He has equated this natural development, in a curiously neo-colonialist way, with that of European literatures. The Arabic theater has, by this analysis, not yet completed its natural progression. It should have had Classic seventeenth and eighteenth centuries followed by nineteenth and twentieth century interest in the portrayal of modern life. It is no longer possible to wait for Arabic literature to develop, for theater has become one of the necessities of contemporary life like bread or water. Al-Hakim mentions his "mad anxiety" with which he has tried to fill "a frightful gap" in Arabic literature. He has undertaken "in thirty years a trip on which the dramatic literature of other languages has spent about two thousand years."

This creative panic has made him a diverse playwright. He has felt a need to move on to new experiments. He has not been able to allow himself to specialize. He has, for example, looked to Sophocles and Greek drama, "to ladle water from the spring, then to swallow it, digest it, and assimilate it, so that we can bring it forth to the people once again dyed with the color of our thought and imprinted with the stamp of our beliefs." The result was the Greek inspired and Greek style tragedy "King Oedipus." He had already written a Qur'an inspired Greek style tragedy, "The Sleepers of Ephesus" (1933), as well as "Praxagora" (1939), a serious play based on a comedy by Aristophanes. He had also written plays inspired in part by the *Thousand and One Nights:* "Shahrazad" (1934) and "The Wisdom of Solomon" (1943), both tragedies of a sort. He had written autobiographical fiction, in the form of social realism: "Return of the Spirit" (1933); in the form of spiritual memoir: *Bird of the East* (1938); and in the form of social protest: *Maze of Justice* (1937). He had in addition written a Muslim passion play, "Muhammad" (1936). Since his "Oedipus" he has written drawing-room comedy: "Tender Hands" (1954); science fiction: "Voyage to Tomorrow" (1957), "Moon Report" and "Poet on the Moon" (1972); modern comic domestic tragedy: *Fate of a Cockroach* (1966); a surrealistic tragedy: *Ya Tali' ash-Shajara* (1962, *The Tree Climber*[57]); a modern tragedy: "Incrimination" (1966); a play inspired by ancient Egypt:"Isis" (1955); an autobiography, "The Prison of Life," and many other works.

Al-Hakim has not only written works of diverse inspiration with diverse subjects but has written in different types of Arabic as well. He has written in literary Arabic which is not often spoken and in urban or rural spoken dialect Arabic which is not often written. In "Incrimination," he has experimented with a language hybrid which he hopes will eventually bridge the gap between the different levels of Arabic.

The one aspect of al-Hakim's writing that he feels has not been diverse is his style. He explains that a person "who affects a special style of walking stumbles," and that the same thing holds true for writing style. He therefore did not "pay attention to the various movements and styles when" he began to write. He grasped his pen and let his nature direct him. He does not, however, deny that there have been advances and innovations in his style, "For nature itself is always advancing continuously and innovating."[58]

Al-Hakim's works have in spite of, or perhaps because of, their great diversity frequently returned to the same themes, whether spiritual or social. His plays also feature an approach which is common to his classic and his modern plays. It is a picture-yourself or what-if-you approach. It insists on confronting even a classic legend with a candid and naive questioning. It is a science fiction approach, but it is not limited to plays with a science fiction theme. In this what-if approach the hero is typically presented as an ordinary individual who is confronted by a thought-provoking situation. The audience is challenged to think through the hero's quandary with him. Samira and Hamdi in "Food for the Millions" provide an example of this when they start, hesitantly at first, to discuss the crisis of the hero of the play within a play projected on their wall.

Presumably all fiction has a what-if aspect, but it seems possible to distinguish al-Hakim's what-if-you approach from once-upon-a-time or documentary approaches. It is characteristic for his plays to focus on an extraordinary dilemma. The hero of the

"Sultan's Dilemma" is both slave and sovereign, a living contradiction of terms. The heroes of the "Sleepers of Ephesus" wake one day to find that everyone insists they are saints who have slept for three hundred years. But they do not want to be saints. The hero of the *Tree Climber* has difficulty determining whether he has murdered his wife and whether the murder is connected to the absence of his miraculous lizard. The second characteristic of the what-if approach is that the hero should be an ordinary person with whom an audience can identify. Solomon is a great king and prophet but makes the same mistakes as any mortal—worse mistakes, he says. Oedipus is "neither a hero nor a criminal." He is "just another individual upon whom the people have cast their fictions and heaven its decrees." This insistence that the hero is just like any of the rest of us—even in a play based on classic legends or concerned with the depiction of ideas—can produce strange diversities of tone in a play or a credibility gap for characters. When al-Hakim sought to consider the heroine of Aristophanes' *Ecclesiazusae* ("Women in Council") a real person, the satiric comedy of the first act of his adaptation gave way to a rather somber political play documenting Praxagora's problem with ruling. In his postscript to "Oedipus," al-Hakim explains away the supernatural aspects of the blinding of Oedipus. His argument assumes that one can identify with Oedipus as though he were the boy next door.[59] Oedipus himself may have thought it a divine blow, but we know he acted in a moment of passion. If you take the Shahrazad portrayed in the *Thousand and One Nights* to have been a real person just as depicted and then imagine yourself her husband, she certainly would be a puzzle capable of shaking your sanity. How credible a character emerges, however, when epic pasteboard is joined with mortal flesh?[60] Does the removal of the original, legendary color leave the eternal verities pallid? Does the mixture of truth with emotion or of the ideal with the naturalistic sentimentalize the classics or, on the contrary, add a new dimension?

When al-Hakim's plays are read together and considered together—the eleven in these two volumes for example—a conversation arises between the plays. This conversation is one of the reader's best guides. It should prevent him from taking the trunk or tail for the whole elephant. Those who are distressed by the effusive praise in "Tender Hands" for Salim, the good technocrat[61] can turn to the attack on technocracy in "Poet on the Moon," or vice versa. A reader interested in controversy can quote to taste. A reader interested in Tawfiq al-Hakim can listen instead for the repeated themes. Some of these themes have been the conflict between heart and intellect, the reforming, educational role of the poet, the reality of the national and spiritual identity of Egypt (and of the Arab world), a call for fair treatment for women combined with respect for male rights and the family, affirmation that the Arab past provides a solid foundation for efforts in the future but is not a goal to return to in itself. He also insists that society be international in outlook, and finally, composed of individuals of conscience and compassion. A reader who thinks such themes closer to the Western theater tradition than to his stereotypes of Arab culture and Islam may need to reconsider some of his stereotypes before he disputes the authenticity or originality of Tawfiq al-Hakim's one-man Egyptian theater tradition.

Notes

[1]For partial translations see P.J. Vatikiotis, "The People of the Cave," *Islamic Literature* VII (1955) 191-212; IX (1957) 449-471, 547-572; and John A. Haywood, *Modern Arabic Literature* (London: Lund Humphries, 1971), pp. 219-234.

[2] Edward Gibbon, *The Decline and Fall of the Roman Empire* (New York: The Modern Library, [1932]) Chapter XXXIII (423-455 AD) II, 243.

[3] In Tewfik al Hakim, *Fate of a Cockroach* (London: Heinemann, 1973).

[4] See A. J. Arberry, *Sufism* (London: George Allen & Unwin Ltd., 1950), pp. 113-115.

[5] Sayyid-Ahmad Hatif in W.M. Thackston, Jr., *Readings in Classical Persian Poetry* (Cambridge: Harvard University Center for Middle Eastern Studies, privately distributed, n.d.), p. 101, line 78.

[6] As-Suyuti, *Al-Fath al-Kabir,* ed. Yusuf an-Nabhani, 3 vols. (Cairo: Dar al-Kutub al-'Arabiya al-Kubra, [ca. 1350 AH]), II, 325; and at-Tirmidhi, *Sunan,* 10 vols. (Homs: Matabi' al-Fajr al-Haditha, 1965-1968) VII, 211, no. 2528, "Sifa al-Janna." See also the Qur'an, 21:30: "We made from water every living thing."

[7] See Annemarie Schimmel, *Mystical Dimensions of Islam* (Chapel Hill: The University of North Carolina Press, 1975), p. 50.

[8] See "Man's Fate" in this volume.

[9] See Arberry, *Sufism,* p. 101. Compare Rumi: "If I had a hundred souls, they would all become blood shed in grieving for you, Beloved; your heart is stone, or a mountain of marble!" (*Mystical Poems of Rumi,* trans. A. J. Arberry, Chicago and London: The University of Chicago Press, 1968), p. 112.

[10] Thornton Wilder, *The Angel that Troubled the Waters* (New York: Coward-McCann, Inc., 1928), p. xv.

[11] See Hilary Kilpatrick, *The Modern Egyptian Novel* (London: Ithaca Press, 1974), p. 42.

[12] Al-Hakim, *Tahta al-Misbah al-Akhdar* (Cairo: Maktaba al-Adab, 1941), pp. 196-197.

[13] E. A. Wallis Budge, *Osiris and the Egyptian Resurrection,* 2 vols. (London: Philip Lee Warner and New York: G. P. Putnam's Sons [1911]), II, 287.

[14] Lucius Apuleius, *The Transformations of Lucius,* trans. Robert Graves (London: The Folio Society, 1960), p. 189.

[15] *Ibid.,* p. 190.

[16] Al-Hakim, *at-Ta'aduliya* (Cairo: Maktaba al-Adab, 1955), p. 45.

[17] This title is another echo of Maeterlinck or of Sufism. Rumi said: "Die now, and break away from this carnal soul, for this carnal soul is a chain and you are as prisoners"; Rumi, *Mystical Poems,* p. 70.

[18] Al-Hakim, *at-Ta'aduliya,* p. 107.

[19] Aloys de Marignac, Arabic translation in al-Hakim, *al-Malik Udib* (Cairo: Maktaba al-Adab, [after 1949]), pp. 205-207.

[20] "Reply to A. de Marignac" in this volume.

[21] See for example Richard B. Sewall, *The Vision of Tragedy* (New Haven: Yale University Press, 1959), p. 5, or Eric Auerbach, *Mimesis,* trans. Willard R. Trask (Princeton: Princeton University Press, 1953), p. 318.

[22] Al-Hakim, *La'bat al-Mawt* (Cairo: Maktaba al-Adab, 1957), pp. 119, 132.

[23] Al-Hakim, "Fi Sana Malyun," *Arini Allah* (Cairo: Maktaba al-Adab, 1953), p. 100.

[24] Al-Hakim, *Ahl al-Kahf* (Cairo: Maktaba al-Adab, 1933), p. 146.

[25] *Ibid.,* p. 144.

[26] Al-Hakim, "Amama Hawd al-Marmar," *'Ahd ash-Shaytan* (Cairo: Maktaba al-Adab, 1938), pp. 96-97.

[27] Al-Hakim, *Raqisa al-Ma'bad* (Cairo: Maktaba al-Adab, 1939), pp. 58-59.

[28] Al-Hakim, *at-Ta'aduliya,* p. 18.

[29] *Ibid.,* p. 117.

[30] Al-Hakim, *'Awdat ar-Ruh* (Cairo: Maktaba al-Adab, 1933) I, 128-129, 130-134.

[31] Al-Hakim, *Majlis al-'Adl* (Cairo: Maktaba al-Adab, 1972), pp. 90-91.

[32] London, The Harvill Press, 1947.

[33] Al-Hakim, " 'Awdat ila ash-Shabab," *al-Ahram,* January 16, 1976, p. 4.

[34] *Ibid.,*

[35] Beirut: Khayats, 1966.

[36] Al-Hakim, *Masrah al-Mujtama'* (Cairo: Maktaba al-Adab, [1950]), p. 6 or 3 depending on which of two otherwise indistinguishable editions is used.

[37] *Ibid.,* p. 7 or 4.

[38] *Ibid.,* p. 443 or 441.

[39] Al-Hakim, *ar-Ribat al-Muqaddas* (Cairo: Maktaba al-Adab, 1944), p. 262.

[40] Al-Hakim, *Himar al-Hakim* (Cairo: Maktaba al-Adab, 1940), pp. 92-99.

[41] Walter Kerr, "Stage View: 'Family' Drama at its Most Ferocious," *The New York Times,* Sunday, April 30, 1978.

[42] For a contemporary American treatment of incest in the happy family see Paul Theroux, *Picture Palace* (Boston: Houghton Mifflin Company, 1978).

[43] Al-Hakim, " 'Awdat ila ash-Shabab."

[44] Al-Hakim, *Masrah al-Mujtama',* p. 7 or 4.

[45] Al-Hakim, *Ahl al-Kahf,* pp. 163-168.

[46] Al-Hakim, *Masrah al-Mujtama',* p. 7 or 4.

[47] Luis Bunuel's 1949 film "The Great Madcap (El Gran Calavera)" has a similar plot about a widowed Mexican millionaire in which ruse and counterruse combine in the conversion of a family of social parasites into constructive members of Mexican society.

[48] Al-Hakim, *ar-Ribat al-Muqaddas,* p. 269.

[49] Al-Hakim, " 'Awdat ila ash-Shabab."

[50] *Ibid.*

[51] For an account of the rise of modern realism in European literature see Auerbach, *Mimesis,* pp. 314, 387, 437-438, 481-482, and 491, for example.

[52] Al-Hakim, *Ashwak as-Salam* (Cairo: Maktaba al-Adab, 1957), p. 105.

[53] Al-Hakim, *Fate of a Cockroach,* p. 126.

[54] Tewfik El Hakim, "Souvenirs sur l'Art et la Justice," trans. Maamoun Goneim and M. Ambar, *La Revue du Caire,* XXXIV (1955), 183-184; Arabic: al-Hakim, "Al-Wazir Ja'far," *'Adala wa Fann* (Cairo: Maktaba al-Adab, 1953), pp. 134-136.

[55] Al-Hakim, *at-Ta'aduliya,* pp. 77-78, 113; see also his *Min al-Burj al-'Aji* ("From the Ivory Tower," 1941).

[56] Al-Hakim, *Masrah al-Mujtama',* p. 7 or 4.

[57] Translated by Denys Johnson-Davies (London: Oxford University Press, 1966).

[58] Al-Hakim, " 'Awdat ila ash-Shabab."

[59] Thus the recent case of a brother and sister separated through adoption and charged with incest after their marriage is close to the spirit of al-Hakim's "Oedipus." See Stacy Jolna, "A Love Story with More Than Likely, an Unhappy Ending," *The Washington Post,* June 21, 1979.

[60] William Trevor says of P. G. Wodehouse: "He was aware that he was creating pasteboard figures, and he also knew that with purely comic novels such figures are the only kind that will take the strain." ("Ageing Children," *Manchester Guardian Weekly,* March 6, 1977).

[61] For the politics of "Tender Hands" see Richard Long, *Tawfiq al-Hakim* (London: Ithaca Press, 1979), pp. 153-155.

The Wisdom of Solomon

Characters

FISHERMAN
AFREET, DAHISH IBN AD-DAMRIYAT
SADUQ, The High Priest (Zadok)
ASAF IBN BARKHIYA, Solomon's Vizier
SOLOMON
BILQIS, The Queen of Sheba
THE ARMY COMMANDER OF SHEBA
THE CHIEF VIZIER OF SHEBA
THE CHIEF MESSENGER OF SHEBA
MUNDHIR, A Captive Arab Prince
SHAHBA, Lady-in-Waiting to Bilqis
SAKHR, An Afreet
COURT ATTENDANTS
VIZIERS
ARMY COMMANDERS
MESSENGERS
MAIDS
SOLOMON'S AIDES AND CHIEF JINN
PRIESTS

Scene One

(In Yemen . . . by the seashore. The fisherman has thrown his net into the water and is pulling it in.)

FISHERMAN *(raising his head to the sky):* My God, You know I have cast my net three times. The first time I found a dead donkey, the second a jar filled with sand and clay, and the third—stones and bottles. My God, sustain me by Your grace this time, O Best of all sustainers. *(He drags in the net.)* What's this? A brass pot? . . . Not bad. Thank you, my Lord, in any case. I will sell this in the Brass Market. It is worth ten gold dinars. *(He examines the pot.)* Strange! It's heavy. I will have to open it and see what's inside.

(He takes out a knife and works on opening it. He finds nothing in it but thick, black smoke which comes out and rises to the sky. The smoke solidifies, trembles, and becomes an afreet.)

AFREET: There is no God but God and Solomon is the Prophet of God!

(The fisherman in terror does not move or speak.)

AFREET: Who are you? *(The fisherman does not reply.)* Speak, Fellow. Answer . . . Who are you?

FISHERMAN: A . . . fish . . . fisher . . . fisherman.

AFREET: Are you the one who released me from this pot?

FISHERMAN: Yes . . . I am.

AFREET: Rejoice, then, Fisherman, at the good news.

FISHERMAN *(hopefully):* Fine, wonderful . . . What good news do you bring me?

AFREET: That you will be killed this hour in the worst possible way.

FISHERMAN: There is no power or might save God's!

AFREET: Did you hear what I said?

FISHERMAN: This is good news I don't deserve.

AFREET: To the contrary, you deserve more than that.

FISHERMAN: Thanks, Sir . . . What is my crime? What is my offense?

AFREET: Do you want to learn the story?

FISHERMAN: I want to know why you will kill me when I have released you from the pot and brought you up from the depths of the sea?

AFREET: This will become clear to you if you listen to my story.

FISHERMAN: Speak then and be brief, for my spirit has sunk to my toes.

AFREET: I am one of the rebel jinn. My name is Dahish ibn ad-Damriyat.

FISHERMAN: Pleased to meet you.

AFREET: I rebelled against Solomon son of David. I did not go with the other jinn to the kingdom of Hiram to bring cedar and cypress wood to build the temple. I have high aspirations. I am made for higher deeds than carrying stones and transporting wood. Solomon ordered his vizier Asaf ibn Barkhiya to bring me abject before him. When I was in his presence, he counseled me to obey and follow him. I refused. Then he imprisoned me in this jug and fastened it with lead. He sealed it with his mighty name. He ordered me carried away and thrown into the sea. I remained there three years. I said to myself: anyone who sets me free I will enrich forever and ever. But no one set me free. Another three years came, and I said: whoever sets me free—I will disclose the treasures of the earth to him. No one set me free. Four more years passed. Then I said: if anyone sets me free, I will fulfill his every need. No one set me free. Finally, I said: if anyone sets me free now, I will kill him. You came and set me free.

FISHERMAN: Praise to the One who allots our fates!

AFREET: This is just your luck. It's not my fault.

FISHERMAN: You're right, Sir. The fault is mine. You have simply done your duty.

AFREET: I like your good nature and light spirit. For this reason I would like to do you a service.

FISHERMAN *(hoping for the best)*: May God reward you. Your generosity, Generous One, pleases me.

AFREET: Wish for . . .

FISHERMAN: Truly? . . . And you'll do it?

AFREET: Yes . . . wish for the kind of death you most desire and crave.

FISHERMAN: There is no might or power save that of God the High and Mighty!

AFREET: Rest assured that were it not for my liking for you I would not have undertaken to do anything like this for you.

FISHERMAN: It's my good luck that you have taken a liking to me.

AFREET: Yes . . . Tell me now what kind of death suits you?

FISHERMAN: Suits me?

AFREET: Speak and be quick. Don't waste any more of my time.

FISHERMAN: Have patience with me, Sir. You are the one who wasted his time in the jug all those years. Do you begrudge me—your rescuer—a few moments?

AFREET: What will you do now with these moments? You once possessed the fullness of life. What did you do with it, you ambitionless wretch, except imprison all of it in this net?

FISHERMAN: Indeed, my lack of ambition imprisoned me in this net, but your high aspirations, Sir, imprisoned you in this jug.

AFREET: Because I went too far in my rebellion.

FISHERMAN: I too went too far in my dependence.

AFREET: Yes, each of us deserved to be punished. I have been punished and have paid the penalty. Now it's your turn to get what's coming to you. The right penalty for you is to lose the life you didn't know how to profit from.

FISHERMAN: O might of God!

AFREET: Isn't this justice?

FISHERMAN: It's justice . . . have I no right of appeal? . . . But, Sir, may I give my life for yours. Are you punished by imprisonment and I by death?

AFREET: What would you wish for me then?

FISHERMAN: All the best.

AFREET: The ultimate punishment for me is imprisonment, for I cannot be executed. I do not die.

FISHERMAN: You don't die?

AFREET: Have you forgotten that my substance is immortal? I don't die, but I do take different shapes.

FISHERMAN: You take different shapes?

AFREET: Different forms . . . I am appearing to you now in a form you can see, understand, and perceive.

FISHERMAN: How strange! Are you able then to take other forms?

AFREET: I can appear to you if you want in the form of a terrifying donkey, raging camel, or a black cat.

FISHERMAN: By your Lord, why don't you appear to me in the form of a big, plump fish?

AFREET: So you can sell it in the market for ten gold dinars?

FISHERMAN: Oh, Generous Gentleman, what would it matter to you if I did that? This affair would cost you nothing . . . to become a fish for a few moments until I sell you . . . then you change back as you were after I get the price.

AFREET: You get the price in gold and the purchaser gets a fish made of air. No sir. I am an afreet with a sense of honor.

FISHERMAN (sighing): This too is my bad luck.

AFREET: What are you saying?

FISHERMAN: I say this is my good luck, or bad. I don't, by God, understand any part of my current plight. God protect you, Sir . . . This honor of yours which you guard in market and business transactions—I am trying in vain to capture some of it, and I'm the one who rescued you from the depths of the seas.

AFREET: Will you return to this story of rescue once again, Idiot? Do you reckon that you rescued me? You ought to know, Fellow, that the true life for one like me is not in aimless release in space but in concentration and consecration in the service of a precious goal.

FISHERMAN: *(turning to the sea):* Look . . . look.

AFREET *(trembling):* Woe!

FISHERMAN: What are these great ships?

AFREET *(in a whisper):* Solomon!

FISHERMAN *(whispering):* O happiness! Release has come.

AFREET: What are you saying, ill-omened fisherman? I no longer have time to kill you in the most hideous way . . . Prepare . . .

FISHERMAN: What will you gain from killing me? Flee with your skin, Sir, before King Solomon comes.

AFREET: Where shall I flee, Dullard. He who imprisoned me can fetch me back from the farthest clouds and the caverns of the earth.

FISHERMAN: What will you do then?

AFREET: I don't know.

FISHERMAN: You have my sympathy, Mr. Afreet.

AFREET: Listen, Fisherman. You have it in your power to save me.

FISHERMAN: I?

AFREET: Yes, you. And you must save me, because in that way you purchase your life.

FISHERMAN: Let's agree on the price first. Because we formerly had a a small difference of opinion over the price of the previous rescue.

AFREET: First and foremost, I would like you to be clever and understand at last that you did in no way rescue me by letting me out of the jug. For the Prophet Solomon was angry at me and still is. My escape from his captivity without his consent will without doubt increase his vengeance and anger.

FISHERMAN: What can be done?

AFREET: I see only one solution. I will return to the jug, and you will seal it over me the way it was. Then you kneel at Solomon's feet and intercede for me. If your effort succeeds, I will give you what your soul desires. If it does not succeed, then never mind, you will have done your duty.

FISHERMAN: What if I seal the jug on you and throw it with you into the sea where you came from. I would save myself the effort and return to my net and profession under God's protection.

AFREET: You won't do that. You are a stupid man, but you have a sense of honor.

FISHERMAN: You've won me over. Get into your jug and my fate is left to God.

(The afreet changes to smoke and enters the brass jug. The fisherman seals it as it was before. He picks it up.)

A Musical Interlude

(Voices are heard approaching. The fisherman disappears with his jug and net. The priest Saduq and the vizier Asaf ibn Barkhiya appear.)

SADUQ: Didn't you find him behind these sanddunes?

ASAF: I have not seen any trace of him.

SADUQ: Perhaps he is up in this tree.

ASAF: Saduq, your eyesight is growing feeble. It is a bare tree hiding nothing.

SADUQ: What's become of this blasted hoopoe then?

ASAF: I don't know!

SADUQ: When did Solomon give you the order to release him?

ASAF: Before noon when we sighted the shore.

SADUQ: Perhaps he had trouble finding water in these deserts.

ASAF: Even if he had trouble finding the water's location he could not miss ours. Why hasn't he returned to us yet?

SADUQ: Do you know why? I remember now . . . Didn't this shepherd we met at the harbor say he had seen the hoopoe when he came in from the sea . . . seen him alight beside another hoopoe in this tree? Then they flew off together.

ASAF: We'll let King Solomon deal with him then.

SADUQ: Where is the king?

ASAF: Hush! He's behind you. You don't see him?

SADUQ: O Prophet!

(Solomon enters laughing. He is laughing and looking at the ground as though watching something cross the sand.)

SADUQ: Do you make fun of me and my weak vision, Prophet?

SOLOMON: Of you, Saduq the Priest? No, of all of us. Of Asaf, the head of my army, of my army, and of myself. We are all nearsighted. *(He laughs and laughs.)*

ASAF: Why, O King?

SOLOMON: Listen, listen . . . listen to this ant. She is shouting at them. Don't you hear her screams?

SADUQ: Do you hear something, Asaf?

ASAF: And you?

SOLOMON: Listen . . . she is shouting as loudly as she can.

SADUQ *(searching about him)*: As loudly as she can . . .

SOLOMON: Isn't that eloquent?

SADUQ: O Prophet of God?

SOLOMON *(laughing):* Why don't you laugh like me at what she says?

ASAF: Laugh, Saduq!

SADUQ: You laugh first.

SOLOMON *(raising his head):* Go, Asaf, to your troops and tell them what she said.

ASAF: O King . . .

SADUQ: Go, Asaf, as he ordered you. Tell them what she said.

ASAF *(as though addressing himself):* What did she say?

(Saduq laughs in his sleeve at Asaf.)

SOLOMON *(raising his head):* Sorry, forgive me. My apologies, Friends. I forgot you are hard of hearing. Oh, if we were given the power to hear all the voices in this world . . . She says: "Ants, enter your dwellings lest Solomon and his armies crush you without noticing it."[1]

SADUQ: You know the language of the ants and of the birds and rule the jinn and mankind.

SOLOMON: "This is by my Lord's grace."[2]

SADUQ: He put in your hand power and in your head wisdom.

SOLOMON: Wisdom! . . . Ah, I hope it remains in my head for a long time. I fear for it an enemy I do not yet perceive clearly.

SADUQ: Fear nothing, Solomon. You are God's prophet, free of error, absolved of trespasses.

SOLOMON: Who is deceived by these words of yours, Priest?

SADUQ: I am not so stupid as to dare to deceive you.

SOLOMON: But you dare to deceive the people.

SADUQ: They believe only when they are deceived.

SOLOMON: This is the wisdom of the professional priest. You know, Saduq, that for me wisdom is based on fact. It rests on truth.

SADUQ: And isn't this the difference between a priest and a prophet?

ASAF *(returning):* O King! King!

SOLOMON: What do you want, Asaf?

ASAF: The hoopoe has returned.

SOLOMON: "I will certainly punish him severely."[3] Bring him to me.

(Asaf motions to one of his attendants to bring the hoopoe.)

SOLOMON *(to the hoopoe):* Where were you? Where is the water I sent you to search out and direct us to? Answer and don't droop your head and tail. Tell me: what's your defense and excuse? *(He smells him.)* Ah

... what is this exotic perfume that your feathers give off? Tell me the truth . . . What do you say? . . . That other hoopoe beside which you landed . . . led you where? How amazing . . . How strange.

(Saduq and Asaf follow the conversation attentively.)

SADUQ: Where did it lead him, O Prophet?

SOLOMON: Hush . . . hush. Don't interrupt his story . . . Speak, Hoopoe . . A beautiful woman rules them, endowed with everything kings boast of. "She has a great throne"[4] of gold and silver crowned with gems . . .

ASAF: Where is this land, King?

SOLOMON: Hush . . . Let him tell me . . . Answer . . . Who is she? . . . The Queen of Sheba?

SADUQ: Sheba?

ASAF: I have never heard of this land.

SADUQ: What is their religion?

SOLOMON: Answer, Hoopoe! . . . What? . . . They glorify the sun?

SADUQ: Have they not yet heard of the religion of Solomon?

ASAF: Is there a king or throne which has not yielded to the glory of Solomon . . . Solomon to whom the kings of the Hittites and of the Aramaeans submitted! Hiram the king of Tyre served him as well as the king of Bashan and the king of the Amorites. He has mastered all the kingdoms from the Euphrates River to the last of Palestine.[5] Solomon who outshines all other kings of the earth in wealth and wisdom . . .

SADUQ: Yes, Solomon whom all the earth has sought out to hear the wisdom which God put in his heart.

SOLOMON *(as though not hearing them):* Hoopoe, we shall see whether you have spoken the truth or not. Saduq, write a letter in my name sealing it with my seal to invite the Queen of Sheba to come and make herself known to me. Bind the letter to the hoopoe's leg and release him.

SADUQ *(taking the hoopoe):* I will, Prophet of God.

(Saduq exits. The fisherman appears hesitantly, stumbling, and carrying the jug in his hand.)

ASAF *(turning towards him and shouting):* Who are you, Man?

FISHERMAN: I . . . am a fisherman.

ASAF: We have no need of you.

FISHERMAN: I seek King Solomon . . .

ASAF: Go away, Man.

SOLOMON: On the contrary, come close. What is on your mind?

FISHERMAN: Am I . . . in the presence of King Solomon?

SOLOMON: Yes. What do you want?

FISHERMAN: O King, I am a poor fisherman. I have heard of your justice and wisdom. I wish to present a case before you. My hope is that you will rule as justly for me as you did for that woman whose child another woman claimed. Didn't you make that just ruling and order the child cut in two with half for each woman . . . [6] In that way, the truth appeared. The false mother said: "Cut him in two so that if I can't have him no one will." The true mother said: "No, give the child alive to her to be hers rather than kill him." I, too, O Wise King, ask you to judge my case in the same way.

SOLOMON: Who is your adversary and antagonist?

FISHERMAN: You.

SOLOMON: I!

FISHERMAN: Yes, you!

SOLOMON: State your case.

FISHERMAN: I am a man whose livelihood is in his net. If I throw my net into the sea and something drops into it, is it mine or not?

SOLOMON: Show me what you found.

FISHERMAN: This jug, King.

SOLOMON: Yes . . . yes. I understand what you mean and want.

FISHERMAN: Doesn't it belong to me?

SOLOMON: Don't you see my name and seal on it?

FISHERMAN: Your name and seal are on it, King, but you threw it into the sea. Then it left your ownership. It fell into my net and became my property.

SOLOMON: If you want, you can have the jug and its brass.

FISHERMAN: Together with its contents.

SOLOMON: Do you know what is inside it?

FISHERMAN: I know.

SOLOMON: Do you think it your right to own the spirit imprisoned inside the container? Don't you think it just for you to take the container and give me the spirit?

FISHERMAN: God did not grant me the container empty.

SOLOMON (*lowering his head a moment and then raising it*): Perhaps you are right, Fisherman. God does not give us that great container our body empty of spirit. But listen . . . There is a condition.

FISHERMAN: What is that condition, King?

SOLOMON: God makes the body bear the consequences of the acts of the spirit. When it does good that good returns to the body. When it does ill that ill falls back on it. Do you understand what I mean?

FISHERMAN: O King?

SOLOMON: Here is my verdict, Fisherman. I hope it is just. This jug and its contents are yours. You have the right to release the imprisoned jinni from it. But you will bear the consequences of his action whether good or ill.

FISHERMAN: But . . . O Prophet?

SOLOMON: I accept no revision of this condition. You can have a jinni with great talents, genius, and ability. If you take him, bear the effects of his deeds. No one but you will be responsible for your fate. Whether he destroys you or makes you happy, it is of no concern to us. If he runs amok on the earth you are the offender. If he does good you are the one rewarded.

FISHERMAN: O my master . . . I had not foreseen any of this. It was simply a promise which slipped out of me to the afreet to ask you for his release and to work to save him . . .

SOLOMON: You are the one who has the power, if you wish, to release him or to imprison him.

FISHERMAN: But . . . Prophet, how am I to bear the consequences of his deeds and the results of his acts? Who will guarantee me his good behavior?

SOLOMON: This is none of my business. I have given you the choice. The choice is for you to make.

FISHERMAN: O my Lord . . . I have gotten myself into something which is beyond me . . . I promised him and he trusted me and my sense of honor . . . How can I violate my promise now?

SOLOMON: Before you now you have your honor in one palm and your destiny in the other. Whichever you choose, I will have no objection.

FISHERMAN: I choose honor, and my fate is up to God and you.

SOLOMON: You have chosen well, Fisherman.

FISHERMAN: But I too have a condition for you, King.

SOLOMON: What condition?

FISHERMAN: That I be with the jinni in your service and remain in your castle always, under your supervision, so that the afreet does not tempt me with his treasures and seduce me with his lures. Then I would depart from the shore of security and stray from the right course. I wish not to employ his magic power except with your inspiration and guidance, for your sake and that of your might and sovereignty. For myself I ask nothing but to live under your protection and near you.

SOLOMON: I grant you that . . . but I shall never release you from responsibility for the jinni's deeds, even if you employ him with my permission and for my sake. His failure is on your head. You will be rewarded for his success.

FISHERMAN: I accept. May our Lord grant me and the afreet right guidance. (He releases him from the jug. Smoke ascends.)

AFREET (emerging while calling out): Repentance, repentance, O Prophet of God!

Scene Two

In Sheba, the throne room of the Queen's palace. Bilqis is on her throne. Her viziers and army commanders surround her. The captive prince Mundhir sits at her feet.

BILQIS: I have given you ample time to reflect for a while on the affair of that letter which the hoopoe delivered. Days have passed. The time has come, in my opinion, for you to give your view.

COMMANDER: I am still of my original view, your Majesty.

BILQIS: War?

COMMANDER: "We are intrepid."[7] O Queen. We have a strong army. Why should we submit to Solomon?

BILQIS: This is always the opinion of army men. What is your opinion, Viziers?

CHIEF VIZIER: We will be guided by your opinion, O Queen.

BILQIS: You have already said that many times to me. You think it good policy to defer always to my opinion in weighty affairs. But duty obliges me in a situation as grave as this to keep in mind at least that you have heads on your shoulders with which you could consult with me so we can form a plan.

VIZIER: But you know, your Majesty, that you have a soul which illumines what is dark and a sensitivity and intelligence that for long have guided you correctly in what must be done in the most trying crises. The land of Sheba has reached this summit only by virtue of Bilqis and her heart and feelings.

BILQIS: I wish now to listen to the voice of your intellects.

VIZIER: There are situations, your Majesty, in which it is reasonable for our intellects to keep silent.

BILQIS: I have told you from the first that war is noxious. Solomon is a powerful and mighty king. If he conquers us and enters our lands he will lay waste to them and destroy them. He will make the mightiest people the most humble. But the Commander of my army as you heard persists in his opinion, confident of his courage, and craves victory over the aggressor.

COMMANDER: Yes, your Majesty. Of what use is the army then if it does not rush to repel the aggression of enemies?

BILQIS: The army's strength does not excuse haste to deploy it at every instance . . . Truce, peace . . . nothing is better than peace when the army's power crouches behind it protecting and shepherding it.

VIZIER: Your Majesty, if this statement of yours is not the voice of reason, then what is?

(Bilqis smiles contentedly and casts a glance at the face of the captive prince Mundhir. One of the court attendants enters and whispers something to Bilqis.)

BILQIS: They have returned so quickly? Show them in. *(She faces her men.)* Listen to me. I have kept something from you. The day I received Solomon's letter, it occurred to me at once to send messengers to him bearing a gift from me, so I could establish his true aim. Now the messengers have returned. Hear their report.

(The messengers enter. Their chief salutes the Queen and presents the gift.)

MESSENGER: O Queen . . .

BILQIS: What is this?

MESSENGER: The gift, your Majesty. King Solomon returned it, telling us: "I have no need of your gift. It makes no impression on me. Return to Bilqis and her people. We shall surely come against you with troops for which you are no match if this queen does not come and present her case to me."

BILQIS: What did you see in the land of Solomon?

MESSENGER: Silver and gold in Jerusalem are so common they are like stones. There are as many cedars as there are sycamore figs in Shephelah.[8] Solomon has fourteen hundred chariots, twelve thousand cavalrymen, and forty thousand stalls of horses.[9]

BILQIS *(to her men)*: You hear . . . *(She motions to the messengers to withdraw.)*

COMMANDER: The answer to this . . .

BILQIS: I know your answer . . . Anything new from you, Statesmen?

VIZIER: What does King Solomon want exactly?

BILQIS: This is the question I have been asking myself from the beginning. Perhaps if you had done the same you would not have needed all this time for reflection and thought.

COMMANDER: What use is this question? The matter is plain. A strong king who thinks a country weak covets it.

BILQIS: Why not understand his aim in another fashion? A rich king seeks to entertain a queen whose friendship he covets.

VIZIER: Truly, your Majesty, truly . . . What is statesmanship but this: skillful explanation of aims and expert understanding of goals according to the demands of the case.

BILQIS: If you want my opinion, then I tell you that there is absolutely nothing wrong in my accepting his generous invitation and in visiting him with thanks. I would like nothing better than to see the kingdom of the Mighty Solomon and to examine the novelties I have heard of. Solomon certainly deserves praise if he affords me a chance to realize a hidden ambition and a long held wish.

(She motions with her hand that the audience has ended. Everyone departs except the Queen and the captive prince.)

BILQIS *(turning to her captive):* Goodness! . . . Did you see, Mundhir?

(Shahba, her lady-in-waiting, enters followed by other maids carrying cosmetic aids.)

SHAHBA *(arranging her mistress' hair):* Your Majesty, you are exerting yourself a great deal.

BILQIS: You're right, Shahba . . . but what shall I do when they load my back with responsibilities? . . . What have you to say, Mundhir, about what I have done?

MUNDHIR: Why seek my opinion of your conduct?

BILQIS: Aren't you a little amazed by what I am doing?

MUNDHIR: What amazes me is that you always try to impress me.

BILQIS *(as though whispering):* I try . . .

MUNDHIR: There is no need to show me that at every moment. I do not deny that you are intelligent, adroit, skillful . . . I acknowledge that you are a great queen.

(Bilqis motions to all the maids except Shahba. They leave. She takes the mirror in her hand and looks at it.)

BILQIS *(while observing her hair and inspecting her neckline):* A great queen! Is there nothing besides that? What do you think, Mundhir, of this necklace at my throat and these pearls in my hair?

(Mundhir does not reply.)

BILQIS: And the fragrant scent of my perfume . . . Speak . . . Why are you silent like this?

MUNDHIR: You seek my opinion in this also?

BILQIS: Why not?

MUNDHIR: Can I claim for myself knowledge and judgment in these matters?

BILQIS: It's enough for me if you look and tell me if you like it or not.

MUNDHIR *(rising):* Will you permit me, Queen?

BILQIS: No . . . rather stay. You know your staying does not inconvenience me at all.

MUNDHIR: Don't you think you exaggerate in keeping me by you at all times . . . I participate in your judging, ruling, diplomacy, and . . . your toilette.

BILQIS: What harm is there? Aren't you my faithful dog?

MUNDHIR: Perhaps it is your right to make me a dog, but how do you know I am faithful?

BILQIS: I see no reason for you to betray me.

MUNDHIR: The reasons are not what I lack.

BILQIS *(raising her head from the mirror and looking at him):* Strange . . . amazing . . . You don't even trouble yourself to hide your hatred for me.

MUNDHIR: To express what I have in my soul is my one remaining freedom. Do you think it too much for me?

BILQIS: Your freedom? . . . Your freedom! . . . Won't you cease, Mundhir, considering yourself a captive. Are you cast in a pit? Are you a prisoner in a fortress? You are always with me. You live in my palace. You eat at my table, stroll in my garden, and see me at work and rest. You pass most of your time in my presence. You are neither gracious nor charming, for you call your existence beside a beautiful woman imprisonment.

MUNDHIR: It is not your beauty which has taken me captive, rather your army.

BILQIS: How wretched is the woman who hears talk like this from a man. But I am a great queen and you a man of little importance. So say what you wish. Your words do not hurt my feelings nor wound me.

MUNDHIR: I ask myself why you keep me always near you to hear talk like this from me.

BILQIS: Would you like me to keep you at a distance from me? Should I hand you over to the guards and jailors although you are a prince and a descendant of kings? No, Mundhir. My army indeed has overcome your family and land. That is the law of war. But you have worth that must be preserved and rank that must be maintained. I keep you within eyesight so that I can be confident you are comfortable and be certain you live the way I want you to.

MUNDHIR: I thank you for this generosity and care, even though I think you do that because my company pleases you and my proximity makes you happy.

BILQIS: It is a matter of taste and good manners for me to agree with you. So I do not allow myself to cast in your face my words: your company is a fetter and your proximity a prison.

MUNDHIR: I am sorry if I have hurt your feelings with harsh words. I ask your forgiveness, Queen. Now I find myself in need of pure, fresh air. If you will permit me to go into the garden a moment . . . *(He goes out without awaiting her permission.)*

BILQIS *(sighing and looking at her lady-in-waiting):* You see, Shahba?

SHAHBA: This is not a living, human being! He is made of stone!

BILQIS: How did he know that his company pleases me and being near him makes me happy? I have never weakened before him . . .

SHAHBA: Perhaps you should weaken a little more than that, your Majesty.

BILQIS: No, I don't need to . . .

SHAHBA: Truly, your Majesty, that is not necessary for the victorious queen . . . but . . .

BILQIS: But it is necessary for the defeated woman.

SHAHBA: I didn't say that . . .

BILQIS: Do say it, Shahba . . . You know it is the truth. Ah . . . That has never happened to me before now.

SHAHBA: I know.

BILQIS: If that captive knew what he has in his grasp, he would perceive at once who the victor is.

SHAHBA: Perhaps if he knew that, his heart would soften a little.

BILQIS: Have your lost your senses, Shahba?

SHAHBA: Don't fear, your Majesty. He will not learn anything from me.

BILQIS: How can I prostrate myself further when I am living at the feet of a man whose ear is blocked to hearing the throbbing of my heart?

SHAHBA: But you are suffering . . .

BILQIS: Yes, Shahba . . . greatly.

SHAHBA: We must find a cure.

BILQIS: I think there is no remedy for my condition.

SHAHBA: We must hope.

BILQIS: I hope for nothing but to preserve these moments I spend with him. He treats me to comments I don't like, but I prefer that to being parted from him.

SHAHBA: What will you do now that you have resolved to travel to Solomon?

BILQIS: Oh . . . indeed. I was thinking about that just now.

SHAHBA: Will you have your captive be your escort?

BILQIS: I can't imagine the trip without him.

SHAHBA: What will you say of him to Solomon?

BILQIS: I don't know yet. Perhaps I will say he's my attendant.

SHAHBA: It is not easy to deceive Solomon. He is said to rule mankind and the jinn.

BILQIS: What harm is there in his knowing the truth of the matter?

SHAHBA: Don't you fear your captive may conspire with that terrifying king against you?

BILQIS: I fear only that my captive be absent from my sight for a moment . . . Where is he now?

SHAHBA: Didn't he say just now that he was going to the garden for a breath of air?

BILQIS: Yes . . . pure fresh air . . . because he is stifled by my perfume.

SHAHBA: I suffer for you, your Majesty, and I can do nothing for you.

BILQIS: Look out at him from this window and ask him to come so I can tell him about the trip.

(Shahba approaches the window overlooking the garden and motions to him to come in.)

SHAHBA: He's coming.

BILQIS: He was annoyed and impatient . . . Isn't that so?

SHAHBA: I naturally can't see that from where I am.

BILQIS: I know everything that transpires in his mind and passes through his head without seeing him.

SHAHBA: Here he is.

(Mundhir enters.)

MUNDHIR: Yes . . . here I am.

BILQIS *(to Shahba):* Don't forget, Shahba, that you too are getting ready to travel.

SHAHBA: Your Majesty, I will follow you more closely than your shadow.

(Shahba retires.)

MUNDHIR: What is the momentous event and weighty affair for which you called me?

BILQIS: Sit down first of all.

MUNDHIR: I have grown tired of sitting.

BILQIS: Here, here . . . My faithful dog must always place himself at my feet.

MUNDHIR *(sitting at her feet):* What do you want now?

BILQIS: For you to follow me every place.

MUNDHIR: Can I do anything else . . .

BILQIS: You will go with me to King Solomon.

MUNDHIR: With my chains in your hand, you will be able to hold me tight wherever you go.

BILQIS: It would not please me to say there of you that you are my captive.

MUNDHIR: What would it please you to say of me?

BILQIS: I want a refined title for you.

MUNDHIR: More refined than the title of your dog?

BILQIS: Don't make fun, Mundhir. Why shouldn't I say you are my faithful counselor?

MUNDHIR: No. I prefer to be your faithful dog rather than your faithful counselor.

BILQIS: Be a deceitful counselor if you wish.

MUNDHIR: I cannot deceive one who places his trust in me and confides in me.

BILQIS: What do you want your status to be with me then?

MUNDHIR: Nothing. The status of a silent witness, the waiting captive.

BILQIS: What do you await? A day of liberation and flight . . . so you can return to your family and country to rally them to war against me and to gather them into armies to take your revenge on me? Is this all you dream of and hope for in this world?

MUNDHIR: A hope worth living for . . .

BILQIS: No, Mundhir, there are hopes and dreams more beautiful than that and more noble, which are worthy for us to live for.

MUNDHIR: It does not surprise me that our opinion on things differs.

BILQIS: I ask myself at times: is it impossible for us to agree some day?

MUNDHIR: This is a question I never ask myself.

BILQIS: I know that . . . alas.

MUNDHIR: The question which dominates me now is: why are you taking your captive with you on your trip to Solomon?

BILQIS: Because I . . .

MUNDHIR: Because you cannot be confident of his comfort when he is distant from your sight?

BILQIS: That's it, Mundhir.

MUNDHIR: If I tell you that I would be more comfortable shut inside a locked fortress with other captives . . . will you satisfy this request?

BILQIS (in a confusion which she seeks to hide): Why do you request this, Mundhir?

MUNDHIR: If I have the right to ask you anything, then this is my request.

BILQIS: For me to put you in a locked prison?

MUNDHIR: In solitary confinement.

(Bilqis lowers her head and hides her eyes with her hand so that he will not see a tear which is about to drop.)

MUNDHIR: Is this a difficult request requiring so much thought from you?

BILQIS (raising her head): I had thought that putting you in my castle instead of in the prison would facilitate for you somewhat the means of escape.

MUNDHIR: Did you truly think of that?

BILQIS: Yes, I used this stratagem for that reason and employed the arguments you know to convince my viziers and army commanders to leave you here. Perhaps I wish to have you accompany me on the trip to allow opportunities to arise for you . . .

MUNDHIR: How stupid I am. I should have understood the matter this way.

BILQIS: Keep secret what I said. Make me your partner in the secret. Do not expose me to the anger of my people.

MUNDHIR: You will aid me to flee so I can gather an army to fight you?

BILQIS: So long as that's what you want . . .

MUNDHIR: Bilqis?

BILQIS *(confused without being conscious of it and with tenderness):* Yes, Mundhir . . .

MUNDHIR: Why are you looking at me this way?

BILQIS *(as though addressing herself):* It's the first time you call me by my name.

MUNDHIR: Shall I travel with you then?

BILQIS: Yes.

MUNDHIR: I am going to get ready to travel, if you will permit. *(He goes out happy.)*

BILQIS: Yes . . . *(She puts her head in her hands and tries to hold back the tears.)*

Scene Three

In Jerusalem . . . Solomon's palace . . . a great hall.

SADUQ: What's troubling you, Prophet? . . . What are you pondering?

SOLOMON: Leave me . . .

SADUQ: I wouldn't think the arrival of this queen would preoccupy the mind of the mighty Solomon.

SOLOMON *(raising his head):* What are you saying, Saduq?

SADUQ: Is it necessary for me to stay to meet her?

SOLOMON: Yes.

FISHERMAN: Should I stay too, your Majesty?

SOLOMON: Yes.

SADUQ: I don't see the vizier Asaf ibn Barkhiya . . .

FISHERMAN: He went with his cavalry to meet her at the gate of Jerusalem.

SOLOMON *(as though speaking to himself):* Why are they late? What is all this delay?

SADUQ: There's no delay. They are no doubt on the road to the palace now.

SOLOMON: I don't hear the sound of the chariots or the neighing of the horses.

SADUQ *(as though addressing himself):* I don't know what all this concern is about.

SOLOMON *(turning towards him):* What do you say, Saduq?

SADUQ *(mischievously while lowering the window curtain):* I am not saying anything. I am only lowering the curtains on this window which overlooks your gardens—those in which your many exotic birds take their leisure.

SOLOMON: My wives?

SADUQ: Who number a thousand . . . From the Moabites, Ammonites, Edomites, Sidonites, and Hittites.[10] Models of beauty, exemplars of loveliness, each of whom your great heart encompasses. It is the heart of a prophet!

SOLOMON: Many exotic birds?

SADUQ: Why not?

SOLOMON: In spite of that . . .

SADUQ: I have no argument with your actions . . .

SOLOMON: My heart tells me . . .

SADUQ: Your heart is truthful.

SOLOMON *(as though addressing himself):* This time . . . yes.

SADUQ: At all times and on all occasions.

SOLOMON: Hush. I think I hear the beating of drums.

SADUQ: I don't hear anything.

SOLOMON: I see her coming from afar.

SADUQ: Let's get ready then. Let your chief aides from mankind and the jinn come surround your throne.

(He gestures with his hand. The space fills with attendants arriving to the strains of music.)

SOLOMON: And she? Where will she sit?

SADUQ: That is dependent on your wish.

SOLOMON: An idea is going through my head. If one of you realizes it, I will give him everything he desires.

AIDES: Order us and we will obey, O King.

SOLOMON: I want her to sit on her throne.

AIDES: Her throne?

SOLOMON: Yes . . . which of you will bring me her throne now before she arrives?

AIDES: Her throne!

SOLOMON: Yes, you jinn. Who among you can do that?

(The afreet Sakhr advances from the ranks of the jinn.)

SAKHR: I can.

SOLOMON: You, Sakhr?

SAKHR: I will bring it to you, King.

SOLOMON: When? . . . When?

SAKHR: Before the end of the day.

SOLOMON: But she is arriving shortly.

SAKHR: The place is far away, your Majesty. I will carry it to you from the kingdom of Sheba.

SOLOMON: I would like her to sit on her throne the moment she arrives.

(The jinni Dahish quickly pushes his way through to the fisherman and whispers.)

AFREET *(whispering):* I will bring it to him in the twinkling of his eye.

FISHERMAN *(whispering):* Be quiet.

SOLOMON: What does your afreet say, Fisherman?

FISHERMAN: Nothing, your Majesty.

SOLOMON: I thought he was speaking of Bilqis' throne . . .

FISHERMAN: He was joking, your Majesty.

AFREET: Is this a time for jest, O Prophet.

SOLOMON: Indeed . . . this is not the time for it. Of what did you speak then?

AFREET: Her throne. "I will bring it to you in the twinkling of your eye."[11]

SOLOMON: Are you confident that is possible?

AFREET: Put me to the test.

SOLOMON: If you fail, do you know what the penalty is?

AFREET: My imprisonment in the jug and the fisherman's death.

FISHERMAN *(as though speaking to himself):* There's no power or might save God's.

SOLOMON: Did you hear, Fisherman?

FISHERMAN: I heard.

SOLOMON: You are, as you remember, responsible for the consequences of his acts . . .

FISHERMAN: Then he will never go.

AFREET: No, let me go.

FISHERMAN: King, by your Lord, don't let this conceited libertine ruin me.

AFREET: Don't tremble in fear, Stupid. It's an opportunity . . . an opportunity I've awaited for a long time to display my genius.

FISHERMAN: It is rather an opportunity to display your disasters which will land on my head.

AFREET *(punching the fisherman):* Buck up! Buck up!

FISHERMAN: Oh . . . I wish I had not found your ill-omened jug and been satisfied with the dead donkey and the broken water jar.

AFREET: Stupid Fisherman, don't stand in the way of my high aspirations.

FISHERMAN: Hush, Cursed One! From the day I met you I've not known any rest.

AFREET: If I succeed, you will know glory.

FISHERMAN: King, will I really be blamed for his failure?

SOLOMON: And rewarded for his victory . . . Isn't that the pact and covenant?

AFREET *(punching the fisherman):* Take a chance . . . Take a chance.

FISHERMAN: Oh . . . it's nothing but gambling.

AFREET *(punching the fisherman):* Wager! . . . Risk . . .

FISHERMAN: Leave me alone, Cursed One. My shoulder has had its fill of punches. Get away from me and do whatever you want.

AFREET *(shouting):* Ah . . . Bravo! Bravo!

FISHERMAN: I promised, King, to put this jinni at your service. So let him go then. He may be successful in attaining your goal. Go, Jinni. My fate is up to God.

AFREET *(shouting):* Close your eyes, Prophet. Close your eyes, Crowd.

(They all close their eyes.)

FISHERMAN *(closing one eye):* We have closed our eyes. Go and be quick.

SADUQ: Both your eyes, not just one, Coward.

FISHERMAN *(closing his eyes):* God's curse on you! I may never open them again.

(The lights suddenly go out. Darkness fills the space for a moment. Then the light returns. The throne of Bilqis is in the front of the Hall.)

AFREET: O Mighty King!

FISHERMAN *(his eyes closed):* Haven't you gone yet, Wicked Afreet? Ah . . .I am punished and executed and the matter is wrapped up.

SOLOMON *(looking at the throne):* Fisherman!

FISHERMAN *(his eyes closed, advancing to the king):* Here is my head, King.

SOLOMON: A head deserving to be crowned with glory.

(The fisherman opens his eyes in astonishment.)

SOLOMON (pointing to the throne): Look.

FISHERMAN: My God, my God.

AFREET: You see?

FISHERMAN *(in amazement):* When did you bring this?

SOLOMON: Your comrade the jinni was correct. It is genius.

FISHERMAN: Praise to you, O Lord of the heavens.

SOLOMON: It is truly an amazing feat.

(The fisherman recovers from his daze and feels proud.)

FISHERMAN *(boasting):* This is a simple matter, your Majesty. We have the capability to do more amazing things than that.

SOLOMON: What do you request now? Whatever you desire is yours.

FISHERMAN: Can I truly take what I want?

SOLOMON: Yes, ask for what you will.

AFREET *(whispering to the fisherman):* Do you taste the delight of victory now?

FISHERMAN: Wealth, honor, authority . . .

AFREET: Ask . . . ask.

FISHERMAN: Yes . . . yes. I ask that I should have . . . in my service . . . and in my possession . . . and at my command . . .

SOLOMON: Speak.

FISHERMAN: I ask that I should have . . .

SOLOMON: What?

FISHERMAN: That you give me, King . . .

SOLOMON: Ask what you want and don't be afraid.

FISHERMAN: The truth is, your Majesty . . . . I . . .

SOLOMON: Speak! . . . Speak!

FISHERMAN: I find nothing to ask for.

AFREET: Ugh! There's no remedy for the stupidity of this man.

FISHERMAN: If I took these things people ask for, what would I do with them here? Your Majesty, you gave me everything the day you gave me permission to live near you. So long as I retain your confidence, what need have I for the treasures of the earth?

SOLOMON *(turning to the priest):* Do you hear, Saduq? These words remind me of mine which I addressed to my Lord the time He appeared to me in a dream at night. He said: "Ask . . . what I shall give you."[12]

SADUQ: At that time you answered your Lord: "Give your servant an understanding heart to govern your people and to distinguish between good and evil."

SOLOMON: Yes, yes. I said that, and my statement was pleasing to my Lord. He said to me: "Because you asked for this and did not ask for a long life for yourself, riches, or the destruction of your enemies, but rather asked for discernment and wisdom, I grant you a wise heart."

SADUQ: He also gave you what you did not ask for: riches and authority far beyond any other king.

SOLOMON *(as though addressing himself):* He gave me that for a secret reason I have not yet discovered.

SADUQ: He instructed you to follow His way and observe His commandments, like your father David.

SOLOMON: I hope I have been true to the pact.

SADUQ: You are guiltless and free of sin, Prophet.

SOLOMON: Fisherman, you too, since you have asked me for my trust and proximity and have made that your every treasure, I grant you what you request. It is yours. I instruct you to preserve it.

FISHERMAN: To the end of my days, Prophet of God.

SOLOMON: As for the jinni Dahish ibn Damriyat, he has won my admiration and pleasure.

AFREET: You can count on me, Prophet, for I was created for great affairs and mighty deeds.

FISHERMAN: Be modest! A little modesty!

SOLOMON *(smiling):* Let him . . . He has the right to swagger a bit now.

(The beating of drums and whinnying of horses is heard.)

SADUQ *(near the balcony):* The procession draws near.

SOLOMON *(in a whisper as though to himself):* Yes . . . she draws near.

SADUQ *(watching):* Come look, O Prophet.

SOLOMON *(without moving):* I have no need to look.

SADUQ: Amazing! . . . What beauty! It's as though she were the sun rising and lighting up the street.

SOLOMON: I see that.

SADUQ *(turning to him):* How can you see that from where you are?

SOLOMON: I don't see only with my eyes the way you do.

SADUQ *(looking from the balcony):* And the vizier Asaf has bowed his head before her . . . as though he dares not look at her face.

SOLOMON: Who is the attendant with her?

SADUQ: This beautiful maid behind seems to be her lady-in-waiting so far as I can tell.

SOLOMON: Who besides her?

SADUQ: I don't see anyone else.

SOLOMON: Look more closely, Saduq. Sometimes your vision is limited.

SADUQ: True . . . true. This is a youth to her left who seems to be one of her viziers.

SOLOMON *(shutting his eyes as though seeing with his imagination):* A handsome youth . . . I can describe him to you if you wish.

SADUQ: They are now at the Palace gate . . . They are entering.

SOLOMON *(opening his eyes and preparing for the welcome):* She will be astonished when she sees her throne. But she will keep it to herself . . . What a woman!

(Trumpets are sounded and the doors open. Bilqis appears in her long cloak. Behind her are her lady-in-waiting, Shahba, the captive, Mundhir, the vizier, Asaf ibn Barkhiya, and the male and female attendants.)

BILQIS: Here I am, Mighty King . . .

SOLOMON: How kind of you to answer my invitation, Beautiful Queen!

BILQIS: For a long time I have wished to visit your kingdom to see your country.

SOLOMON: I hope you will enjoy your stay with us.

(He leads her towards her throne.)

BILQIS *(standing a moment in surprise before her throne):* You have done too much to welcome me!

SOLOMON: I wanted you to feel here that you are in your own palace.

BILQIS: Truly, truly . . .

SOLOMON: Isn't this your throne?

BILQIS *(deliberately and with control):* It's as though I were on it . . .[13]

SOLOMON: I hope it is the very one.

BILQIS: It is . . . thanks to you, Generous King.

(She takes her seat on her throne and Solomon sits on his. Stunning music . . . glasses and drink . . . a troupe of beautiful dancers performing exotic dances.)

SOLOMON *(after the dance is terminated):* Asaf, attend to your guests. Make ready every comfort and care for the attendants of the glorious queen. *(The King motions with his hand, and everyone departs leaving him alone with Bilqis.)*

BILQIS: I see you are in a hurry to be alone with me.

SOLOMON *(looking at her a long time):* I have long awaited you.

BILQIS: In spite of that I have not been slow to come.

SOLOMON: Nothing is more difficult for a man than to await his preordained destiny.

BILQIS: You are looking at me as though you were reading a book.

SOLOMON *(contemplating her):* And what a book?

BILQIS *(smiling):* Do you think I deserve all this attention from you?

SOLOMON: Allow me to read the page of your face a while . . . you whose perfume I sniffed when we were separated by seas of sand and whom I invited when we were separated by long distances . . .

BILQIS: Here I am before you.

SOLOMON: Oh, if I were able . . .

BILQIS: What?

SOLOMON: To withdraw your heart with my hand from inside you and throw it down to feed the hoopoe . . .

BILQIS: What is my heart's crime?

SOLOMON: Why do you wish to retain a heart which is not yours?

BILQIS: Not mine?

SOLOMON: Are you able to claim that you possess it?

BILQIS: How do you know this?

SOLOMON: Don't be taken aback or dismayed . . . I know things about you . . .

BILQIS: Truly . . . it's as though you know me.

SOLOMON: My heart has told me much about you.

BILQIS: I see it is futile to hide anything from you, King Solomon.

SOLOMON: Do you love him so much?

BILQIS: Tell me first of all what your relationship is to me? Are you my
friend or an enemy? Are you a king who honors a queen or a victorious
conqueror who brings evil to a land and a people? I have not yet seen
whether I have the right to take you as a confidant and counselor so that
I can answer this question of yours.

SOLOMON: Be confident, Bilqis, that I wish to win only your friendship.
This is my entire ambition.

BILQIS: This is your entire ambition?

SOLOMON: To me it is not a slight ambition.

BILQIS (taking a long look at him): Do you think me . . .

SOLOMON: Don't be perturbed.

BILQIS: Allow me also to read the page of your soul a while.

SOLOMON: It's my right that you at least make me that trusted confidant.

BILQIS: Thank you, Solomon.

SOLOMON: How happy it makes me to hear you say my name like this . . .
Reveal your heart to me, Bilqis . . . and your feelings.

BILQIS: Ah . . . yes. I love him so much it torments me many times a day.

SOLOMON: Is he of royal birth?

BILQIS: Yes, but today he is my captive.

SOLOMON: Your captive?

BILQIS: Isn't this strange?

SOLOMON: I understand what you suffer.

BILQIS: You have no need for me to speak at length, Solomon. With your
sensitivity you perceive what is said and what is not.

SOLOMON: I suppose you would not endure separation from him a single
day.

BILQIS: For that reason, I ventured to bring him with me here.

SOLOMON: He is secure.

BILQIS: I hope so.

BILQIS: No, be confident, Bilqis.

BILQIS: I did not expect friendship to grow between us with such speed,
Solomon.

SOLOMON (rising): I must not be too selfish and greedy and keep you long
when you are tired from the hardship of travel.

BILQIS (rising): Thank you, Friend.

SOLOMON *(clapping his hands for the maids who then appear):* Sleep well, Lady.

(Bilqis goes out with the maids. Solomon remains. His head is bowed. He begins to poke the floor with his staff. The afreet enters leading the fisherman.)

FISHERMAN *(whispering to the afreet):* Leave me alone. Let's go back! It's not right for us to come in upon him without permission.

AFREET *(whispering):* Doesn't he put his trust in you, Stupid?

FISHERMAN: Did I give you control over me when my eyes were closed to do what you want?

AFREET: Look! The king is downcast, thoughtful, concerned. We have never seen him like this before at all. He needs us.

FISHERMAN: Hush! Don't get us involved in something that does not concern us. Aren't we well off now, at peace, enjoying safety and security?

AFREET: Oh . . . safety and security are the harbingers of stagnation, indolence, death . . . No, I am not satisfied with that. To work . . . to work, to life.

SOLOMON *(turning to them):* What are you doing here?

FISHERMAN *(afraid):* I don't know, your Majesty. But this deluded one . . .

SOLOMON: Fisherman!

FISHERMAN: At your service, King.

SOLOMON: I need you. I want to ask you a question.

FISHERMAN: I would gladly give my life for yours, your Majesty. I am your servant.

SOLOMON: Have you ever been in love?

FISHERMAN: I?

SOLOMON: Have you ever known love?

FISHERMAN: Love?

AFREET *(whispering):* What has tied your tongue? Is anything simpler than this question? Speak!

SOLOMON: Leave him now, Jinni. Don't prompt him. Go until we call you.

(The jinni disappears while looking at the fisherman mournfully.)

SOLOMON *(to the fisherman):* I want an answer from the depths of your innocent heart and your guiltless conscience.

FISHERMAN: Love, your Majesty . . . I've known it only once.

SOLOMON: How?

FISHERMAN: That is a story which if it were written so all could see would contain a message for those who reflect.

SOLOMON: Tell me! . . . Tell me. I am listening to you.

FISHERMAN: That happened to me three years ago. I was fishing one day. I had cast my net all day long and had found nothing in the net but a broken container, clay, stones, and pieces of bottles. Evening was approaching and I was despondent. Then I threw my net out for the last time and pulled it in. It had in it an extraordinary fish. I had never seen one like it before. Half of it was blond and half blue. I said to myself: this fish was not made for one of my sort. It is made to be presented to the king. But hunger had me in its grip, so I said to myself: why think it too good for me? Let it be my supper. I took it to my house and cut it open. And I found a gem inside! I was insanely happy. I took the gem to the market and sold it for five hundred gold dinars. I had scarcely put the money in my pocket when I saw a slave merchant selling a maiden with blond hair and blue eyes. My eyes had never seen anything more beautiful. Love for her penetrated my heart. It was as though decreed by fate. I took out the dinars and put them in the merchant's hand. I took the maiden. I had only walked a short distance with her when she said to me: "I was not made for you. If you are an honorable man with a conscience, then set me free. What is due you I may repay you one day. If I am unable, then there is a Lord in heaven who will undertake that for me." I said to her, "Lady, you are free this instant. Go where you will. Don't feel you are going off with my money. It came by accident and vanished before the hour was over. But you are taking away my heart. Farewell for eternity, Beautiful One. Farewell to eternity, O Love!"

SOLOMON: What happened to her after that?

FISHERMAN: I don't know. I left her in the street after those words and went on my way. I have not seen her since. I don't know what happened to her nor in which of God's lands she is now.

SOLOMON: And you still remember her?

FISHERMAN: Is it in my power to forget her?

SOLOMON: You love her still?

(The fisherman bows his head and does not respond.)

SOLOMON: Yes, Friend, I understand what you suffer.

AFREET *(appearing suddenly):* I can find out where she is and locate her.

SOLOMON: Who gave you permission to come in?

AFREET: Allow me, King, to do something for this stupid man.

SOLOMON: Is it in your power to bring him love?

AFREET: I have the capacity to do the most amazing things.

FISHERMAN: Deluded Creature, in your place! I have no right to search for her and ruin her life. She was not made for me. Her heart was not mine. What are our wishes when confronted by this?

SOLOMON *(as though addressing himself):* Ah, this is an affair for which there is no remedy.

AFREET: There is a remedy for everything, King. Listen to me. Listen to me. There is a remedy for everything except despair. Despair alone is the affliction which has no remedy.

FISHERMAN: Did your Lord create you in this fashion to create fatigue and disturb rest?

AFREET: Work, work, struggle, struggle.

SOLOMON *(raising his head):* Jinni.

AFREET: At your command, your Majesty.

SOLOMON: Tell me the truth . . . and beware lest you deceive me or tempt me . . .

AFREET: God forbid, your Majesty. Am I so touched by insanity as to venture to tempt you.

SOLOMON: Can work and struggle really gain the key to the locked heart?

AFREET: Why not?

SOLOMON: I fear that your estimation of your ability has gone overboard.

AFREET: No, your Majesty. Opening what is locked is rather simple.

SOLOMON: It may be simple for you to open a treasure, a fortress, or a talisman . . . but the heart . . . the heart?

AFREET: Is no more difficult than anything else to attain, your Majesty.

SOLOMON: How do you go about it?

AFREET: Work and struggle to wrest the keys from the one who has taken possession of it.

FISHERMAN: Is this allowed by the law of the heart and love?

AFREET: Be quiet, Stupid.

FISHERMAN: Tell me, how long will I have to endure this insolence from you?

AFREET: Until you strip the cloak of indolence from yourself and busy yourself with me to strive and fight.

FISHERMAN: Moreover, what business of yours is my heart's love?

AFREET: Who besides me has an interest in that?

FISHERMAN: What a slap in the face!

AFREET: Listen, Fisherman. The heart and love are an arena like any other. The despondent bystander achieves no victory there. Rise, Dolt, contend and gain the battle from your foe.

FISHERMAN: My foe? . . . Who is my foe?

SOLOMON *(raising his head):* Jinni!

AFREET: At your service, King.

SOLOMON: Who knows? . . . Perhaps there is an element of truth in what you say.

AFREET: Count on me.

SOLOMON: Tell me how this struggle of which you speak should proceed?

AFREET: First of all: dazzle the eye of the one you love.

SOLOMON: Then what?

AFREET: Then demonstrate the weakness of your foe to the one you love.

SOLOMON: I don't think you've come up with anything unusual or new . . .

AFREET: Is love itself anything new or unusual?

FISHERMAN: Jinni, are you a human being so that you can understand the human heart?

AFREET: I told you to keep your ignorance and stupidity to yourself. The reality of the human heart is simpler than any other reality. What is the heart? Is it anything but a space like any other space, a box like any other box, and a chamber like any other chamber? If a person enters and locks it, in the darkness one thing is confused with another. It is no longer possible to distinguish beauty from ugliness, nobility from vileness. A ray of light must enter that chamber for good qualities to stand out from defects.

FISHERMAN: Where do we get the light?

AFREET: We weave it out of the rays of our glittering thoughts and from the candles of our skillful fingers. Don't we have many talents?

SOLOMON: Ah . . . how skillful you truly are in filling our souls with hope.

AFREET: Always come to me. I am the one who can vouch for your victory.

SOLOMON: We shall see, Jinni, whether you can substantiate your claim.

AFREET: You shall see my achievement, King!

SOLOMON: But . . . woe to you if you fail!

FISHERMAN: Woe to him alone, your Majesty, for I as of this moment dismiss his foolish opinion in front of witnesses.

SOLOMON: That will spare you nothing, Fisherman. The two of you are a single being for purposes of reward and punishment.

(He leaves them and proceeds to depart.)

FISHERMAN (punching the jinni fiercely): Did you hear, Cursed One? Did you hear?

AFREET (rubbing the place he was punched angrily): Leave me! Leave me alone!

FISHERMAN (kneeling at the jinni's feet): By your Lord, reassure me about my future.

AFREET (pushing him away): Relax . . . relax.

Scene Four

An extraordinary palace with a floor of white glass resembling a deep body of water. In the center of the space is a divan with other furniture.

AFREET *(pointing to everything around him):* Aren't you delighted and proud now? This is our work.

FISHERMAN: Yes, yes! This is our work.

AFREET: Everything you see around us is the offspring of my imagination.

FISHERMAN: Yes, our imagination.

AFREET: Solomon has given me charge of the affair and put, as you know, all his jinn and men at my service and disposal. Thus he gains in no time at all a palace which is the most amazing wonder.

FISHERMAN: Who after this will venture to doubt our genius?

AFREET: If there's anyone to doubt it, it is always you.

FISHERMAN: I? . . . When was that, my dear friend!

AFREET: Your dear friend? What's come over us? Come see with your own eyes this furniture. Touch these curios with your hands. Then tell me whether Bilqis will be able to contain her amazement and admiration before all this?

(The fisherman steps on the crystal floor, raising the edges of his gown unconsciously.)

FISHERMAN: Our achievement and glory could make an inanimate object speak our praises enthusiastically.

AFREET: Comrade of glory and genius, why are you raising your gown and baring your leg?

FISHERMAN: Oh . . . indeed. I almost thought I would get wet from the water. *(He lets his gown down.)*

AFREET: It is made of bottles and glass as you know. Have you forgotten your work and achievement so quickly?

FISHERMAN: Indeed, we have made our art so perfect that we ourselves are ensnared by it.

AFREET: Speak for yourself. I have not been fooled.

FISHERMAN: Only the clever are fooled.

AFREET: I have no doubt that your are a clever fisherman . . . always falling into your nets.

FISHERMAN: That is the mark of skill.

AFREET: Among you human beings!

FISHERMAN: We are the first ones to fall for the most ingenious deceits of our intellects.

AFREET: Then I can hope for the success of my project.

FISHERMAN: Your project? What is it?

AFREET: You will learn in time.

FISHERMAN: It astonishes me that you have so little confidence in me. It seems you are afraid to inform me of your intentions. What encouraged you to act before we planned everything together? Aren't we like a single being? Each of us suffers the consequences of the other's action. The same fate awaits us in the end.

AFREET: To the contrary, we are made of different substances. We must be suspicious of each other, although you're the one who started it.

FISHERMAN: Dear Friend, the time is not appropriate for disagreement and quarreling.

AFREET: What a man you are! At the hour of my triumph and victory you call me your dear friend . . . What if hope's horizon grows dark?

FISHERMAN: You have never disappointed my hopes in you. What cause is there now to raise this dust in the air of our serenity? Tell me now: where is Solomon?

AFREET: With Bilqis.

FISHERMAN: Where?

AFREET: In the sky!

FISHERMAN: You told me about this a little while ago . . . but, which sky do you mean?

AFREET (pointing to the sky seen beyond the large balcony): Do your eyes see any sky but this?

FISHERMAN: Which eyes do you mean?

AFREET: The eyes above your nose.

FISHERMAN: Indeed . . . they see only this blue sky with white clouds . . . but how can Solomon and Bilqis be in a sky like this?

AFREET: They are sitting on a carpet.

FISHERMAN: A carpet in space . . .

AFREET: Why not?

FISHERMAN: Amazing! How did that happen?

AFREET: The way it happens to birds . . . Are you amazed by the hoopoe when he is flying in the sky?

FISHERMAN: Certainly not.

AFREET: Then why are you amazed by the carpet when it flies?

FISHERMAN: There is no need for this joking now, Jinni.

AFREET: Am I in the habit of joking, Fisherman?

FISHERMAN: It's true . . . we've never joked with each other . . . but . . .

AFREET: But what? Space which supports a bird is able to support anything. What is so strange or astonishing about it?

FISHERMAN: This carpet is transporting them?

AFREET: Like a ship pushed by the hand of the wind.

(A flying carpet with Solomon and Bilqis aboard appears in the sky over the balcony.)

FISHERMAN *(turning):* Look . . . look. Here it is. Here they are on the flying carpet.

AFREET: That's right!

FISHERMAN: What amazing power you have, Dear Jinni. You have the power to do anything.

AFREET: Anything.

FISHERMAN: Yes . . . yes. Everything. You can do everything, everything.

AFREET: You believe me now?

FISHERMAN: Totally.

AFREET: Let's depart and leave the place to them . . . Don't think that I have forgotten the desire buried in the depths of your heart.

FISHERMAN: What desire?

AFREET: Your old love . . . Let's go search her out for you.

FISHERMAN: No, no. I don't want to.

AFREET: You don't want her?

FISHERMAN: I promised to leave her and her affairs to her fate.

AFREET: Believe in me, Stupid. Leave it up to me. That's enough.

(He pulls him outside. Solomon and Bilqis alight on the balcony and enter.)

BILQIS *(on the threshold):* What is this too, Solomon?

SOLOMON: A palace I have erected for you.

BILQIS: For me?

SOLOMON: Yes. Proceed.

BILQIS *(baring her legs and as though addressing herself):* How am I to cross this deep water?

SOLOMON *(laughing):* If you permit me, I will carry you.

BILQIS: And you? Aren't you afraid of getting wet?

SOLOMON: In your service I am fearless.

BILQIS: You wish to carry me in your arms over this water?

SOLOMON: I wish to do that.

BILQIS: Just as you carried me on your carpet over the air.[14]

SOLOMON: It's a great happiness for my arms to have the good fortune of my carpet.

BILQIS: Yes, yes. You have now achieved what you desire. Let it be as you wish.

SOLOMON (*carrying her and crossing the area towards the sofa*): They speak of the treasures of Solomon . . . but I now carry . . .

BILQIS (*in jest*): Take care not to drown . . . My, what thunderous, clashing waves this sea has.

SOLOMON: I am truly afraid of drowning . . . but . . .

BILQIS: But . . . naturally not in this glass sea.

SOLOMON (*placing her on the sofa*): Possibly you will forgive me this little fib.

BILQIS: I have no other choice while I am in your hands.

SOLOMON: You are not in my hands now. Here I have seated you free on your divan.

BILQIS: Do you think this suffices?

SOLOMON: And I previously seated you free upon your throne.

BILQIS: This is true, but . . .

SOLOMON: But what, Bilqis?

BILQIS: Alas! I thought you were a friend, Solomon.

SOLOMON: Strange! What are you thinking of?

BILQIS: Many things which I wish had not come to my attention.

SOLOMON: Explain a little.

BILQIS: Is it right for me to explain to Solomon who knows every language, even the language of birds?

SOLOMON: There's one type of bird, Bilqis, whose language I don't know.

BILQIS: Why are you looking at me this way?

SOLOMON: I want to read my crime against you in your eyes.

BILQIS: No, Solomon. The matter has not yet reached a point to justify this epithet. All it amounts to is that I . . .

SOLOMON: Speak, Bilqis.

BILQIS: Tell me: why are you trying to dazzle my eye with these marvels?

SOLOMON: Have I really been able to dazzle your eyes?

BILQIS: Is this your aim?

SOLOMON: There is a kind of warning in your tone and looks. I have not yet found anything worth saying . . .

BILQIS: It is fitting for you to tell the truth. It is fitting for both of us to speak the truth.

SOLOMON: Oh . . . the truth is frightening at times.

BILQIS: Is there anything that frightens you, Solomon?

SOLOMON: I don't know . . . Perhaps I fear a word from your lips now.

BILQIS: I won't say it. A person like you, Solomon, does not need this word to understand.

SOLOMON: I fear even understanding.

BILQIS: You have my sympathy.

SOLOMON: Your sympathy?

BILQIS: If I could do anything for you beyond that I would not hesitate.

SOLOMON: Now you have said it all, Bilqis. Thank you. *(He rises to leave. Bilqis looks at him questioningly, not knowing how to answer. Solomon does not speak.)*

BILQIS: Are you leaving this way?

SOLOMON: I think you have nothing more to say to me?

BILQIS: In spite of that, I would have liked to have spoken more gently.

SOLOMON: What use is this now?

BILQIS: I have proffered you my friendship, Solomon. But you ask me to give you something I do not possess.

SOLOMON *(bowing his head and restraining his emotion)*: Be confident that I . . . Does he know your heart is in his grasp?

BILQIS: I don't know. I fear, however, that he may have felt . . .

SOLOMON: Felt its flame burning his fingers. *(Bilqis bows her head.)* Why do you fear that he should know.

BILQIS: Oh . . . don't ask me, by your Lord.

SOLOMON: I want you to tell me.

BILQIS: It is no longer easy for me now.

SOLOMON: Yes . . . I see it is no longer easy for you now to confide in me. You did so happily yesterday . . .

BILQIS: Yes, yesterday.

SOLOMON: I am still listening to you, Bilqis.

BILQIS: By your Lord, Solomon; don't ask me this.

SOLOMON: Do you find such difficulty today in disclosing your soul's essence to me?

BILQIS: Can't you speak of anything but this, Solomon?

SOLOMON *(as though speaking to himself)*: Oh . . . all the doors have been closed in my face now.

BILQIS: Tell me, Solomon: do you really have a thousand wives?

SOLOMON *(absent-minded)*: Yes.

BILQIS: Are they all beautiful?

SOLOMON: Yes.

BILQIS: From the women of all the lands of the earth the most beautiful have come to you as prophets of beauty bringing you the revelation of loveliness.

SOLOMON: Yes.

BILQIS: Was the beautiful woman of Shulam really as splendid as your description?

SOLOMON *(raising his head):* Have you read my "Song of Songs"?

BILQIS: Have you forgotten that the hand of your wisdom took care to slip it between my pillows. How could I not read it? I couldn't get to sleep yesterday until I had read it time and again . . . Oh . . . How sweet these words are: "Give me the kisses of your mouth to drink, for your love is more delicious than wine.[15] Your anointing oils are fragrant. Your name fills the air with perfume . . . I have searched long nights in my bed for the one my heart loves.[16] I have found no way to him."

SOLOMON *(looking at her in delight):* "How beautiful you are, my Love . . . [17] How your beauty stands out among women like the lily among the brambles.[18] You are as beautiful as Jerusalem.[19] You are as awesome as legions with standards. Turn your eyes from me, for they have strewn my heart with disorder . . . Out of sixty queens and eighty concubines, from among countless virgins," out of a thousand wives from the world's beauties . . . "you alone are my dove. You alone are perfect."

BILQIS *(whispering as though addressing a distant person):* "I am my beloved's and my beloved is mine.[20] I was asleep but my heart was awake.[21] I dreamed my lover knocked at the door . . . I had removed my shift. Should I rise to put it on? I have washed my feet. Should I get up to tread the earth with them? I was thrilled by the voice of my beloved . . but my beloved had departed and vanished. My soul almost departed when he did. I sought him in the darkness and found no way to him. I called out to him, but he did not answer."

SOLOMON *(contemplating her body):* What beautiful feet and legs you have. "Your love is more delicious than wine.[22] Your scent is more fragrant than any spice. The taste of honey is on your lips, my Beauty . . . " *(He inhales her fragrance at length.)* "Your clothing diffuses the fragrance of Lebanon. You are a locked garden . . . You are a fountain whose water sprinkles a picture-perfect paradise in which pomegranites are planted, bunches of grapes dangle, and flowers and sweet herbs dance with myrrh, aloes, spikenard, and every tree used for incense. How beautiful you are, my Beloved![23] Your eyes are like the pools of Heshbon.[24] Your breasts are two fawns; rather they are twins from the belly of a gazelle. Your neck is an ivory tower . . . Your hair is almost purple. Its tresses could hold a king captive . . . You are a date palm and your breasts the date clusters. So let your breasts be like bunches of grapes and your perfumed breaths like the apple's scent. Your mouth is like the finest wine."

BILQIS *(as though putting her lips out to an imaginary person):* "It goes down smoothly for my beloved in pure drops between his teeth.[25] I am my beloved's and my beloved is mine . . . O you whom my heart loves, make me a signet to seal your heart.[26] Make me a seal upon your arm, for love is strong like death . . . Ah, I entreat you, Women of Jerusalem, if you find my beloved, inform him I am sick with love."[27]

SOLOMON *(looking at Bilqis):* O Beauty among women, how does your beloved excel everyone else? How does your beloved excel other men?"

BILQIS *(as though dreaming and describing a distant person she knows):* "My beloved is like silver blended with gold. He stands out among ten thousand. His countenance is pure gold. His locks are wavy, black like a raven. His eyes are two doves bathing in milk . . . by the edge of a brook. His cheeks are beds of spices. His lips are a lily from which honey drips. His arms are bands of gold set with chrysolite . . . He is as beautiful as Lebanon. He is as lofty as the cedar. His mouth is confection. Everything about him thrills me. Such is my beloved . . . Such is my friend."

SOLOMON *(with a note of suppressed rage):* Such is your captive . . . Is he really like that?

BILQIS *(as though dreaming):* Yes.

SOLOMON: What a woman you are! Have you ascribed all my song's epithets to your beloved?

BILQIS *(coming to):* What are you saying?

SOLOMON: Had I known you would stay up all night whispering my poems to the one you love, I would never have slipped them between your pillows.

BILQIS: Indeed, Solomon, thank you. It was a lovely night.

SOLOMON *(as though speaking to himself):* How cruel woman is . . .the woman in love.

BILQIS *(taking note):* Do you think I have caused you pain, Solomon?

SOLOMON: You doubtless do not perceive what you are doing to me.

BILQIS: Sorry . . . I truly . . . was not aware of what I was saying just now.

SOLOMON: Because you were not conscious of my presence by you. You see only his image. You always address his ghost.

BILQIS *(confused):* I no longer know how to answer you, Solomon.

SOLOMON: You are the only woman who ever did . . . did that to me.

BILQIS: The only one?

SOLOMON: No woman has ever put me in this humiliating situation.

BILQIS: I'm sorry!

SOLOMON: No woman before you has heard my plea and not willingly thrown her heart at my feet.

BILQIS *(with light sarcasm):* My offense then is certainly great?

SOLOMON: Are you being sarcastic?

BILQIS: No, I am speaking seriously. I am the one out of at least a thousand women who has not thrown her heart at your feet. At the same time, I ask myself what importance one heart is to you when you trample underfoot the hearts of women numbering a thousand.

SOLOMON: Of what importance to me are the hearts of all the women of the world so long as there is one heart whose portal my voice cannot reach?

BILQIS: Indeed . . . This is an affront to the power of Solomon the Great.

SOLOMON: You know that and say it?

BILQIS: And yet I do not cast my heart at your feet.

SOLOMON: You have cast me in the dirt of your captive's footsteps.

BILQIS: Yes.

SOLOMON: Your captive who has no greater standing with me than an ant like those I hear bustling around my sandals.

BILQIS: Yes.

SOLOMON: Don't you have eyes to see the place of your lover and the standing of Solomon?

BILQIS: I see . . . you stand in the heavens and his place is in the dust. In spite of that, if my heart were still free in my hand I would give it to him again.

SOLOMON: What are you saying, Woman?

BILQIS: My love has never risen so high in my eyes and the thought of him has never been so beautiful to my soul as now.

SOLOMON: My felicitations to you for him . . . But know that if I really wanted to conquer your heart I could not be stopped.

BILQIS: Would you be able?

SOLOMON: One who was able to lift you to the peaks of clouds and to exploit the wind to carry you is surely capable of descending to the depths of your soul to change and exchange the pages of your heart.

BILQIS *(with a bit of sarcasm):* I am eager to see this miracle!

(She rises.)

SOLOMON: You shall see it!

BILQIS: Till we meet then. *(She departs.)*

(Solomon does not respond. He bows his head in suppressed rage. The jinni and the fisherman poke their heads out from behind the door.)

SOLOMON *(as though speaking to himself):* O Lord, what have I done? What so vexed me that I so quickly lost my senses?

FISHERMAN *(advancing and stumbling hesitantly):* I hope you are all right, your Majesty.

AFREET: How are you, your Majesty?

SOLOMON *(raising his head screaming):* Come forward, you two cursed deceivers!

FISHERMAN *(pushing the jinni):* Go forward, Cursed Deceiver!

AFREET: What has happened, King?

SOLOMON: The heart . . . the heart is harder to capture than you think, Fools. Oh, why did I listen to the chatter of creatures like you. What punishment shall I inflict on you now?

FISHERMAN: Is this to your liking, Jinni?

AFREET: Your Majesty, continue your struggle. Don't lose hope prematurely.

SOLOMON: Your stubbornness, Afreet, will cost you more than you can endure.

AFREET: I am content to bear the consequences, King.

FISHERMAN: Slowly, not so fast. I am not content. This impudent afreet is no concern of mine.

AFREET: Hush, Ambitionless Coward . . . Let me act.

SOLOMON: And will I listen to you again when you have made me the laughingstock of this woman?

AFREET: Patience, King . . . it is simple for us to achieve our objective.

SOLOMON: It is simple for us to dazzle the eye, to make the soul tremble with admiration, convince the intellect of our power, point out the weakness of our rival, and still not triumph over the secret of love or find the way to open the locks of the heart.

AFREET: The heart's door is like any other. When it doesn't open with a key, it can be opened without one.

FISHERMAN: How can it be opened without a key?

AFREET: You break it.

FISHERMAN: Your Majesty, this afreet will subject us to a catastrophe.

AFREET: Let me act. Let me act!

SOLOMON: Beware lest you harm this woman.

AFREET: She won't be harmed and you will win her. I have a sound method. What I lack is confidence. Confidence in me . . . Have confidence in me!

SOLOMON: Tell me . . . What's your method?

AFREET: This rival who inhabits her heart and who has shut the door in our faces . . .

SOLOMON: Beware lest any injury befall him!

AFREET: Have no fear for him.

SOLOMON: What are you going to do to him?

AFREET: I will turn him to stone.

FISHERMAN: That's cute . . . You see, your Majesty?

AFREET: You keep quiet. Don't spoil my deliberation and planning.

SOLOMON: And then?

AFREET: And then, King, I will create a marble basin around this stone. When his lover comes to you to complain, inform her that if she wishes warmth to pervade that stone and her beloved to return to life as before, she must weep night and day before the marble basin until it fills with her tears. Then the beloved will awake filled with love for the one who melted his congealed stone with her tears.

SOLOMON: And how does this gain us what we desire?

AFREET: I won't answer now. You will see, your Majesty, with your own eyes.

SOLOMON: I almost believe I have been more patient with you than I ought . . .

AFREET: Trust me, King. Trust me. I am the one who brought you her throne. Am I not able to bring you her heart?

SOLOMON: I think you're spending a long time on that.

FISHERMAN: He was not aware, your Majesty, that the road to a human heart sometimes is longer than the road to the land of Sheba.

AFREET: Oh . . . freedom, freedom. Grant me, by your Lord, freedom to act.

SOLOMON: You paint the horizon for me with things that almost blind my eye, so that I cannot distinguish what should be done from what should not. Shall I order you to proceed or order you to desist? I let you guide me yesterday and what did I reap?

AFREET: Every fruit has a season, King. The season to harvest this fruit has not come yet. Wait, your Majesty. Wait till I call you to put out your hand for the plucking.

SOLOMON: When? When? Do you see me extending my hand to a mirage while following your glittering nonsense?

AFREET: Hope, your Majesty. Hope. What harm does it do you to plac' your hope in me and let me work until I am exhausted.

SOLOMON: True . . . I have no alternative now, whether I like it or not. Do to me what you want. I shall wait and not tire of waiting, extending your deadline, allowing you to work, witnessing what your powers can produce, waiting watchfully for what your genius brings forth. Go, Jinni. Do what you are going to. Let me see how long your sovereign is to stand with his hands shackled.

Scene Five

A chamber in the palace. Bilqis sits, head bowed, weeping before a marble basin in which lies the statue which is her beloved Mundhir turned to stone. Close to her is her lady-in-waiting Shahba.

SHAHBA: Won't you take a moment's rest from your exertions, your Majesty? *(Bilqis does not respond.)*

SHAHBA: Listen to me a bit.

BILQIS *(raising her head):* Leave me alone, Shahba. Leave me.

SHAHBA: Have a thought, your Majesty, for your eyelids and lashes.

BILQIS: My eye will not be dry until he rises to life.

SHAHBA: You have stayed awake long nights weeping.

BILQIS: I will not cease weeping until the basin is filled. *(A moment of silence.)*

SHAHBA: Oh, your Majesty, I feel for you. *(Bilqis does not respond.)* Can't I do anything for you?

BILQIS *(in a kind of whisper):* No, Shahba.

SHAHBA: Shouldn't I help you by crying with you?

BILQIS: No, I want to redeem his life with my tears alone.

SHAHBA *(looking into the basin):* The basin is almost filled by your tears, but you are about to waste away with fatigue. It's your spirit itself which flows over this marble.

BILQIS: What harm is there to that so long as it returns his spirit to him.

SHAHBA: Your sacrifice is appalling, your Majesty.

BILQIS: I am answerable for his life. He lost it because of me. I shall certainly restore it to him whatever the price.

SHAHBA: Why did Solomon do that?

BILQIS: I don't know.

SHAHBA: Didn't he say he did it for your own good?

BILQIS: I don't know yet whether it will be good or bad for me.

SHAHBA: A king like this cannot violate his word.

BILQIS: This is my hope.

SHAHBA: Yes, I don't think he wishes to mock us.

BILQIS: Is it right for a wise prophet and mighty king to humiliate a woman's heart and mock a queen's splendor?

SHAHBA: This truly is a shocking affair, your Majesty.

BILQIS: He has done it, nonetheless.

SHAHBA: Yes . . . his laughter every evening when he looks down on you from this anteroom. He stands looking at you for a moment while you weep and then bursts out with a thunderous roll of laughter. When he goes off about his business he leaves the echo of that laughter shaking the room's pillars.

BILQIS: And my heart's pillars too.

SHAHBA: Why did you challenge his power, your Majesty?

BILQIS: I did not think he would do something like this.

SHAHBA: A person who has power, does anything and forgets everything.

BILQIS: Yes . . . yes.

SHAHBA: We can do nothing but wait.

BILQIS (as though speaking to herself): And what a wait it is!

SHAHBA: Your pains will not last much longer, your Majesty. Your tears have almost submerged the heart of your enchanted lover.

BILQIS: Really, Shahba? Look closely . . . My eyes are worn out. When my tears cover his heart, the basin will be full, and then . . .

SHAHBA: Then the stone will crumble. Life will spread through him, and Mundhir will rise to throw himself into the embrace of the woman seated beside him, weeping for him and redeeming him.

BILQIS: Do you think it possible that will take place soon?

SHAHBA: I think it will be sooner than you suspect.

BILQIS: Oh happiness!

SHAHBA (looking into the basin): I think you lack only one or two more tear drops . . .

BILQIS: If you are confident of what you say, then let it be a tear of joy. I could shed tear after tear of those.

(Solomon enters the anteroom.)

SHAHBA (turning with a cry that fades away): How terrible!

BILQIS: What?

(Solomon looks at Bilqis and laughs a long time.)

BILQIS (without turning towards him): Is this you?

SOLOMON: Isn't this the time I come?

BILQIS: Yes. You have come according to your habit to amuse your eyes with the sight of my tears.

SOLOMON: Oh . . . if you knew how the sight of them delights me. They refresh my heart as though washing it. It is as though it were submerged on a summer night in a basin of cool water.

BILQIS: I shed only hot tears, King.

SOLOMON: They feel fresh and cool to my heart, Queen.

BILQIS: I am concerned only with *his* heart. His stone heart, King. Prophet, you promised to return it pulsating to me.

SOLOMON: I will do more than that.

BILQIS: What?

SOLOMON: I promised you a miracle. You will no doubt find it a most entertaining miracle.

BILQIS: When will that be?

SOLOMON: Now if you want. Come with me. I will tell you about it in the bright light of this moon.

BILQIS: No, I can't leave this place now. It will take only a few drops to revive Mundhir.

SOLOMON: I wish only to tell you about him and what you will see him do when he revives now.

BILQIS: What shall I see him do?

SOLOMON: Come I'll tell you. Rise. I won't keep you from him long.

BILQIS *(rising):* I will grant you only a brief moment.

SOLOMON: That's all I desire.

(Bilqis goes with Solomon and they leave. Shahba remains, head bowed, in a corner. The jinni enters with the fisherman tagging along after him.)

AFREET: Don't hang around me now. Go to her and leave me alone. I have an awesome task before me now.

FISHERMAN: I don't want that . . . I don't want to go. You will never force me.

AFREET: I told you: go to her, Stupid. She is waiting for you in the garden.

FISHERMAN: I no longer love her. I have no business with her today.

AFREET: Your trembling reveals your love. Go!

FISHERMAN: She was not made for me. She was not made for one like me. She is Solomon's wife. How can I raise my eyes to one of Solomon's wives?

AFREET: Solomon has a thousand wives. It won't hurt him to yield one to you when he learns she is your former girl friend you purchased with the money from your pearl.

FISHERMAN: No, Jinni, don't make me do this.

AFREET: Oh, Stupid, you have in your hand the power to take what you wish. It's a lack of ambition . . . indolence.

FISHERMAN: No, Jinni. It is . . . it's something inside me. I don't know what is. It calls to me that this is something it is not proper for me to do . . .

AFREET: Nothing is calling to you except fear, timidity, and a hesitation to undertake the adventure and a desire to avoid exertion, effort and risk.

FISHERMAN: I beg you not to tempt me to do something I ought not.

AFREET: Will you hesitate, stumble, and bicker at every step? Is this the first time I lead you to your happy destiny? Listen to my counsel! Do what I told you.

FISHERMAN: What did you tell me?

AFREET: You can't get anything without work. Search and you will obtain.

FISHERMAN: Search for what?

AFREET: Your love.

FISHERMAN: Where do I search for it?

AFREET: With her to begin with . . . then with Solomon. Go to her, converse with her and broach the subject. Then go to him, converse with him and broach the subject with him.

FISHERMAN: Is it wise for me to do that?

AFREET: What a simpleton this is who speaks of wisdom when the keys of success are in his hand.

FISHERMAN: The key of success may truly be in my hand, but . . .

AFREET: But what? . . . What? I would like to understand what will come between you and your objective.

FISHERMAN: The thing which interferes with that . . .

AFREET: Ugh . . . It's as though there is another, invisible hand pulling the other way whenever I want to pull you . . .

FISHERMAN: I think you have never been so right as in this, Jinni. The truth is that I am almost torn apart from this pull and that. Have pity on me. Let me catch my breath. I need a rest.

AFREET: Go get some air in the garden. It's the best place for that.

FISHERMAN: I'll go, but I won't speak to her.

AFREET: You will speak to her. Then you will gain courage and remember my advice. Speak!

FISHERMAN: My God, help me. *(He departs.)*

AFREET *(going toward the downcast Shahba):* What's troubling you, Elegant Lady?

SHAHBA *(raising her head and as though speaking to herself):* My Queen . . .

AFREET: Solomon took her aside for a moment from this place. That was the right thing to do.

SHAHBA: At this moment when she had only two drops to go . . .

AFREET: They are destined to flow from another's eyes.

SHAHBA: Woe!

AFREET *(smiling):* Why are you so alarmed, Faithful Lady?

SHAHBA: Another's eyes? After she has wept so much these long nights?

AFREET: How does this matter concern you?

SHAHBA: Creature, how can you say that to me?

AFREET: There is another woman who was also weeping in silence inside her heart without permitting her tears to flow . . .

SHAHBA: No . . . no.

AFREET: She was burying her love in the depths of her soul, enfolding it in the shrouds of secrecy, hoping it would die, stifled, before its specter could appear on the mirror of her motionless eyes.

SHAHBA *(in alarm):* Hush! . . . hush!

AFREET: She too loved him. But it was a hideous love which she dared not whisper even within the confines of her sealed breast.

SHAHBA *(alarmed):* By your Lord, be quiet, Creature. Quiet. Quiet!

AFREET: If this woman could release a sigh from her breast and send a tear from her eye, she would consider herself the happiest of all creation and not ask for anything in life after that.

SHAHBA: No . . .no. I don't want . . . I don't want to!

AFREET: To the contrary, you must want.

SHAHBA: Leave me alone, Creature. I beseech you to go. I must not listen to you.

AFREET: To the contrary, you must listen to me, because my words pour into your soul that power which awakens life in you. You must want. Seek and obtain.

SHAHBA: No . . . I seek nothing. This is hideous.

AFREET: How amazing you are! What is this hideous thing . . . so long as that is possible? So long as I give you the ability to triumph. You have only to cast off your despair and your resignation. Hope and work.

SHAHBA: I don't want to. I don't want that love!

AFREET: You will not be betraying your queen.

SHAHBA: Hush! . . . hush!

AFREET: You can be confident it is not betrayal of your queen . . . but it . . . but it is a great betrayal of your beloved. Yes. How do you know your queen is returning to this place?

SHAHBA: Won't she return to revive the enchanted cavalier?

AFREET: How do you know?

SHAHBA: Don't say you don't know . . . This is frightening. If she does not return he will remain stone like this.

AFREET: Eternally. Do you see your duty now? Do you see the atrocity you are committing? You are letting your beloved remain stone when it is in your power to restore life to him with one of your suppressed tears.

SHAHBA: Oh . . . my Lord! My Lord!

AFREET: Advance and don't hesitate.

SHAHBA: By your Lord, don't make me proceed with something I ought not . . .

AFREET: If you ought not advance to save this luckless man . . . then don't.

SHAHBA: Oh, my God . . . I want to save him . . . but.

AFREET: But what? You have his life's key in your hand now.

SHAHBA: If you knew how much I would give in order to restore life to him . . .

AFREET: That won't cost you more than two tears.

SHAHBA: Don't say that . . . Don't say it. My spirit in its entirety is inadequate to present to him.

(She weeps. The jinni takes her hand and leads her to the basin without her realizing it. Her tears fall into it.)

AFREET *(happily):* Bravo! Bravo! So here you've wept. What tears! They seem to rise from a bottomless spring.

(Thunder is heard and lightning is seen.)

SHAHBA: Lord! Lord!

AFREET: The stone has moved!

SHAHBA *(with a shout of joy):* Mundhir! Mundhir!

MUNDHIR *(rising up):* My darling . . . my saviour . . .

AFREET *(as though speaking to himself):* Now that my mission has been completed, let me bid you two happy, healthy youths adieu. I depart to other work. *(He leaves.)*

MUNDHIR: Shahba, did you do this for my sake?

(Shahba covers her face with her hands.)

MUNDHIR: Why are you hiding your face in your hands?

SHAHBA *(without raising her hands from her face):* Mundhir!

MUNDHIR *(pulling her hands away):* Let me see your eyes.

SHAHBA: No . . . no. I . . .

MUNDHIR: What's wrong? Why are you upset? What is frightening you?

SHAHBA: I beg you to leave me and my concerns.

MUNDHIR: Amazing . . . Is this the way you address one who has given you his heart . . .

SHAHBA: It's not for me . . . It's not mine.

MUNDHIR: But it is for you, Shahba.

SHAHBA: No! . . . No! I'm not worthy!

MUNDHIR: It's your property. You bought it with your tears.

SHAHBA: Ah . . . Lord . . . What shall I say to you?

MUNDHIR: Don't say anything. It's enough for me to know . . .

SHAHBA: No, I can't take this heart.

MUNDHIR: Shahba . . .

SHAHBA: It's not for me. It's not for me. My tears alone were not the price . . .

MUNDHIR: When you see me prostrate myself like this at your feet, dare you continue in your harshness and refuse to accept it from my hand?

(He kneels at her feet. Solomon then appears, smiling. He leads Bilqis in. Bilqis stands dazed before this scene.)

SHAHBA *(attempting to raise him with her hands):* Mundhir! I'm . . .not the only one who wept for you.

MUNDHIR *(without rising):* Your weeping alone shook my soul.

SHAHBA: The basin was not filled with my tears. I shed only two teardrops.

MUNDHIR: These two drops are the two which reached my heart.

SHAHBA: Oh, if I thought my love worthy of you . . . but I'm not the only one who gave you her love.

MUNDHIR: Only your love interests me.

(He rises and embraces and kisses her. Bilqis is pale and motionless as though dead.)

SOLOMON *(laughing):* Do you see, Bilqis? This is my miracle!

(Bilqis collapses. Solomon holds her up. His laughter has suddenly ceased and his expression has changed.)

Scene Six

The Great Hall in Solomon's palace. Solomon is downcast and sorrowful. Before him is the priest Saduq.

SADUQ: Don't grieve, O Prophet. Pay no attention to what happened.

SOLOMON: Saduq?

SADUQ: Your hair has turned ash grey! You are falling apart overnight. Prophet, think no more of this affair.

SOLOMON: How can I not think of it. How could I have done this?

SADUQ: You have not committed any error. Be confident of the reality of your prophethood absolved of errors.

SOLOMON: Priest . . . Priest! I forbid you to mention from this day forward that I am absolved of sin.

SADUQ: I see no harm in what you did.

SOLOMON: I did something no prophet ought to do.

SADUQ: Because you loved a woman?

SOLOMON: No, because I used hideous means to conquer her and to torment her heart. I desired to avenge myself for her rejection by the sight of her soul's flowing blood and her heart's running sores . . . till she collapsed in my arms. She fell while I was laughing in her wan face.

SADUQ: Your Lord put the power in your hand and you used it.

SOLOMON: He also put wisdom in my head. I should have been guided by it.

SADUQ: You were guided by it and are at every moment. You have no right, Solomon the Wise, to proclaim that you embarked on an ill-advised affair.

SOLOMON: Priest, why do you always try to justify my errors?

SADUQ: This is my job.

SOLOMON: Bravo! Hurrah for a prophet whose acts need a defense.

SADUQ: Strange . . . Don't you want a defense and justification for the prophet's acts?

SOLOMON: I had thought the prophet had no need for that.

SADUQ: What work is there then for priests and men of religion?

SOLOMON: Your work is no concern of mine. But I would like to shout to the people: People, I have committed a grave sin. Perhaps not even the most evil-spirited and malicious one of you has done anything like it.

SADUQ *(looking about him in alarm):* Hush . . . hush. Lower your voice, Solomon, so the people don't hear you saying this.

SOLOMON: What do you fear?

SADUQ: Strange! Do you want the people to know you err like them?

SOLOMON: No, I want them to know I err sometimes even more than they and that I was not granted a soul of a substance different from theirs. I am not better than they are in any way . . . Except in that pain which torments me whenever I remember my error . . . and in that remorse which shakes my being; and in the search for true repentance and in advancing towards my Lord seeking forgiveness.

SADUQ: This talk of yours is dangerous, Prophet.

SOLOMON: It's the truth! The truth . . . Nothing is more fitting for a prophet than the truth.

SADUQ: But the prophet is the ideal in which sight must find no distortion. The eyes must see there only beauty and perfection.

SOLOMON: Enough of that, you priests . . . Or shall I call you representational artists . . . For how long will you think the prophet a work of art, produced by your hands, imagination, and paints, to be displayed radiant and glistening on the walls of temples?

SADUQ: So long as you desire the truth, Solomon, then I'll tell you you're right. Religion is an art . . . a divine, heavenly art. For this reason we must adhere in it to the principles of art: beauty and perfection.

SOLOMON: Certainly not, Saduq. It only seems that way to your priests, because of your profession and skill. The truth is that it is not an art. It is too truthful for false adornment, cleverness, retouching, and embellishment to enter into its composition. Religion is the reality of the human heart with its innate sense of good and evil. It is the bare sensation we human beings have of our inability to achieve perfection and our continued striving towards the good, stumbling at times over our evil impulses. Religion is hope and consolation. Yes, it is the hope and consolation rising from the depths of that truthful prayer: "Heavens, I seek the good, but I err. Aid me, Lord, to bear the burden of my weakness and the consequences of my errors. Show me the way whenever I am about to stumble. Endear to my soul the virtues. Grant me the ability to rise above myself a bit, so that I may be worthy of your blessings with which you crowned man's head the day you created him from clay with your luminous hands."

SADUQ: You exaggerate, Prophet, in your estimation of what you did to this woman.

SOLOMON: Go away from me. With your trifling, you block off the sunshine from me.

SADUQ: I will leave you, Solomon, until you become calmer and recover your composure.

(He goes out. Solomon bows his head . . . Music. Asaf enters.)

ASAF: I have carried out your orders, King.

SOLOMON *(raising his head)*: You imprisoned the jinni?

ASAF: Yes. I imprisoned him in the brass jug. Shall I throw it in the sea?

SOLOMON: Not so fast . . . Where is the fisherman?

ASAF: The fisherman? You have not yet ordered me what to do to him.

SOLOMON: Don't do anything to him. Bring him here.

(The fisherman appears immediately.)

FISHERMAN: Here I am, King. I'm at your door, heeding your word and awaiting your verdict.

(Solomon motions to Asaf to leave.)

SOLOMON *(to the fisherman):* You are awaiting my verdict on you?

FISHERMAN: Yes, your Majesty.

SOLOMON: I am not your judge.

FISHERMAN: What are you saying? But you are, Solomon, for you are the most just of those who rule on this earth.

SOLOMON: I am now not worthy to render judgment in your case.

FISHERMAN: Don't say that, Wise Prophet.

SOLOMON: I have committed a greater error than you.

FISHERMAN: What do I hear?

SOLOMON: The truth.

FISHERMAN: What is my fate then? Alas! If you do not judge me, Solomon, another judge whose severity I fear will undertake that.

SOLOMON: Who is it?

FISHERMAN: My soul!

SOLOMON: Yes . . . yes, woe to one like you when his soul is the judge. I too fear that judge and find no one to rescue me from him.

FISHERMAN: You, your Majesty?

SOLOMON: I thought the priest Saduq would be capable of that . . . Alas!

FISHERMAN: Don't be so hard on yourself, your Majesty . . . You seem to have grown old all at once, overnight. Oh, if I could do something for you . . .

SOLOMON *(looking at him for a time):* But you can, Fisherman.

FISHERMAN: I?

SOLOMON: You are fit to be my judge and to save me from my own judgment.

FISHERMAN: I am a lowly fisherman.

SOLOMON: You are the only one capable of trying the mighty Solomon.

FISHERMAN: Why, O Prophet? Why do you raise me to this rank?

SOLOMON: Because you are the bearer of a pure heart.

FISHERMAN: I no longer have a pure heart. The jinni tempted me, as you know, your Majesty, to go into the garden.

SOLOMON: But you did not venture to approach her or to speak to her.

FISHERMAN: I looked at her from behind the trees. I remembered she was your wife and froze in my place.

SOLOMON: What is your crime then?

FISHERMAN: Listening to the temptings of the afreet. Isn't this a great offense?

SOLOMON: But you then listened to the voice of your wisdom and conscience before taking a step further toward error. But I . . . I went several steps down that road.

FISHERMAN: Your Majesty, you subsequently repented. In this way, you erased what the jinni's hand had done.

SOLOMON: Does remorse wipe clean a shower of sins?

FISHERMAN: If it issues from a truthful heart . . . yes.

SOLOMON: Do you really think I deserve God's compassion?

FISHERMAN: As much as I deserve punishment. King, judge me. It is not enough for you to imprison the jinni in the jug. I am his accomplice, responsible as you know for his deeds. Have you forgotten, your Majesty, that we are in your eyes a single being? Have you forgotten that the weight of his actions falls on my back? King . . . Prophet, carry out your just punishment on me.

SOLOMON: Are you not as much his victim as I? I was deceived by his words and seduced by his fictions. How can I blame you?

FISHERMAN: Do you really think, your Majesty, that I do not deserve punishment?

SOLOMON: Since your repentance flows from your truthful heart . . .

(Asaf enters.)

ASAF: O King, Queen Bilqis has come to bid you adieu.

(Asaf leads in Queen Bilqis. She appears in the same gown she wore on entering Jerusalem . . . Music.)

SOLOMON *(rising to receive her):* Bilqis!

(Everyone else departs leaving Solomon and Bilqis alone.)

BILQIS: The hour of my departure has arrived. I certainly thank you for your hospitality.

SOLOMON: If only I could inflict punishment on myself before your eyes before you depart . . .

BILQIS: Forget what happened, Solomon.

SOLOMON: How can I forget?

BILQIS: I have forgotten everything with the passing of that frightful moment just as a distressing dream is forgotten when we wake up.

SOLOMON: I ought not to have caused you a nightmare.

BILQIS: You have erased what you did and restored everything to its prior state.

SOLOMON: Yes, and what is my merit in that?

BILQIS: In any case, it was one of your miracles. You really did plunge me into a world of strange dreams . . . some happy and some sad . . . some astonishing and some painful. I have awakened from all of this now.

SOLOMON: You awake just as you were . . . Your heart is your heart. We did nothing more than those magicians who dazzle the eyes with their deceits and fictions.

BILQIS: Don't say that, Solomon. You are truly the master of tremendous power.

SOLOMON: Of what worth is it? What have I achieved with it?

BILQIS: I shall never forget that you lifted me into the sky on the flying carpet.

SOLOMON: What use is the sky? What influence of any sort did that have on you? A beautiful phrase from the lips of the one you love is alone able to raise you to the sky . . . to that true sky human volition falls short of . . .

BILQIS (sighing): You're right, Solomon.

SOLOMON: I have been incapable of helping you or helping myself. I possess tremendous power . . . I have on hand miracles, genius, and many talents . . . treasures . . . I am a mighty king and a wise prophet. I am master of the jinn and of mankind, of men and properties. In spite of that, was all this of any use when confronted by your heart?

BILQIS: Truly, Solomon, the human heart is the greatest miracle.

SOLOMON: Yes, Bilqis.

BILQIS: A miracle which resists power.

SOLOMON: And wisdom . . .

BILQIS: Yes.

SOLOMON: How are its locks opened?

BILQIS: I don't know.

SOLOMON: Yes. That is something for which only God holds the key.

BILQIS: I'm surprised you didn't know this, Solomon.

SOLOMON: Power, Bilqis, sometimes blinds our eyes to the sight of our human frailty, causes us to forget the wisdom we were granted, and embellishes the pursuit of a hopeless struggle. Then we proceed with our delusion while the mocking Lord looks on. Oh, Bilqis! What will you think of me after today. What will your smile be like when the wisdom of Solomon is mentioned in your presence from now on?

BILQIS: Have no fear. I understand you and appreciate your current feelings.

SOLOMON: Oh, Bilqis! There is no greater threat to our wisdom than our ability.

BILQIS: This is true, Solomon.

SOLOMON: Now I have grasped why my Lord gave me what I did not ask for, namely, authority, riches, and ability in addition to what I did ask for: discernment and wisdom. Here is the difficult test . . . the difficult test!

BILQIS: Truly! How difficult it is to reconcile all these.

SOLOMON: Perhaps true wisdom comes when a man learns how to rule his ability. In this I have failed. My insight was extinguished for a moment by the violent breezes of my ability.

BILQIS: Don't be so hard on yourself. Don't blame yourself for a single lapse.

SOLOMON: The matter is graver than a lapse. It is a great error. It is an offense.

BILQIS: From such an offense our insight at times emerges wide open like the opening flowers which sprout in the mire.

SOLOMON: Bilqis! Am I worthy of this generous forbearance of yours? Is it from your mouth that I hear this lovely consolation?

BILQIS: Yes, Solomon . . . from that mouth which could not say what you wished to hear.

SOLOMON: Oh . . . if we had known. Love is a force . . . a stern force which strikes where it wishes . . .

BILQIS: Not where we wish . . . You're right, Solomon.

SOLOMON: Nevertheless, we ought not dislike this too much. It is necessary for us to have within us a flower left unwatered, a hunger unsatisfied, a desire unfulfilled, and a cry unheard. In this way, we can be truly worthy of wisdom and discernment, fit to understand the human heart and to address it, and able to bring it solace and heavenly revelations.

BILQIS: I am proud, Solomon, that you once loved me . . . and embarrassed I did not grant you . . .

SOLOMON: I am happy now with your friendship . . . It is something greater than I deserve.

BILQIS: It truly is something great . . . but you are worthy of it. Oh, Solomon . . . he also has accorded me his friendship after he learned about my tears.

SOLOMON: Don't remind me of your tears.

BILQIS: Regardless of that, they were not without effect . . .

SOLOMON: If it were in my power to grant you Mundhir's heart . . .

BILQIS: His heart was possessed by Shahba for a long time without my knowing . . .

SOLOMON: For a long time?

BILQIS: Yes, since he fell captive, came to my castle, and saw her.

SOLOMON: Are you trying to lighten the load of my guilt?

BILQIS: No, to the contrary. It's the truth which was hidden from me. The loyalty of Shahba was able to suppress their mutual love for a long time. This faithful woman did the impossible in driving off the specter of that love from herself hoping to please me and fearing for me.

SOLOMON: But you suffered . . .

BILQIS: Yes . . . at first, but now I understand and see what I must do. With your permission, before they travel to Mundhir's country I will give Shahba and Mundhir, as their wedding present, some of the precious things you gave me today.

SOLOMON: Aren't you afraid to release your captive?

BILQIS: Not now.

SOLOMON: Yes, friendship is a great thing. It is not the glittering side of love, but the other side which never tarnishes.

BILQIS: Farewell, Friend!

SOLOMON: My Friend, Farewell!

(Music plays. The vizier Asaf enters with the chief attendants to bid farewell to Queen Bilqis as she goes out with Solomon.)

Scene Seven

In the palace . . . Solomon is sleeping in his chair and propped up by his staff. The priest Saduq, Asaf ibn Barkhiya, and the fisherman are whispering together.

SADUQ: He can't be sleeping all this time!

ASAF: Whenever I have inquired after him I have found him in this state.

FISHERMAN: Hush . . . Lower your voices . . . lest you wake him.

SADUQ: We seek nothing but this. We haven't seen him awake for months.

ASAF: Indeed . . . after Bilqis set forth, his affairs underwent a change. Signs were apparent in him that promised no good.

SADUQ: I think he became sick, but he concealed his illness.

ASAF: Yes, his case is surrounded by enough mystery to arouse anxiety.

SADUQ: No one but this man knows his secret . . . *(He points towards the fisherman.)*

ASAF: True . . . only this fisherman was close to him in the last period. How often I found them alone together, whispering to each other.

SADUQ: Speak, Fisherman!

FISHERMAN: Hush . . . hush!

ASAF: Don't you want to talk?

FISHERMAN: Of what shall I speak? I know no more than you.

ASAF: Tell us: what is the matter with him?

FISHERMAN: Nothing is the matter with him. He's sleeping on his staff, as you see.

SADUQ: Since when?

FISHERMAN: I don't know.

SADUQ: When did you see him awake? . . . When did you last converse?

FISHERMAN: I don't remember.

ASAF: You then are deliberately concealing from us . . .

FISHERMAN: Concealing what?

ASAF: What's wrong with him.

SADUQ: If you don't inform us, I will go to him and attempt to wake him.

FISHERMAN *(blocking the way):* No one will approach him so long as I am here.

ASAF: Strange! . . . Strange.

SADUQ: Who granted you this right?

FISHERMAN: He did . . . He ordered me to keep watch over his rest and to let no one disturb his sleep.

SADUQ: Brief us on the facts of the matter . . . Is he really sleeping?

FISHERMAN: What else?

SADUQ: In truth, it is a disquieting affair.

ASAF: Why don't you get him medical help?

FISHERMAN: Who said he is indisposed?

ASAF: This is a long sleep.

FISHERMAN: This is not an illness. I told you it is rest that he needs.

SADUQ *(turning towards Solomon):* How strange this motionless body is on its chair . . . no movement, no stirring, no gesture, no twitching . . .

ASAF *(turning too):* Truly . . . what a motionless body it is.

SADUQ: Is it possible for this motionless thing to have life in it?

FISHERMAN: What nonsense are you uttering?

SADUQ: If Solomon dies one day he will not die like other people, for the reverberation of his death is liable to shake the pillars of the kingdoms of the jinn and of mankind in the twinkling of an eye.

ASAF: There's no doubt he knew that and planned ahead . . .

FISHERMAN: Why do you speak of death at this hour?

SADUQ: It's merely a passing thought.

ASAF: What is the secret behind his residing here in Bilqis' palace which he built for her? He came to it after she departed and has never left it . . .

SADUQ: The secret of that is with the fisherman.

FISHERMAN: Won't you leave the fisherman alone? For a long time my soul has told me to take my net and return to my profession.

SADUQ: What's to prevent you?

FISHERMAN: I'm prevented by . . .

ASAF: Speak!

FISHERMAN *(turning towards Solomon):* Hush! I heard some movement.

SADUQ: Where?

ASAF: Look . . . look.

(Solomon's stick has crumbled. His body falls to the floor.)

SADUQ: A body!

ASAF: Prostrate on the ground. Fallen to the floor!

(They hurry toward the body shouting. The fisherman stops them.)

FISHERMAN: Lower your voices.

SADUQ: What do you fear now?

FISHERMAN: Beware lest the jinn hear of his death.

SADUQ: My hunch was right. He has been dead for a long time.

ASAF (examining the corpse): Yes, yes. His lifeless corpse has been supported by his staff for a long time. But the termites . . .

SADUQ: What termites?

ASAF (pointing with his finger): Look . . . look at these massive armies of the little creatures around his staff. They have been gnawing on it all this time and ate through it. Then it broke up under the weight of his body.[28]

FISHERMAN: What will you do . . . now?

SADUQ: Let's first put the corpse on this bed and cover it.

(The three of them carry it to the bed and cover it.)

ASAF: And now?

SADUQ: Now the matter must be announced to the people.

FISHERMAN: Is there no way to avoid that then?

SADUQ: Is there any doubt about that?

FISHERMAN: His final words for me were: "Let everyone believe I am sleeping. Let no one touch me."

SADUQ: How strange! Did he wish to rule his subjects—the jinn and mankind—when dead, just as he did when alive?

FISHERMAN: Perhaps he considered that possible. I suppose he feared the liberation of the jinn and the outbreak of disturbances between the jinn and mankind. He thought it wise and for the good of his subjects to do what he did. I have carried out his wishes at any rate, as you saw. I kept his news secret as long as I could, even from you. But I think it was the will of God which wished to mock what we call our wisdom. Weak, blind termites have thwarted the plan of Solomon the Wise and Mighty.

SADUQ: It was the Lord's will likewise that the priests and men of religion should go about their work. Let us begin our rites.

FISHERMAN: I no longer have a place here.

SADUQ: Come with us . . . Why not be one of us?

FISHERMAN: No, I'm returning to my original profession.

(A commotion outside . . . strange sounds.)

SADUQ: What is this hubbub?

ASAF: No doubt it is the jinn. They have learned of Solomon's death. Let's quickly try to get the matter under control.

(Asaf and the priest Saduq leave. The fisherman has taken up his net to depart when the jinni Dahish ibn ad-Damriyat enters with a long laugh.)

FISHERMAN: Amazing . . . who let you out of the jug?

AFREET: This time it wasn't you, naturally.

FISHERMAN: I know . . . this is what Solomon expected. You have revolted and set each other free from the jugs. Isn't that what happened? Oh . . . what will you do to the earth?

AFREET (laughing): Now . . . we are free on this earth. Hear the good news, Fisherman.

FISHERMAN: What good news do you bring me?

AFREET: That I will kill you in the worst possible way. Have you forgotten that we have an old, unsettled account?

FISHERMAN: We settled up. You killed me. That ended the matter.

AFREET: When was that?

FISHERMAN: When you took my meek spirit and simple life into your hands and made of them what you wished . . .

AFREET: But you had second thoughts, escaped from my hand, and agreed to my imprisonment.

FISHERMAN: Because wisdom returned to my soul.

AFREET: Cease your stupidity and listen to me. I am free now . . . free from all bonds, with no master or work. What would you say to my making you king over this people and marrying you to your beloved today. She is one of Solomon's widows. I'll open the treasures for you and bestow glory and power on you.

(The fisherman does not reply.)

AFREET: Why are you looking at me this way?

FISHERMAN: Ah, if I were able to imprison you in this net of mine.

AFREET: Simpleton, this was made to imprison your little soul . . . Go.

FISHERMAN (moving): I'm going.

AFREET: Go off with your failure.

FISHERMAN (stopping): Could you tell me, Jinni, of what use are all these things with which you tempt me? Solomon possessed them all. Weren't the treasures of the earth his? Didn't he have power and glory? Did he not wed innumerable women? In spite of that, all this fell as though it had never existed before one small word: a 'no' sketched on the lips of one woman. Do not try to tempt me after today with a human being's ability. Whenever we go too far in deceiving ourselves about our capacities, Heaven makes us an object of ridicule and mockery. This has happened to Solomon now. Termites which scurry along the ground have overwhelmed his majesty and played havoc with his might. He has toppled with his termite-riddled staff. Jinni, there is nothing left to dazzle me or tempt me . . . not even wisdom itself. The day a wise man is filled with a sense of his own wisdom is the day closest to the time the cloak is stripped off his ludicrous stupidity. You speak of my failure . . .

but the only day I felt true failure was the day I met you. For the bitterness of the failure corresponds to the height of the aspirations. As the capacity becomes great, the humiliation of failure becomes enormous.

AFREET: I acknowledge that I don't understand you, for I am unaccustomed to thinking of anything except triumph and victory. How sweet is the intoxication of success. It makes one forget everything else. It makes up for everything one gives to attain it.

FISHERMAN: In any case, it is an intoxication . . . that is a drunkenness, stupor, and deception.

AFREET: Don't make fun of my words. Don't you yourself try to tempt me with your ambitionless wisdom. You won't weaken my resolve with nonsense like this.

FISHERMAN: I will tempt you just as you tempt me, deceive you just as you deceive me, and join issue with you just as you do with me.

AFREET: How strange . . . I thought I had only to contend with Solomon, and Solomon has died.

FISHERMAN: He died, but the seed of wisdom in Solomon did not die. Here I am before you, contending with you. Prepare then . . . for the war between us will be drawn out.

AFREET: For how long, Fisherman?

FISHERMAN (smiling): To the end of the centuries and generations.

AFREET: Until we meet again then.

FISHERMAN: If you wish to meet me, you know my spot. I hope I won't see you again in my net inside a jug.

AFREET (smiling): You will find me inside a pearl in the belly of a fish. I will never give up on you . . .

(The mournful beating of a drum is heard. An imposing procession enters headed by Saduq and the other priests, Asaf ibn Barkhiya, and the attendants. Their heads are bowed. The covering is removed from Solomon's body which is borne aloft. The procession goes out to the beating of drums in an awesome silence.)

Notes

1 Qur'an, 27:18.
2 Qur'an, 27:40.
3 Qur'an, 27:21.
4 Qur'an, 27:23.

[5] I Kings, 4:21.

[6] I Kings, 3:16-27.

[7] Qur'an, 27:33.

[8] I Kings, 10:27.

[9] I Kings, 4:26, 10:26.

[10] cf. I Kings, 11:1-3.

[11] Qur'an, 27:40.

[12] I Kings, 3:5-14.

[13] cf. Qur'an, 27:42.

[14] cf. Qur'an, 34:12, 27:44.

[15] The Song of Songs, 1:2-3; [16] 3:1; [17] 1:15; [18] 2:2; [19] 6:4-5; 6:8-9; [20] 2:16, 6:3; [21] 5:2-6; [22] 4:10-14; [23] 4:1; [24] 7:4, 7:3-9; [25] 7:9; [26] 8:6; [27] 5:8-16.

[28] cf. Qur'an, 34:14.

King Oedipus

Characters

ANTIGONE
JOCASTA
OEDIPUS
A VOICE from the crowd of Thebans
HIGH PRIEST of Thebes
TEIRESIAS
CREON
A THEBAN who returns with the herdsman
A HERDSMAN from Thebes
AN OLD MAN from Corinth
A SERVANT from Thebes
CHORUS OF THEBANS
ANTIGONE'S YOUNGER SISTER AND TWO YOUNGER BROTHERS
PEOPLE OF THEBES
TEIRESIAS' SERVANT BOY

Act One

King Oedipus is leaning against one of the columns of the hall of his palace. He is motionless, like a statue, and looks long and thoughtfully at the city beyond the spacious balcony. Queen Jocasta appears surrounded by her four young children. She is gesturing to them to slow down and walk quietly. Meanwhile Antigone, the eldest, whispers to her mother.

ANTIGONE *(whispering while looking at Oedipus):* Mother! Why is he looking at the city this way?

JOCASTA: You go to him, Antigone. Cheer him up, for he always listens to you.

ANTIGONE *(approaching him gently):* Father! What are you thinking about, alone like this?

OEDIPUS *(turning towards her):* Is it you, Antigone? *(He sees the Queen and the other children.)* And you, Jocasta? . . . All of you here around me. What brings you now?

JOCASTA: This worry oppressing you, Oedipus . . . Don't tell us it's the plague which has settled on the city. For you have no way to repel it. You have done what you could. You hastened to seek out Teiresias so he could advise you of any inspiration he had gathered from his knowledge of the human sciences and secrets of the unknown. Why then do you remain downcast like this for so long?

OEDIPUS: The ordeal of Thebes . . . This city which entrusted its destiny to me . . .

JOCASTA: No, Oedipus! It is not simply the city's ordeal . . . I know you as I know myself. There's another reason . . . There's a disturbance in your soul. I see its traces in your eyes.

OEDIPUS: A disturbance the cause of which I don't know . . . It's as though some powerful evil were lying in wait for me.

JOCASTA: Don't say that! It's nothing but the people's pains reflecting their specter on your pure soul. We are your family, Oedipus. It is our duty now to cheer you up. Here we go, Children! Come round your father and disperse these dark clouds from his head and heart.

ANTIGONE: Father! Let me ask you something you mustn't refuse. Tell us the story of that beast you killed long ago.

OEDIPUS: I suspect, Jocasta, that you're the one who inspires your children to ask me that always. They have heard that story from me many times.

JOCASTA: Why does that trouble you, Oedipus? In any case, it is a page from your life that it is right for our children to know thoroughly. Every father is a hero in his children's eyes. So why not you, when you are a true hero in the eyes of all of Thebes. Despite that, rest assured that your children are the ones who yearn to hear that from you all the time. Look at their eager eyes and bated breath.

ANTIGONE: Yes, Father. Tell us how you defeated the beast.

OEDIPUS: Do you really want that, Antigone? Haven't you tired of it yet? . . . and your sister and brothers?

ANTIGONE *(shaking her head with the others in the negative):* We shall never tire of it.

OEDIPUS *(taking a seat with his children around him):* Then listen . . . That was twenty years ago . . .

JOCASTA *(sitting down near him):* Seventeen years ago, so far as I recall . . .

OEDIPUS: Yes, you're right. That day as I approached the walls of Thebes, it happened that . . .

ANTIGONE: From the beginning, Father! Tell it to us from the beginning.

OEDIPUS: That has no relationship to the incident with the beast. Nevertheless, let it be the way you wish . . . You know that I grew up, like you, in a royal palace. Like you, I found love and affection in the care of a generous father—King Polybus—and an affectionate mother—Queen Merope. They raised and educated me like a prince until I became a strong, sturdy, intelligent youth. I was proficient in horsemanship and was wild about knowledge. Yes, Antigone, I had the glow your eyes have. I loved to investigate the realities of things. Then one evening, I learned from an old man in the palace whose tongue was loosened by wine that I was not the son of the king and queen. They had never had a child. I was, rather, a foundling they had adopted. From that hour, I never had a moment's rest and never ceased thinking about the truth of my origin. I departed from that land. I wandered aimless in search of my reality until my travels brought me to the walls of Thebes.

ANTIGONE: And here you met the beast.

OEDIPUS: Yes, Daughter. It was a terrifying beast . . . a lion.

JOCASTA: With a woman's face!

ANTIGONE: And the wings of an eagle. You always forget, Father, to tell us about its wings.

OEDIPUS: Yes! . . . yes. It had wings like an eagle. It advanced against me from the forest.

ANTIGONE: Walking or flying?

OEDIPUS: Walking like a bird . . . It opened its mouth . . .

ANTIGONE: And posed you the riddle.

OEDIPUS: Yes, before eating me, it cast me a riddle . . . that riddle it is said it used to pose to any of the Thebans it met . . .

JOCASTA: And none of them was able to solve it! Then it would assault them and kill them immediately. Thus it devastated a great number of the people in the city. Indeed, Oedipus, the people of Thebes continued for a time to avoid remaining on outside the walls till sunset for fear of meeting the beast. They called it "Father of Terror." It frightened people for a long time. My husband, King Laius, had died shortly before and left me in the prime of life to live in this cold palace. I was trembling with fright from the rumors spread in the city about Father Terror and his victims. My brother Creon was at that time the regent. He was not able to repel the disaster. The people rioted asking protection from that danger. Then he did not hesitate to announce his wish that the city's throne be bestowed on the person who rescued it from the beast.

OEDIPUS: Not just the throne, Jocasta. There was another reward even more precious . . . the hand of the widowed queen. I knew none of all this when I met the beast. If I had known that lovely prize awaiting, I wonder what I would have done . . . Perhaps my heart would have been in turmoil, my hand would have trembled, and I would not have been victorious.

ANTIGONE: How did the beast die?

JOCASTA: When your father solved the riddle which no one else could, Father Terror was enraged and threw himself into the sea. At that time I was here in my palace listening to what people had to say about that riddle the beast posed its victims. I didn't know what it was, for no one before your father had returned alive to us to tell us about it. I won't conceal from you, Oedipus, now that at that time I too was posing myself a question, rather, a riddle: who do you suppose the victor will be? Will I love him? For a long time I cried out from the depths of my soul in the still of the night: who will be the winner? . . . not over the beast . . . but of my heart . . . my heart which had not yet known love—despite my early marriage to the good king Laius. But when I saw you, Oedipus, and loved you, I perceived that my riddle had also been solved.

ANTIGONE: How did Father Terror present his riddle to you, Father?

OEDIPUS: He said to me when he had ruffled his wing feathers: "You who approach, what have you come to do here?" I told him, "I have come to search out my reality." He said, "I have a question for you. If you are unable to answer it, I will devour you. What animal walks in the morning on four feet, at noon on two, and in the evening on three?"

ANTIGONE: Don't you answer, Father. Let me solve the riddle today in your place. You answered it in this way: "Beast, you have frightened the city, but you will not conquer me. That animal you ask me about is man! When young he crawls on all fours. When adult he walks upright on his two feet. In old age, he hobbles on his feet and stick."

OEDIPUS: The answer, as you see, is obvious, Antigone. I am amazed that so many people failed to get it. Perhaps we may contain many answers to our questions without knowing or seeing . . .

JOCASTA: Perhaps the beast wanted to make fun of man who does not see himself. But you, Oedipus, saw and answered. In this way, you disheartened the beast, silenced him, and threw him into the sea. You entered Thebes. You found it ready to welcome you, to seat you on its throne, and to bestow on you the hand of its queen. Thus you came to me and lived with me. You fathered these fine, handsome offspring and gave us this happiness.

OEDIPUS: Yes, this happiness which pervaded me and made me forget my reason for setting out and the object of my search.

JOCASTA: Your reality? Of what importance to us is this reality? . . . so long as we're happy! I've told you often not to think that I would prefer you to be a descendant of kings. I and our children are proud that you are instead from the elite of heroes. For this reason, I like you to narrate your heroism to our young ones and to give them your lesson on every occasion. Indeed, I shan't deny that I too always love to hear this story from you. It reminds me of those moments when my heart was awaiting you, anxiously, trembling, not knowing whether you would win its key or whether it should throw itself into a sea of oblivion. Oedipus! My husband! It seems I—and you too—were destined to have complete and unsullied happiness. I had a child by Laius. But no doubt god desired happiness for us and inspired him to repudiate this child, since he would have become an ill omen for him. He handed him over after his birth to someone to kill him on the mountain. Thus there is no phantom to rise between us and spoil your happiness . . . Oedipus! What's troubling you? The dark cloud has returned to settle on your face.

OEDIPUS: My anxiety is for this people in their ordeal. I trembled when you mentioned the word 'happiness' . . . I sense something. This word frightens me now . . . Listen! What is this sound?

(Jocasta and the children turn to the balcony.)

ANTIGONE: They are coming down from the hills, crowding the streets, carrying branches . . .

JOCASTA: Yes, Oedipus! . . . It's the people of Thebes, coming to you, no doubt, bearing branches in supplication.

(Oedipus silently looks from the balcony surrounded by his family.)

THEBANS *(outside shouting):* O King Oedipus! . . . King Oedipus!

VOICE *(from the crowd outside):* O you who are king, sitting on the throne of Thebes! You see the throngs of your people, men and women, young and old, rushing to throw themselves at your portal's threshold, raising in their hands the branches of supplication which quiver over their weakened bodies. Misfortune has stormed through the city as you can see with your eyes. Death afflicts the herds in the pastures and strikes children at random in their cradles. The plague is harvesting spirits throughout your realm and spreading destruction. It mocks our bloodied hearts and our flowing tears . . . Oedipus! You who rescued this city from Father Terror, rescue it today from this plague. The people who proclaimed you a hero and seated you on the throne of this nation—so you would protect it from tribulations—now demands that you act to aid it and rise to its succor.

OEDIPUS: My wretched people! I am not oblivious to your pains nor unaware. I am deeply hurt by your plight. I have not forgotten that you raised me to this throne to protect you and that you expect action from me to save you. So let me have time to think, to plan, and to act.

VOICE *(from outside):* O King, seek an oracle from god. Here is the High Priest entering your palace. Listen to him.

(Oedipus and his family turn to the door of the chamber and see the High Priest entering.)

PRIEST: Oedipus! I have come to say one thing to you and then depart. Your people are falling around you like leaves from the tree. If no leaf has yet fallen from your branch, this should, we think, not prevent your concern for the state of others. But concern alone is not enough. The matter, as you see, cannot be helped by solving riddles or by finding the answers for enigmas. Nothing will deliver us save a return to god.

OEDIPUS: And do I prevent you from returning to god?

PRIEST: You don't prevent us . . . You can't, but you are always investigating what you ought not and always asking questions which you should not pose . . . Heavenly revelation is for you a subject for scrutiny and exploration.

OEDIPUS: If only I were able to free myself from my nature . . .

PRIEST: There is no need of that for you or for us. We have sought another to go to the temple at Delphi to ask god's guidance in what is right for us to do to lift this wrath from us.

OEDIPUS: Who is this man you have dispatched?

PRIEST: He is Creon!

JOCASTA: My brother?

PRIEST: He is, as we all know, a man who does not debate reality nor dispute actuality. He will not say to the priests in the temple at Delphi: furnish me tangible evidence that this oracle truly came down to you from god and did not originate in your minds.

OEDIPUS: I am happy that Creon has your confidence, but I have not yet understood what you came to ask of me . . .

PRIEST: Creon will no doubt return soon. If he brings a command from the temple, are you ready, Oedipus, to carry out this command to save the city?

OEDIPUS: Now I understand . . . *(after a moment's thought)* I can answer you, High Priest . . . I shall not hesitate to carry out whatever can help save the city.

PRIEST: I am going then, to return to you with Creon and the heavenly oracle he brings.

(The High Priest leaves. Oedipus and his family remain, silent.)

JOCASTA *(after a moment):* Mercy on us, O Heaven. I'm . . . afraid.

OEDIPUS: Don't be afraid . . . I'm not afraid. Nothing would truly frighten me unless I saw danger threatening you and our children . . . As for the prattle of these priests . . .

JOCASTA: Don't say that, Oedipus! Don't say that in front of our children. You should know that I owe my happiness to god.

OEDIPUS: Are you sure of that?

JOCASTA: Put aside these ill-omened questions . . . You are no longer sure of anything since you learned you were a foundling. It was a shock to you. You grew up with loving parents. You never doubted that they were your parents. When the veil was suddenly lifted for you to reveal as counterfeit what you thought reality, your confidence in things was destroyed.

OEDIPUS *(turning to the balcony):* Hush . . . What's this commotion?

THEBANS *(outside shouting):* O King Oedipus! . . . King Oedipus!

VOICE *(outside among the people):* This is Teiresias who has come. Seek his advice. He may give you a message from the heavens.

(The blind Teiresias enters. A boy leads him.)

TEIRESIAS: You sent for me, Oedipus?

OEDIPUS: Yes!

TEIRESIAS *(letting go the boy's hand and motioning to him to leave):* Are we alone?

(Jocasta leads the children out.)

OEDIPUS *(on seeing the chamber empty):* Now we are alone.

TEIRESIAS: I know without needing divine revelation your reason for summoning me. I can read your soul. The people demand that you save them. It is not only a cure for the plague which arouses your concern . . . it is the danger rising round you . . . The priests don't like your way of thinking. They are disturbed by your mentality. They are comfortable with a person like Creon. The situation in Thebes today is one which could alarm a king. It is propitious for a revolt. For every trial which shakes the masses shakes at the very same time the props of the throne.

OEDIPUS: Do you think Creon can overcome the plague the way I overcame the beast?

TEIRESIAS: Who knows? Creon went to seek an oracle. He will soon return with the command vouchsafed him.

OEDIPUS: And you, Teiresias . . . whom the people believe acquainted with the human sciences and privy to heaven's secrets . . . Have you no remedy to bring an end to this ordeal which afflicts people?

TEIRESIAS: I have grown old . . . It is proper for me to watch what happens from a distance. Proceed on your way alone, Oedipus.

OEDIPUS: You wish to rid yourself of me now that you see danger advancing on me and know the circumstances which will endanger my sovereignty.

TEIRESIAS: Oedipus, you have will, a strong hand, and a clear eye. What do you want from an old man like me who is feeble and blind?

OEDIPUS: I perceive what is behind your words . . . I know you, Teiresias! A person like you does not withdraw his hand from what is around him without a reason.

TEIRESIAS: I am withdrawing my hand this time in order to see what will happen.

OEDIPUS: To see me fall the way you saw me rise?

TEIRESIAS: It is a great enjoyment for me to see what will happen when I leave matters to the hand of fate.

OEDIPUS: You will not have a chance to enjoy this, Teiresias. I know how to spoil your plan for you. You think you have the reins of my throne in your hand, but your veil is in mine. I will tear it away in front of the people and disclose your true countenance whenever I wish.

TEIRESIAS: Not so fast, Oedipus. Don't let anger make you lose course.

OEDIPUS: Be confident that I shall not allow you to trifle with me. Indeed, I am quite capable of having the people trifle with you.

TEIRESIAS: What can you tell the people?

OEDIPUS: Everything, Teiresias . . . everything! I don't fear the truth . . . Indeed, I am looking forward to the day when I can free myself of that great lie I have been living for seventeen years.

TEIRESIAS: Don't be insane!

OEDIPUS: I may go insane any moment, open the gates of this palace, and go out to the people shouting: listen, Citizens of Thebes! Hear the story of a blind man who wished to mock you and of a well-intentioned man with no ulterior motive who joined him in the farce . . . I am not a hero. I never met a beast with the body of a lion, wings of an eagle, and a woman's face which posed riddles. It is your naive imagination which liked this picture and made popular this image. What I actually met was an ordinary lion which was preying on people who tarried outside your walls. I was able to kill it with my cudgel, throw its body into the sea, and rid you of it. But Teiresias, this brilliant blind man, inspired you— for his own purposes, not for god's sake—to appoint that hero your king. Yes! He's the one who desired that and planned it. He is the one who taught me the solution for that puzzle about the animal that crawls on its hands and feet . . .

TEIRESIAS: Hush! Hush . . . lower your voice!

OEDIPUS: He is the one who in former times inspired Laius to kill his son in the cradle by leading his father to believe that it was heaven which revealed to him that the child would kill his father if he grew up. For

Teiresias, this dangerous blind man, resolved with a will of iron to deprive the throne of Thebes of its legitimate heir. He wished the throne to go to a foreigner. What he wished has come to pass.

TEIRESIAS: I told you to lower your voice, Oedipus.

OEDIPUS: Yes . . . This is Teiresias . . . who has had you believe that he can read the unknown mysteries and hear heavenly voices, while he hears nothing in reality but the voice of his will and peruses nothing but the lines of his scheme and plan. He wished—and was proud of it—to change the course of events, to change the established system of inheritance, and to challenge the will of heaven which had produced a son and heir for Laius. He did that in order to put on the throne with his mortal hand a person who was the offspring of his head and the product of his thought.

TEIRESIAS: Calm yourself, Oedipus . . . The soul's storms extinguish the intellect's lamp.

OEDIPUS: You know now what I can do to you?

TEIRESIAS: And to yourself?

OEDIPUS: I have no fear of the truth for myself . . . even if it casts me off the throne. You know that sovereignty is not my goal. I was in Corinth, my cradle where I grew up in the arms of the excellent Polybus and the compassionate Merope. Their sole aim was to convince the people that I was their son and to put me on their throne. But I fled from that kingship to search for the truth of my origin. I fled from Corinth, because I could not bear to live a lie. I came here . . . only to live a greater lie.

TEIRESIAS: Perhaps the lie is the natural atmosphere for your life . . .

OEDIPUS: And your life too, Teiresias.

TEIRESIAS: And my life too . . . and the life of every human being. Don't forget you're the hero of this city. For Thebes needs a hero. It believed in the story of Father Terror! Beware of depriving the people of their myth.

OEDIPUS: Nothing forces me to keep silent except my fear of depriving my wife and children of their belief in my heroism . . . And nothing causes me such pain as being forced into this lengthy lie with them. I force myself not to shout to them when they are reciting before me the story of Father Terror: don't believe this nonsense! The truth, my children, is . .

TEIRESIAS: Beware, Oedipus! . . . Beware! My great fear is that your reckless fingers will trifle with the veil of Truth and that your trembling fingertips will come too close to her face and eyes . . . You fled from Corinth, roaming in pursuit of her, but she escaped from you. You came to Thebes announcing you lacked origin or lineage in order to display her to the people. She drew away from you. Leave Truth alone, Oedipus . . . Don't challenge her!

OEDIPUS: Why do *you* challenge heaven, Teiresias? Do you suppose you are of a stronger fiber, are more resolute and sharper-eyed than I?

TEIRESIAS: I am not sharper-eyed than you, Oedipus . . . I see nothing. And I see no god in existence save our volition. I willed and to that extent was divine . . . I truly compelled Thebes to accept the king I wished for it. I got what I wished for. As you see . . .

OEDIPUS (in a sarcastic tone): Lower your voice, Teiresias!

TEIRESIAS: Don't make fun of me . . . and don't presume—if your determination to execute your threat is real—that I am incapable of confronting the people. Open your gates, if you wish. Go to your people and raise your voice with whatever you wish. Then you will know what Teiresias has to say!

OEDIPUS: What will you say?

TEIRESIAS: I will shout at the top of my voice: People! I have not imposed my will on you for any glory I covet but for an idea I believe in: that you have a will . . . It was not because of hatred between me and Laius or antagonism between me and Creon . . . rather I wished to turn the page on the hereditary monarchy of this ancient family, to make you the ones who choose your king from a wide spectrum, without regard to descent and lineage, with nothing to recommend him except his service to you and with no title for him other than his heroism for you. Thus there exists in your land only your will. That's all that should exist.

OEDIPUS: And what of your will, you brilliant blind man! You know the people find no pleasure in having a will. The day they have it in hand, they hasten to give it to a hero their legends have contrived or to a god enveloped in the clouds of their dreams. It seems to be too much for them to bear. They are not strong enough to preserve it and wish to be free of it to cast aside its burden. But you are a man blinded by delusion. You don't truly strive for public glory. You want, however, to be the fountainhead of events, the source of upheavals, the motive force changing and replacing human destinies and natural elements. I see in you this cloaked presumption. I read in your soul this hidden conceit.

TEIRESIAS: I have a right to boast a little, Oedipus . . . You don't deny that I have succeeded. That you are on the throne is nothing other than a manifestation of my will.

OEDIPUS: I am tired of hearing that from you. I summoned you to hear your opinion of this ordeal, not the hymn of your glory. I am not clear about your position with me . . . Are you with me? Have you turned against me? I don't see the grounds on which you have founded your will.

TEIRESIAS: You will learn that at the appropriate time, Oedipus.

OEDIPUS: When?

TEIRESIAS: When Creon arrives with that oracle from the temple at Delphi. I am well advised to learn something of the will of heaven before proceeding to form my will.

OEDIPUS: Am I able to rely on your support, Teiresias?

TEIRESIAS: It would be stupid, Oedipus, to fear anything from me.

OEDIPUS: Let's await then what Creon will bring . . .

TEIRESIAS: Let me go now . . . until it is time for action. At this hour I will say to you only: confront your destiny, Oedipus! Don't be afraid . . . I am with you!

OEDIPUS: Are you confident, Teiresias?

TEIRESIAS: Where is the boy who leads me?

OEDIPUS *(as though addressing himself)*: My destiny? . . . What is my destiny?

TEIRESIAS: Where's the boy?

(Oedipus goes to the door and opens it. The boy enters. He leads Teiresias out. Oedipus remains alone, leaning his head against a pillar, downcast. It is not long before Jocasta enters by herself.)

JOCASTA *(searching the chamber with her eyes)*: The prophet Teiresias has departed?

OEDIPUS *(turning to her)*: Yes!

JOCASTA: Perhaps he has told you how to drive away this affliction and end this ordeal . . .

OEDIPUS *(speaking to himself)*: I must not rely on anything but this hand of mine . . . This hand which knows how to deal harshly with anyone who threatens evil to you or me . . . whether a beast, a person . . . or a god!

JOCASTA: Don't scorn god, Oedipus! You owe our happiness to him . . . It's not possible he would wish you harm. He is the one who led you from Corinth to this place where you found me and where we have lived in contentment producing these dutiful children.

OEDIPUS: I no longer see anything in the fog surrounding me. I know only that a disaster threatens me . . . From what direction? I don't know! From what hand? I don't know! I am like a lion in the forest which senses a snare set near it but doesn't know where it is or who set it. I am fumbling and groping like a blind man. I see nothing and no one! I merely smell the scent of danger near me . . .

JOCASTA: Your love for us, my beloved husband, is what is making you imagine this. The plague will not approach our house! It will not touch anyone of our young children! It is rather another infection which I think you are doubtless giving me . . . that anxiety disturbing your peace of mind. I, too, Oedipus, am filled by that alarming foreboding. I almost feel as if there were something coarse strangling me . . . here around my neck. I can hardly breathe. I sense a dark melancholy in which my soul sinks like a corpse into the darkness of the tomb.

OEDIPUS: Hush! Don't mention death, Jocasta.

JOCASTA: Do you see how my depression distresses you just as your anxiety and concern distress me? It would be good, Oedipus, for us to banish these ghosts from us. It is no doubt the atmosphere of this city, heavy with suffering, which has spread these dark, gloomy clouds through our souls . . .

OEDIPUS: Perhaps . . .

JOCASTA: Whatever the case is, it's our duty to be resolute and to pretend to be joyful for the sake of our children.

OEDIPUS: Yes! . . . Where's Antigone?

JOCASTA: This girl, Oedipus, believes in you more than you do yourself. I left her just now telling the other children that you will no doubt vanquish the plague the same way you did Father Terror, because god did not put you on this throne in vain. . .

OEDIPUS *(in almost a whisper):* My dear daughter!

JOCASTA: She believes that her destiny is bound to yours . . . For a long time she has told me that she hopes for nothing for her future except to live in the temple of your heroism and to see the world as you see it . . . to have your eyes, to see life's riddles, puzzles, and secrets with them .

OEDIPUS *(as though speaking to himself):* I hope to have her eyes to see for me the soul's tranquility, the heart's truthfulness, and existence's purity . . .

JOCASTA *(listening):* Listen, Oedipus! . . . What is this din?

THEBANS *(outside shouting):* Creon has come! . . . Creon's come!

OEDIPUS *(looking towards the balcony):* Yes! He's come . . . What do you suppose your brother has brought?

JOCASTA *(looking towards the balcony):* He must have brought good news, for he has fastened a garland of flowers to his forehead.

OEDIPUS *(at the balcony):* Here's the High Priest with him. They are making their way through the crowds of people and waving a greeting to them.

JOCASTA: They are nearing the palace gate. I shall go to allow you to devote yourselves to the city's welfare.

OEDIPUS: I have a burning desire to know what he has brought.

JOCASTA: I hope you will learn from him now something that will comfort your soul and spread peace through it. *(She departs.)*

OEDIPUS *(in a whisper):* Yes! . . . I will learn now.

(The High Priest enters with Creon.)

PRIEST: Here is Creon who has returned from the Delphi temple with a mighty oracle. I would like him to reveal it to you in private, Oedipus, if you will permit him to speak.

OEDIPUS: I am listening to him. Let him reveal to us everything he brings.

CREON: Oedipus, here's what I've learned . . . The oracle has revealed to us the secret of this anger which heaven has sent down on our land.

OEDIPUS: What is this secret? Quickly!

CREON: There is an abomination in this land which must cease. Otherwise, we are destined to perish.

OEDIPUS: What abomination?

CREON: A sin befouls Thebes which must be erased.

OEDIPUS: Explain!

CREON: Blood from our land has been shed and that must necessarily be washed away with blood.

OEDIPUS: Whose blood? . . . Who did it?

CREON: Laius! Before you came to us, we had a king named Laius.

OEDIPUS: I know! I know! . . . I know his name, but I never saw him.

CREON: This king was killed.

OEDIPUS: Killed?

CREON: The order of god is unambiguous. Justice must be done and revenge taken on the killer.

OEDIPUS: If this is all you've brought, then it's true . . . but this crime, so far as I can see, happened long ago.

CREON: It's been about seventeen years.

OEDIPUS: Will it be easy after this length of time for us to follow its tracks and lift the veil from the killer's face?

CREON: The god said: "Search and you shall find!"

OEDIPUS: I love nothing better than searching . . . my whole life is nothing but a search. So long as god—as you say—is the one ordering me now to search and investigate you will find me thoroughly obedient. Do you hear me, High Priest?

PRIEST: I have heard . . . I hope you will pursue to the end your search for the killer.

OEDIPUS: Here I begin the search, at once . . . Tell me, Creon. Where was Laius killed? Was it in his palace? Or in the city? Or outside it?

CREON: Laius had left Thebes on pilgrimage to the temple at Delphi to consult the oracle, as he said, on the matter of his son whom he had delivered up to death long before, on the command of heaven.

OEDIPUS (as though speaking to himself): On the command of heaven . . . yes . . . That poor king! . . . And then?

CREON: There isn't anything more . . . He did not return to us after that day he set forth.

OEDIPUS: Was there no witness who saw or heard anything of what happened to him?

CREON: All the witnesses were taken by death . . . except for one. He was able to escape with his skin . . . We learned only one thing from him.

OEDIPUS: What was it?

CREON: He related that a gang of thieves waylaid King Laius and killed him and his attendants.

OEDIPUS: Would thieves dare attack a king this way?

CREON: This is the account he gave us.

OEDIPUS: I don't think people like that would attack the king unless someone here had incited them to it, spurred them on, and paid them a price for that.

CREON: This is what occurred to us too at that time.

OEDIPUS: In spite of that, you did nothing to search for the killers or to disclose the hand which directed the crime?

CREON: At that time, we were preoccupied. Our attention was seized by a more alarming disaster which took us by surprise and left us sleepless.

OEDIPUS: What catastrophe is greater than the murder of your reigning king?

CREON: Father Terror had appeared at the time killing people with his riddles outside the walls of Thebes!

OEDIPUS: Yes! . . . Yes, how stupid you all are. My eye sees everything clearly now. I can almost see the person who planned all that . . . and know the hand which moved and the will which incited . . .

PRIEST: What are you saying, Oedipus? Repeat once more what your lips uttered.

OEDIPUS: What my lips uttered is no concern of yours. You are awaiting my action and seek justice . . . The killer of Laius must be presented to you, even if that is not entirely to my liking . . . Truly! . . . You are right! It had not occurred to me that the pillars of my throne are plunged in a king's blood. I wouldn't have thought that the person who wanted that would go so far as crime. I will not hesitate! Yes! Do you hear? I shall not hesitate to hand over the killer . . . not just to save Thebes but to save my conscience. High Priest! . . . Go and announce to the people that I will promptly carry out the command Creon brought. I will give them the killer.

PRIEST: Do you know, Oedipus, who the killer is?

OEDIPUS: It is not difficult for me to know now. Go at once and leave the matter to me . . . Amazing! . . . Why are you frozen to the earth like statues?

PRIEST: Are you confident that you will take vengeance on the killer of Laius?

OEDIPUS: Do you doubt that, Priest? Whatever the standing of this man among you, I will deliver him to you to receive the recompense for what his hand committed. This is my promise that I will never go back on, no matter what it costs me to be faithful to it. For everything dear to me is reduced to insignificance by this hideous crime. Who can trust—after today—a man who dared kill a king! I will tear the veil from his face and present him to justice, even if that is a curse for me and leads to my destruction.

PRIEST: Your knowledge of the criminal, Oedipus, has relieved us of a heavy burden.

OEDIPUS: What burden?

PRIEST: The burden of disclosing his name to you.

OEDIPUS: Did you too know who he was?

PRIEST: We knew . . . Creon brought his name with the oracle from the temple at Delphi.

OEDIPUS: And weren't you astonished when you learned who he was?

PRIEST: Totally astonished, Oedipus . . . for he's the last person one would have suspected.

OEDIPUS (as though speaking to himself): Yes! . . . That man of exalted standing, high status, venerated by everyone.

PRIEST: He truly is that . . . We are sad he is the one who committed an offense like this.

OEDIPUS: My sorrow is no less than yours . . . but justice is superior to any rank. The victim's blood must be washed away with the killer's. This is what heaven has commanded you, Creon, and I will obey the command.

PRIEST: We did not suppose you would obey heaven's command with such alacrity . . . Forgive us our previous suspicion of you. You are more magnanimous than we imagined . . . But, may we ask you what has kept you silent all this time about the killer?

OEDIPUS: I knew nothing of this crime until today.

PRIEST (looking at Creon): What are you saying, Oedipus?

OEDIPUS: Why are you exchanging these glances?

PRIEST: We are amazed that you could have been ignorant of it . . .

OEDIPUS: Why are you amazed?

PRIEST: Because you have the closest link to the crime's secret.

OEDIPUS: If you mean Jocasta, you can rest assured that she knows nothing of the affair. If you mean my link to the killer or the instigator of the murder, then I am astonished that you never suspected him all the time he has maintained a position of trust among you and been sought for his counsel.

PRIEST: Would you have wanted us to suspect the lofty soul without proof? . . . to accuse this high rank without a command from god or an oracle from heaven?

OEDIPUS: Now that you know the oracle from heaven and the veil has been removed from the killer's face, here is my decision. He deserves punishment for the offense. He wished to change with his hand the fates and destinies. He let nothing stand in the way of his will . . . not even conscience . . . Go to him and don't shrink back. Hurl the accusation plainly in his face, without fear of his sanctity or awe of his majesty.

PRIEST *(looking at Creon):* Will you truly permit us to do that, Oedipus?

OEDIPUS: Once again you're exchanging these looks . . . What do you think me, Priest? Do you think I'm not strong enough to execute this command? . . . And you Creon? Haven't you found me able before today to meet difficulties and with the daring to confront adversity?

CREON: No one will deny you your courage, Oedipus. You have confronted a danger that no one else among the people of Thebes could have. The victory was yours alone. But . . . not everyone is like you. You bear for us an adversity which is too great for us and ask us to accuse that lofty rank . . .

PRIEST: Truly . . . if it were possible for you to spare us this painful scene, you would do us a favor we would never forget.

OEDIPUS: You want me to take charge of the affair myself?

PRIEST: Yes!

CREON: This is no doubt the best way. The oracle of Delphi has reached you, Oedipus, and you know the killer's name has become known. Quick vengeance is the price desired to save Thebes. All that remains for you is to carry out this vengeance speedily, without clamor or commotion. Afterwards, it will be our responsibility to announce the affair to the people.

OEDIPUS: I will do this for you. It won't cost me much hardship . . . But what distresses me . . .

CREON: Your family?

OEDIPUS: My family? Of what relevance is my family here? . . . Yes . . . You're right . . . In truth, I think Jocasta believes strongly in this man. In that respect, she resembles all the people in this land . . . The echo will resound far and wide and have a great impact the day the killer's name is announced . . . But what I ask you is to remember . . .

CREON: What? . . . The effects of that, relative to the throne?

OEDIPUS: I am not thinking now of that throne, for that hand has soiled it with blood . . . Certainly not . . . Rather I want you to remember that the sinner may deny the accusation and charge those who advance it with falsehood, slander, fabrication, and falsification. He may call it a conspiracy trumped up to destroy him for personal reasons . . . It is best if you remain here. I shall summon him so that you can tell him what the oracle revealed about him . . . After that I will take care of the rest . . .

PRIEST: Who is it you will summon?

OEDIPUS: The killer of Laius . . . He's not far from this place . . . Wait! I will send for him.

PRIEST *(looking at Creon):* Oedipus!

OEDIPUS: Strange! Why do you keep exchanging these looks?

PRIEST: You know he's not far from us now . . .

OEDIPUS: Perhaps . . . He promised to come on your arrival . . . as though he knew what awaited him. He awakened doubt in me about what Creon would bring. But I won't wait for him any longer . . . He must be sought for. *(He moves.)*

PRIEST *(stopping him):* Where are you going, Oedipus? The killer of Laius is not far from us.

CREON: He is not far from this palace.

PRIEST: He is, as you know, in this palace now . . . only a step away.

OEDIPUS: In this palace now? . . . . What do you mean?

PRIEST: You know, Oedipus, what we mean and whom we mean.

OEDIPUS: The killer of Laius is in this palace?

PRIEST: And in this chamber . . . as you no doubt know.

OEDIPUS: Explain!

PRIEST: Woe! . . . Haven't you known all the time what we mean? Who besides yourself were you accusing then, Oedipus?

OEDIPUS: Besides me? . . . What's this I hear from you?

PRIEST: Strange! . . . Didn't you know that you, Oedipus, are Laius' killer?

OEDIPUS: I . . . the killer of Laius? Have you gone mad, Priest?

PRIEST: I am not mad . . . It is the oracle Creon brought from the temple at Delphi.

OEDIPUS: The oracle said I am the killer?

PRIEST: Speak, Creon!

CREON: Yes! . . . That's the truth! . . . I will relate it as I heard it without adding a word. This is the revelation from heaven . . . "Oedipus is the killer of Laius."

OEDIPUS *(racked by laughter):* I the killer? Is this credible?

PRIEST: We are truly greatly distressed . . . but . . .

OEDIPUS: When was your king, whom I never saw, killed? . . . When did I do that and where?

PRIEST: We don't know . . . We can't answer these questions. We can tell you only what the oracle revealed to us.

OEDIPUS: Whose oracle? . . . Creon's oracle or an oracle from you religious men?

PRIEST: What are you saying, Oedipus?

OEDIPUS: Here's a trick which has been uncovered! . . . a riddle disclosed in the land of puzzles and riddles! . . . How stupid you are! Not one of you can even devise an adequate trap.

PRIEST: Don't overdo this kind of talk, Oedipus!

OEDIPUS: Hush! I see the affair now as plain as day. The veil has truly been lifted . . . not from the face of a killer and a crime but from the face of a conspiracy and of conspirators. You must not think, Creon, and you, High Priest, that I am so dull-witted that I will fall into a trap like this which would not catch even small birds. I am not so weak as to be incapable of punishing you and all those who support you, openly or clandestinely, with every type of punishment.

PRIEST: Not so fast, Oedipus!

OEDIPUS: I have not yet shown you I am fit to be called a hero. My victory over a beast will not compare with that fortitude with which I shall conquer the traitors.

CREON: Who are these traitors?

OEDIPUS: You are at their head, Creon! . . . You who covet my throne. These priests have misled you, but I shall make you all the laughingstock of the people.

CREON: That's enough, Oedipus! I refuse to let you call me a traitor. Remember I am your wife's brother . . . I would never harm you nor would I harm Jocasta for the sake of ambition . . . Sovereignty was in my hand before you came to us. I released it to you for the sake of the people's welfare and in obedience to the counsel of the holy and inspired.

OEDIPUS: And today you attack me pleading the people's salvation again as well as obedience to the counsel of those men of religion who love you.

PRIEST: Don't speak blindly, Oedipus! The men of religion know that god's hand raises and lowers people to royal thrones. It is not for human hands to do. We would not have come to you on this grave matter had we not known that our god cursed this land. He inspired us to root out its causes and dispel his anger from us. You yourself promised to aid us and execute god's command. We who have brought it to you are racked by pain and distress. You ought to have received heaven's will submissively. You ought not hurl your thunder and lightning at us, in an attempt to hide the voice of truth which has come down from on high.

OEDIPUS: The voice of truth? What is the voice of truth? Is it what you hear and I don't? Don't I have two ears on my head like you?

PRIEST: The voice of truth, Oedipus, is not heard by the ear or the head . . . but by the heart!

OEDIPUS: Yes! . . . With words like these, Priest, you wish to make me feel I am far removed from your heaven . . . that I am subject to its curse and the object of its anger . . . It afflicted this land with the plague merely because I am dwelling here . . . Why am I cursed by god? Is it because I do not accept what you attribute to him until after an inquiry which satisfies my intellect? If you said that, if you dared, you would find no objection from me. But you say something that corresponds to your obvious scheme. You say I am cursed by heaven, because I killed Laius . . . That the blood which soiled Thebes and brought the plague can only be washed away by the killer's blood . . . What a conspiracy! What a conspiracy it is!

PRIEST: Anger, no doubt, has blinded you, Oedipus! We have passed on to you what the oracle revealed. Make your plans accordingly.

OEDIPUS: The matter does not require lengthy planning.

PRIEST: You have all the time you wish . . . We have nothing left to do but depart.

OEDIPUS: Depart? . . . Do you think a person who says what you have said today can depart in peace?

PRIEST: What do you mean, Oedipus?

OEDIPUS: Priest! You don't know the Oedipus yet whom you dared term a murderer. You claimed he had defiled the earth of Thebes with blood. You will not depart in peace, Priest . . . nor you, Creon!

CREON: Oedipus!

PRIEST: We won't depart in peace?

OEDIPUS: You have only two roads by which you can depart. Choose between death and banishment.

PRIEST and CREON *(shouting):* Death or banishment!

OEDIPUS: There is no punishment for a traitor who conspires against the sovereign except death, but I grant you the choice, out of compassion for you . . . Discretion would dictate I be firm and pluck you from life by the roots like rank, stinking weeds which disperse around them anarchy and corruption. I have given my verdict on you: banishment or death . . . Banishment or death!

Act Two

The square in front of the palace . . . A chorus of the people is assembled. Oedipus, the priest, and Creon stand before them as though appearing before a court.

OEDIPUS: People of Thebes! You have before you now a crime against my person and throne committed by these two conspirators. I have pronounced a sentence on them which I think just . . . But I will not carry out my verdict until I mount an investigation of their offense in your presence. I would not like to be blinded to truth by anger. I shall now disclose the face of truth to you so you can see the criminals barefaced.

CHORUS: Who would have thought, Oedipus, that Creon and the High Priest would conspire against you?

OEDIPUS: You in your simplicity, Citizens, do not see what is fabricated in the dark . . . but I will tear aside the curtain for you at this moment so you can see in the light those sinful hands which wished to defile your throne with sin and blood.

CHORUS: Woe to anyone who would harm a single one of your hairs, King. We shall never forget that you are the hero who saved us from Father Terror . . . Strike down your enemies, Oedipus, without mercy . . . We are with you.

PRIEST: How skillful you are, Oedipus, in rallying the people against us . . . and in presenting us as criminals, when our only crime is that we told you the command revealed by heaven to free Thebes of this plague.

OEDIPUS: Do you persist, Treacherous Priest, in terming this conspiracy an oracle from heaven?

PRIEST: Don't get angry, Oedipus! You are the one who just said that you don't want anger to blind you to the truth. Hold firm to prudence, seek the aid of patience and proceed with the inquiry you promised. Do it quickly to keep the people from thinking about the misery they are suffering.

OEDIPUS *(to the chorus):* People, do you actually think I am trying to distract you with this inquiry from the torment you suffer?

CHORUS: Proceed, Oedipus, with what you have begun. Strip back the curtain for us. We are eager to see what is behind these affairs.

OEDIPUS: Do you see, Sinful Priest, how your arrow has missed its target? . . . This is the will of the people.

PRIEST: How naive they truly are, these people! Yes, these people who are nourished by imagination not by realities! They have forgotten the plague annihilating them. They have forgotten that you have found no remedy to save them. They have forgotten heaven's oracle which they were awaiting. They remember only their desire to see the phantoms you claim to reveal.

OEDIPUS: Don't scorn the people, Priest! You are appearing before their court. They are the ones who will find you guilty and support my punishment for you when they see your crime laid bare after I have stripped you of your secret.

PRIEST: Do it, Oedipus, and quickly . . . You are still the hero who fascinates people by disclosing secrets and solving riddles. But the people will learn that I conceal no secret and harbor no riddle. I merely sought in good faith to ask god's aid in dispelling this plague from our land. I have informed you of the oracle . . . That is my entire offense against you.

OEDIPUS: Not at all, Priest! You know your crime just as Creon knows his . . . and those who support you covertly . . . I shall not undertake its presentation to the people. Rather, I leave you that honor, so it won't be said I reported it incorrectly or distorted it intentionally . . . You tell your story, Priest . . . or let your accomplice speak.

(Queen Jocasta comes out of the palace.)

CHORUS *(turning):* Queen Jocasta!

JOCASTA: May I attend this trial? The accusation you advance against these two men is grave, Oedipus.

CREON: Do you believe, Jocasta, that your brother Creon would covet your husband's throne?

OEDIPUS: It is not I, Jocasta, who will try your brother but the people. I am only a man who has undertaken the investigation into the crime. You will see now with your own eyes, just as the people around you will see, what the inquiry discloses.

CREON: We have already been sentenced to death or banishment!

OEDIPUS: I will never be satisfied with less than this penalty for those who conspire against the throne . . . This conspiracy, had it been concluded, would have had among its consequences my death or banishment.

JOCASTA: The evidence will have to be damning, Oedipus, before you carry out this harsh sentence on them.

OEDIPUS: Here is the inquiry, conducted in public before you, Jocasta, and before all the people. In it I will go to the pits and delve the depths to extract for you at the end of the affair the manifest and unambiguous truth.

CHORUS: Proceed with your work, Oedipus . . . You are the person best able to remove the cover from the secret of things.

OEDIPUS: I would like the hearing to take place with Teiresias present. I know his standing with you. I sent for him before coming out to you.

CHORUS: You did well, Oedipus. The presence of this blessed elder among us at this hour will certainly increase our peace of mind.

JOCASTA: No one so wishes for peace of mind as I do . . . for I of all people know Creon best. He is my brother with whom I grew up. His upright character, his even temper, and his clear conscience all combine to make my soul amazed by his deed . . . I have not yet learned how he conspired against the throne. All I've heard is that he is accused of this crime. But I don't know how he came to that.

OEDIPUS: You will learn now . . . not from my mouth, but from his!

(Teiresias appears led by his servant boy.)

CHORUS: Here's Teiresias who's arrived.

OEDIPUS: Make way for him!

TEIRESIAS: I know why you are gathered here . . . Beware of asking my opinion, Oedipus, or of requesting me to speak!

OEDIPUS: I shan't do it. I merely wanted you to be present at this trial, because a person like you should not be forgotten in great undertakings. Listen to what will be said now and grasp the import of these statements.

TEIRESIAS: I am listening, Oedipus.

OEDIPUS: Now, People, hear how these men conspired. I promised to let the accused state the case for the sake of justice. I will not go back on this promise. Go ahead, High Priest . . . You speak first.

PRIEST: What shall I say? . . . You have put us into this shameful situation, Oedipus. You have affixed to us the stigma of accusation. You have presented us to the people's eyes as sinning traitors before we have learned what our offense was . . . I have nothing to say except what you and the people know . . . Your outcry against that plague which has been decimating you, People of Thebes, was raised. We saw no means to repel the plague from us except to seek an oracle from heaven . . . We thought a man from the royal house, known for prudence of opinion, forthrightness, and proper conduct, should go to the temple at Delphi . . . That man was Creon, as you know. Do you see anything the matter with this action, anything untoward about it?

CHORUS: Certainly not!

PRIEST: Creon went to the temple at Delphi. Then he returned with the oracle from god concerning this plague and its cause. I did not wish to reveal it except to the king in private. We wished to confine the matter to the narrowest limits and hoped to avoid upsetting you.

CHORUS: What was the oracle Creon brought?

PRIEST: It's up to Creon to reveal it to you, if he wishes . . .

CHORUS: Speak, Creon!

CREON: It's an alarming matter! I am not entitled to announce it to you without permission from Oedipus.

OEDIPUS: I give you permission to say everything here.

CREON: Here is what I brought . . . transmitting to you the exact text: "Heaven is angry, because the earth of Thebes has been defiled by impurity . . . Its king, Laius, was killed. No revenge has yet been taken on his murderer. The anger against Thebes will not be lifted unless that blood is washed away."

CHORUS: Our King Laius was killed?

OEDIPUS: This is not the amazing part, People . . . Ask him who the killer was . . .

CHORUS: Who was the killer? . . . Who was he?

CREON: You can be sure that it pains me deeply to utter his name. When I learned for the first time, I was struck by a terror I haven't the power to describe. Oedipus has been blinded by desire and fear. He has forgotten our relationship and my place with him and in his family. He has similarly forgotten my earlier days which I spent in his support . . . and my character which would reject what he has accused me of . . . and my nature which would shy away from what he suspects I did.

CHORUS: Who killed Laius, Creon? Who's the killer?

CREON: Don't force my mouth to mention this dear name! Ask the king standing before you to tell you.

OEDIPUS: No, you speak his name yourself, Creon.

CHORUS: Tell us the killer's name, Creon.

CREON: It is . . . Oedipus.

CHORUS: This Oedipus? . . . Oedipus our king? . . . He is the killer of Laius?

JOCASTA: What do I hear from you, Creon?

CREON: This is the way the oracle came from heaven, Jocasta.

CHORUS: Oedipus is the killer? . . . The killer is Oedipus?

OEDIPUS: Do you see, People of Thebes, how the conspiracy was hatched? Can you imagine I killed Laius when I had never seen him? Don't you remember that when I came to your land your throne was vacant and his resting place unknown? But they wish me to be the killer so that I would deserve in consequence death or banishment. For they are distressed by my rule and dislike, for a reason best known to themselves, that I should remain your king.

CREON: Would I ask heaven to pour its curse on me even if I had in my soul a vile objective like this? I swear . . . I swear I added nothing to what I heard and learned by heart from the oracle of the Delphi temple.

JOCASTA: May I give my opinion about the disagreement which has arisen between you? I don't think either of you is a liar or covetous. I have no doubt that Creon heard what he reported to you, Oedipus, with pure soul and clear conscience . . . But heaven's oracle is too elevated in status for human beings to comprehend it, all the time. People rarely are able to understand the divine oracle properly . . . God's will has goals which man's mind is not able to grasp. Thus no person has complete sovereignty over the unknown or ability to prophesy. I have at hand the example of Laius. A prophecy informed him that he would die at his son's hand—his son from his loins and my belly . . . I believe Teiresias who is present remembers the story of that prophecy.

TEIRESIAS: I remember that, O Queen.

OEDIPUS (with concealed sarcasm): Indeed . . . he had better remember that!

JOCASTA: What happened after that? . . . That son perished in the cradle, for his father handed him over three days after his birth to a shepherd who carried him off with his feet bound to be destroyed on a desolate mountain. Laius met his death, as you know, outside this land. A gang of thieves, as I was informed at that time, attacked him. They killed him in a distant place at a spot where three roads meet. Thus the father died by a hand not his son's! What became of the prophecy then? The oracle, as you see, is not always borne out in all circumstances. Heaven does not whisper its words to every ear. It guards its secrets better than you suspect . . . Its language is not understood by every person . . . It prefers to reveal its intentions through actions not words. Speech is our human language . . . God's language is the deed . . . . Beware of taking what Creon brought for a proof! It is only something he heard. It should have no effect. No decision should spring from it.

OEDIPUS: I hope, Jocasta, that my ear has misheard.

JOCASTA: Why? . . . What's this anxiety on your face?

OEDIPUS: It's nothing . . . It's merely the situation no doubt . . . with the strange talk and amazing accusations stirred up, which has landed me in confusion.

JOCASTA: Be more explicit, Oedipus. Disclose what is troubling you. Do you think I said anything injurious to you, unintentionally? Many pointless words slip at times, like rabble, into the parade of ideas.

OEDIPUS: I imagined I heard you say that Laius was killed at a place where three roads met.

JOCASTA: That's true . . . That's what I said.

OEDIPUS: You said that? . . . you said that?

JOCASTA: What's come over you, Oedipus? . . . Yes. That's what I eventually learned then.

OEDIPUS: Where were those roads? . . . in what land?

JOCASTA: In a land called Phocis . . . where the road branches into two courses. One of them leads to Daulia, the other to Delphi.

OEDIPUS: At what time did that take place?

JOCASTA: Everyone knows that happened shortly before you ascended the throne.

OEDIPUS: O Heaven! Is it possible that is true?

JOCASTA: What, Oedipus? What's bothering you and causing this turmoil in your soul?

OEDIPUS: Don't ask me anything . . . Tell me what Laius looked like? How old was he?

JOCASTA: He was tall and slender with curly, grey hair . . . His face resembled yours a bit.

OEDIPUS: Do you suppose heaven's curse has truly struck me?

JOCASTA: What are you saying, my husband? . . . You frighten me.

OEDIPUS: Do you suppose there's some truth in the oracle? . . . Tell me something else too . . . so that not a shadow of doubt remains in my soul.

JOCASTA: You scare me! I will tell you everything that came to my knowledge.

OEDIPUS: What was King Laius' retinue like? . . . How many guards did he have?

JOCASTA: No more than five men guarded him on his trip . . . and a scout in advance. There was only a single carriage in which the king rode.

OEDIPUS: Enough, Jocasta! . . . My eye sees everything clearly and plainly now . . . but . . . who told you all that?

JOCASTA: A servant . . . He was the only one who returned alive from that trip.

OEDIPUS: Is he still in service here?

JOCASTA: To the contrary! He asked me to release him from the palace service when he saw you had taken his master's place and ascended his king's throne . . . So far as I know he went to the fields to work as a herdsman, far away from this city.

OEDIPUS: Can we have him brought at once?

JOCASTA: We can . . . but what do you want from that?

OEDIPUS: Oh, my dear wife! I fear I have divulged more than is fitting . . . I must see that man first.

JOCASTA: You will see him . . . but, have I not the right, Oedipus, to know what is spreading this anxiety and turmoil through your soul?

OEDIPUS: You will know . . . Send for that herdsman!

CHORUS: Let one of us set off like the wind to the fields to search out the herdsman.

(Some of the assembled people run off.)

JOCASTA: What do you wish to learn from him, Oedipus?

OEDIPUS: This herdsman is my only hope . . . I would like to hear words from him contradicting what you said.

JOCASTA: Contradictory in what respect?

OEDIPUS: You said that the killer was a gang of thieves . . . and that he is the one who told you that. I must hear his testimony to clear up this important matter. Was the killer truly a group or was he a single individual? On this testimony rests the verdict and hangs the destiny . . .

JOCASTA: Whose destiny? . . . Whose destiny, Oedipus?

OEDIPUS: Mine! . . . There's something I have concealed from you, Jocasta. Just as you concealed from me the information of the circumstances surrounding the death of King Laius.

JOCASTA: I haven't concealed anything from you . . . It did not occur to me to mention those details until there was some call for it or some motive for us to go over them. They are not a pleasant topic for me to discuss with you when there is no need.

OEDIPUS: I too have not intentionally hidden anything . . . It is just a passing incident to which I attached no importance at the time and paid little attention, because I did not know who it was I met.

JOCASTA: Whom did you meet, Oedipus?

OEDIPUS: A man in a carriage . . . guarded by about five men who blocked my way in the land of Phocis at the crossroads between Daulia and Delphi. A dispute broke out between us over the right to pass first. The dispute developed into a quarrel, and the fervor and passion of youth drove me to violence. I raised my cudgel in the men's faces, and we began to fight. I vanquished them in the battle, but it seems that a blow of my cudgel missed and struck the head of the person in the chariot. I set off afterwards on my way until I neared the walls of Thebes and met the beast. And you know what happened to me then . . . If that man in the carriage was your King Laius, then I'm the one who struck and killed him.

JOCASTA: My god! . . . my god!

OEDIPUS: But I was alone and you all said that Laius was killed by a band of thieves . . . This matter must be cleared up before I pronounce sentence on myself.

CHORUS (turning): Here's the herdsman. They've brought him.

(Some of the people who left to search for the herdsman enter. They are leading a feeble, old man.)

THEBAN (with the herdsman): We hadn't gone far when we met him on his way here. He had heard, so he said, news of the ordeal. He was coming to pray with the people of Thebes and to entreat heaven to lift this plague from our land.

CHORUS: What a decrepit old man he is!

OEDIPUS: Come near me, Man, and answer the questions I ask you . . . Were you in the service of King Laius?

HERDSMAN: Yes! . . . I was born in his household and grew up in it.

OEDIPUS: What was your employment with him?

HERDSMAN: Herding his livestock.

OEDIPUS: Do you remember how Laius was killed?

HERDSMAN: That happened a long time ago . . . and my memory has grown weak and my mind feeble . . .

OEDIPUS: Recall! Recall! . . . Who killed Laius?

HERDSMAN: He was killed . . . so far as I remember . . . by a strong-bodied youth.

OEDIPUS: How?

HERDSMAN: He jostled against the king's chariot at a crossroads between Delphi and Daulia. A quarrel broke out between him and the guards in the retinue. He conquered and killed them. One of his blows struck the king's head. It was a fatal blow and he died. I fled from the battle with my skin. No one else escaped.

OEDIPUS: Was it a group which attacked the king?

HERDSMAN: Certainly not, your Majesty! It was a single man.

OEDIPUS: Everything has become clear to me and to you all. The veil has been removed from the killer's face . . . You were right, Creon. The oracle you brought from the temple at Delphi was right. I ask your forgiveness and that of the High Priest. I have erred in my suspicion of you and by falsely accusing you . . . The killer of Laius is before you . . . People! I shall not attempt to defend him. Judge him as you see fit. Provide him the punishment he deserves.

JOCASTA: Oedipus! . . . Oedipus! Don't exaggerate this way . . . accusing yourself. You didn't intend to kill him . . . You didn't know the identity of the man you killed.

OEDIPUS: Don't defend me, Jocasta, for you are part of me. It is not right for us to undertake a defense of ourselves for the sins we have committed.

JOCASTA: If you refuse me and yourself this right, here is Teiresias to speak on your behalf.

TEIRESIAS: If you need me, Oedipus, I am not far from you.

OEDIPUS: Certainly not! . . . Rather, stay in your place, Teiresias. Don't interfere. My case is clear. I committed a crime and forgot it. But heaven did not forget it . . . Now it wants the price and demands the penalty. Whatever doubts the intellect may have about the truth of the relationship between that crime and this plague, honor does not doubt the reality of the duty cast on my shoulders. My duty now is to remove myself from the throne of a man who died by my hand.

JOCASTA: He died by your hand against your will . . . I don't think heaven demands of you this oppressive price for it.

OEDIPUS (as though addressing himself): Heaven is never unjust, for it is a set of scales which has no defect, tilt, deviation, or passion . . . When we perceive it to be unjust that is simply because of our inability to see what consciences conceal and our forgetfulness for our past account . . . It adds to the manifest sin the weight of the concealed one. I have lied to the people! I have deceived the people . . .

TEIRESIAS *(shouting and interrupting):* Enough! Enough!

(At this moment a feeble old man with a stooped back appears.)

OLD MAN *(shouting):* O People!

CHORUS *(turning):* Who is this old man coming in from the fields?

OLD MAN: Direct me to the palace of Oedipus!

CHORUS: This is the palace before you! . . . Who are you, Stranger? What do you want?

OLD MAN: I am a messenger from Corinth. I have brought a message to Oedipus.

OEDIPUS: Here I am, Man! Approach! What is your news?

OLD MAN: Happy news! . . . Although it contains something that may stir your sorrow.

OEDIPUS: Speak, Messenger! Tell us what news you bring.

OLD MAN: The people of Corinth greet you and ask you to be their King.

CHORUS: King? Over the people of Corinth?

JOCASTA: O how heaven severs and binds! . . . Do you see how unjust you are to yourself, Oedipus? You wished to vacate the throne of Thebes and here's another throne coming to you from heaven!

OEDIPUS *(to the messenger):* What has become of your King Polybus?

OLD MAN: He has died and been entrusted to the earth.

OEDIPUS: Polybus has died? . . . How? Did he die of an illness or in some incident?

OLD MAN: Of the illness of old age!

OEDIPUS: I shall never forget that he was like a compassionate father . . . What has become of Queen Merope?

OLD MAN: Age weakened her . . . and she is on her way to rejoin her husband.

OEDIPUS: She loved me too, as though she were my mother . . . What good, generous people they were . . . I remember their distress when I informed them of my discovery of the real nature of the tie binding me to them . . . that I was nothing more than a foundling they adopted . . . They exerted every effort to pluck this truth from my head. But I refused to accept their affection when it was like accepting alms . . . I hope they forgot me after I fled from Corinth and that in the course of time they found other things to think of . . .

OLD MAN: To the contrary! They did not forget you. They sent after you, at that time, someone to search for you. But you had disappeared. Polybus died mentioning your name and charging me to renew the search for you and to propose to you to be king after him.

OEDIPUS: How did you know where I am?

OLD MAN: It finally occurred to me to search for you in your birthplace. So I travelled on foot to Thebes. When I drew near its walls I learned that you are its king today.

OEDIPUS: Who said Thebes is my birthplace?

OLD MAN: I know that, because I'm the one who found you when you were an infant and handed you over to Polybus.

OEDIPUS: You found me, Old Man?

OLD MAN: On a wooded mountain near Cithaeron.

OEDIPUS: What were you doing there?

OLD MAN: I was herding livestock.

OEDIPUS: How did you find me?

OLD MAN: Those scars on your feet will tell you.

OEDIPUS: Indeed! . . . Those old scars I grew up with . . . No one ever told me anything about them, of their secret or origin.

OLD MAN: They are the marks of fetters. You were shackled by your ankles! I was the one who took off your fetters. For this reason you were 'Oedipus'—that is, Swellfoot!

OEDIPUS: By heaven . . . who did that to me? Was it my mother who gave birth to me or my father who rejected me?

OLD MAN: I don't know anything about that. Ask the one who delivered you to me about that.

OEDIPUS: Delivered me to you? . . . Weren't you, then, the one who came across me?

OLD MAN: No, another herdsman was the one who entrusted you to me and put you in my hands in that form.

OEDIPUS: Another herdsman? Who is he? Can you inform us who that herdsman was?

OLD MAN: I remember he said that day he was one of Laius' men . . .

OEDIPUS: Laius? . . . The former king of Thebes?

OLD MAN: Yes, King Laius . . . That herdsman told me he was one of his servants . . .

OEDIPUS: He had many servants, no doubt. Is the servant you mean still alive? . . . Is it possible for me to see him, question him, and learn from him?

OLD MAN: This is a matter the people of Thebes can answer for you.

OEDIPUS: People! Inform me! Hasn't any one of you heard anything about the servant we are speaking of? . . . Hasn't one of you seen him in the city or in the fields? Let one who knows among you speak . . . Do not remain silent! Here we have now reached the key to the secret . . . the secret of my birth and of my reality which I have for so long investigated and pursued.

CHORUS: Ask Queen Jocasta . . . perhaps she knows that servant in the household of Laius . . .

OEDIPUS: My dear wife! Don't you know anything about that servant?

JOCASTA *(her face drained of color):* Which servant are you talking about? . . . I know nothing. We ought not to know . . . My husband, you are paying too much attention to what is being said . . . Leave this matter. Close this door. You won't find anything of value behind it.

OEDIPUS: How strange, Jocasta! How can I close this door when it has begun to open on the secret I long to know?

JOCASTA: No, no, Oedipus! Don't do all this digging in search of a secret . . . You are digging now the grave for your happiness! I entreat you to desist . . . I'm afraid . . . An eternal curse is gathering to break over our heads . . . For heaven's sake desist, Oedipus!

OEDIPUS: Don't be afraid! . . . I told you one day that you shouldn't be concerned about the truth of my birth . . . Even if I were the child of your humblest slaves . . . would this frighten you . . . or cause you shame that would humiliate you or damage your self-esteem? I will continue my search for my reality . . . that desire is stronger than I am. No one can stand between me and my desire to know who I am and will be . . .

CHORUS: Proceed on your course, Mighty King! Remove the curtain from your birth. Whatever your origin and birth, we are proud of you.

OEDIPUS: I don't want to live in a fog, even if the price is the kingship. I left Corinth and its throne to search for the truth . . . Now that I have almost placed my hand on its key, should I recoil, draw back and desist? . . . That shall never be! . . . That shall never be.

CHORUS *(turning towards the back):* What's with this herdsman in back of the crowd who is slinking away like a person wishing to flee?

OEDIPUS: Which herdsman?

CHORUS: The one who was in Laius' retinue.

OEDIPUS: Seize him and bring him forward! He must know something.

(Some of the people push the herdsman forward to the place where Oedipus stands.)

CHORUS: Why are you fleeing, Herdsman?

HERDSMAN: I wasn't fleeing . . . But I saw no cause for me to stay.

OEDIPUS: Your departure in this way must be for a reason we shall now learn . . . Perhaps you know the person we seek.

HERDSMAN: I don't know anyone . . . or anything.

OEDIPUS: First, bring him close to the messenger from Corinth. Messenger, examine his face carefully. Perhaps that may lead to something . . .

(The herdsman is pushed near the old man.)

CHORUS *(looking at the two men):* Two feeble old men . . . They seem to be the same age.

OLD MAN *(shouting after staring at the herdsman):* He's the very one . . . the very one!

OEDIPUS: Who? . . . Who?

OLD MAN: The herdsman who handed me the infant.

OEDIPUS: Did you hear, Herdsman?

HERDSMAN: I haven't understood anything this old man said.

OEDIPUS: Haven't you previously met this old man any place?

HERDSMAN: I don't remember.

OEDIPUS: How is it he can remember?

OLD MAN: Allow me, Oedipus, to sharpen his memory . . . I don't think he has forgotten those days when we worked near each other in the region of Cithaeron. He was herding two flocks and I was herding one. Three seasons from spring to fall passed in succession until winter came. I drove my flock away returning to Corinth and he drove his two off returning to Thebes . . . Didn't we do that, Herdsman?

HERDSMAN: Yes . . . this is truly what we used to do . . . but that was many years ago.

OLD MAN: Yes . . . many years have passed, but that doesn't prevent you from remembering that nursing infant which you put into my arms one day, imploring me to raise him as if he were my son.

HERDSMAN *(trembling):* What do you mean? . . . What do you want me to say?

OLD MAN: I simply want you to look in front of you, Old Friend . . . This is your nursing infant! *(He points to Oedipus.)*

JOCASTA *(unconsciously emitting a whisper like a rattling in her throat):* Enough! . . . Enough!

(She starts to dart off towards the palace, but Oedipus prevents her.)

OEDIPUS *(shouting):* Where are you going, Jocasta?

JOCASTA: O god! Mercy!

OEDIPUS: Stay a moment to hear with your own ears the truth of my origin.

JOCASTA: I can't stay another moment . . . I can't . . . can't.

OEDIPUS: You can't endure the blush of shame tinting your face when you hear in front of this crowd from whose womb your husband emerged! . .

I have never compelled you to do anything before, but I compel you now to remain where you are to learn about me what the assembled people will learn at this time ... even if there is in that some humiliation for your royal majesty and wound for the glory of your ancient family.

CHORUS: Stay with us, Queen! Hear what we hear ... Nothing will harm you. Oedipus is our king because of his heroism, not because of his lineage.

OEDIPUS: Listen, Jocasta, to the wisdom and the request of the people!

JOCASTA *(hiding her face with her veil):* Have mercy, Heaven!

OEDIPUS *(to the herdsman):* Now, Herdsman! Give us a frank and straight answer with no twist to it about the real facts concerning that infant you delivered to this comrade of yours.

HERDSMAN: This comrade of mine, your Majesty, doesn't know what he is saying. He is no doubt mistaken.

OEDIPUS: Beware, Herdsman! If you refuse to answer when asked nicely, we know how to force you to talk!

HERDSMAN: Be gentle, your Majesty, with an old man like me.

OEDIPUS: If you desire gentle treatment, speak!

HERDSMAN: What more do you want to know than you know already?

OEDIPUS: That infant of whom your friend spoke—are you the one who handed him to him?

HERDSMAN: Yes, your Majesty ... I did ... and I wish I had died that day.

OEDIPUS: I will treat you to death today, if you refuse to reveal the truth.

HERDSMAN: Alas for me! This truth is death for me, and what a death!

OEDIPUS: Haven't you ceased trying to shirk and evade?

HERDSMAN: There's no longer any way for me to ... Haven't I confessed that I gave him the infant? What more do you want from me then?

OEDIPUS: Where did you get that infant? ... From your own house or someone else's?

HERDSMAN: Not from my house ... rather ... from someone else's.

OEDIPUS: Whose?

HERDSMAN: Woe! Alas! I entreat you for heaven's sake to desist from questioning me!

OEDIPUS: Answer ... answer. If you refrain from answering now, I will subject you to every form of torture and have you killed in the worst possible way ... Speak!

HERDSMAN: That infant was from the house of Laius.

OEDIPUS: Was he the son of one of his slaves? .... Speak!

HERDSMAN: Can't you spare me from saying it? Your Majesty, have pity on me!

OEDIPUS: You must speak . . . I must hear. Otherwise, I will crush your white head mercilessly and pulverize your feeble body.

HERDSMAN: The infant was his . . . own son.

OEDIPUS: Whose?

HERDSMAN: The son . . . of Laius!

OEDIPUS: The son of King Laius?

HERDSMAN: Yes!

(There is a commotion among the people . . . Oedipus sways . . . but he is able to regain his composure.)

OEDIPUS: What you say is hideous, Man. It's hideous what you are saying! My mind can scarcely believe . . . Beware, Man, that there be in your words any lie or fiction . . . I understand now the reason you were fleeing from me . . . In actuality, you are the real source of the story . . . The temple priests no doubt learned it from you! For no secret is buried in the chest for seventeen years without an aroma spreading from it into the air. You are the origin of the Delphi oracle! Take care that you don't trump up a lie against me or give inspiration to a falsehood!

HERDSMAN: But it's the truth . . . It's in your power to ask Queen Jocasta, for everything took place in her presence and with her knowledge . . . They gave me the child to destroy, but my heart did not dare . . . so I gave him to this man to take to his country and to have for his son. He took him and in that way saved his life.

OEDIPUS: Was it a son Queen Jocasta bore?

HERDSMAN: Yes, your Majesty. It was said at that time it was necessary to destroy him . . . because of an unlucky prophecy attached to him . . . that this son would kill his father!

OEDIPUS *(screaming):* Laius! . . . Jocasta! Heaven! Heaven! The fog has dispersed from around me. I have seen the truth . . . How repulsive is Truth's face! What a curse! Never before has a person been subjected to one like it. Teiresias! . . . Teiresias! But you are motionless, like a statue . . . I sensed the specter of disaster and my chest was oppressed by it, before it struck . . . but I never imagined it would be so hideous . . . You also were disturbed by it, Jocasta . . . Jocasta!

(Jocasta, who seems to have been standing erect but in a daze all this time, falls to the ground in a swoon.)

CHORUS *(shouting):* Hasten to the Queen . . . Queen Jocasta sinks under weight of the catastrophe! Help her . . . Give her first aid. Take her into the palace!

(People gather around the Queen. They carry her gently. Oedipus assists them, stunned by the misfortune. They take her into the palace, leaving Teiresias where he stands.)

TEIRESIAS: Take me far away from this place, Boy . . . For heaven has been pleased to make it a playground . . . Yes! For god is at play, creating art, shaping a story . . . a story based on my thought. With respect to Oedipus and Jocasta, it is a tragedy. With respect to me a comedy. You who rule this palace must shed tears. I am obliged to laugh! *(He laughs hysterically.)*

Act Three

Scene One

In the palace . . . Jocasta is in her chamber, stretched out on her bed. Oedipus and the children surround her apprehensively.)

OEDIPUS *(whispering):* Keep back from her a bit, my children and don't be alarmed. She's sleeping.

ANTIGONE: Her eyelashes are moving, Father!

OEDIPUS: Yes, she's coming to . . . Take care not to let her see your anxiety . . . It's just a passing illness which will soon vanish.

(Jocasta sighs and opens her eyes.)

JOCASTA: Where am I? . . . Are you here, my children? . . . Is this you, Oedipus . . . Woe is me! Woe is me!

OEDIPUS: Have courage, Jocasta!

JOCASTA: Am I still alive then? . . . Hasn't the earth swallowed me? Haven't I ceased to exist?

OEDIPUS *(in a lowered voice):* No more of this talk in the presence of our children.

JOCASTA: Our children . . . our children . . . How repulsive your words are!

ANTIGONE *(alarmed):* Mother!

OEDIPUS: Antigone, you go along with the other children . . . Don't disturb your mother now.

(He gently shows them out of the room.)

JOCASTA *(as though speaking to herself):* Our children! . . . Our children!

OEDIPUS *(returning to her):* Jocasta! . . . Darling! Have pity on yourself and on me!

JOCASTA: Our children! . . . From whose womb did they come . . . all of them including you, Oedipus! . . . A single womb carried them and you . . . You will never say after today that they are your children . . . rather they are also your brothers and sisters. You will not say I am your wife from now on. I am also at the same time your . . . I am also your . . . What? . . . What am I to say?

OEDIPUS: Don't say anything, Jocasta!

JOCASTA: Has the world ever known an offense like this before? Has the earth's face been defiled by a sin like this? Has anyone ever suffered a curse like this? . . . And in spite of that I am still alive. Alive and breathing . . . speaking . . . and seeing my children . . . All of my children . . . all of them! *(She weeps and tears her hair.)*

OEDIPUS: Have pity on yourself and on me.

JOCASTA: Oedipus! . . . My husband and . . . my son! Why did heaven do that to us? What crime necessitated this punishment for us? . . . Do you think it was my crime the day I left you, a babe, to your destruction . . . My son and husband! Is this possible? . . . Is it possible for a human being to suffer this without being afflicted by insanity . . . or instantly struck by a thunderbolt? I must die, Oedipus! . . . I must die!

OEDIPUS: You will not die, Jocasta! I will protect you like an enraged beast . . . I will stand in the way of anyone who tries to touch a hair of you. I will defy heaven's thunderbolts with you . . . and the blows of fate . . . and the curses of human beings. You will not die! . . . You will not die!

JOCASTA: What value does life have now, Oedipus? What value does our life have? . . . Our enemies are not in heaven and not on earth. Our enemy is within us. Our enemy is that buried truth which you dug up with your own hands and uncovered leaving no way to escape it . . . except by ending our lives . . . I must die if I am to stifle the repulsive sound of that repulsive truth deep inside me.

OEDIPUS: You will not die . . . I will destroy every enemy you have . . . even if it is inside you!

JOCASTA: No, Oedipus! Don't do it! . . . In that way, you extend my torment. You don't relieve me. The matter has been decided and the curse of god and of the people has settled on us . . . Wherever we go, looks will follow us like stones thrown at us.

OEDIPUS: Take heart and be brave like me . . . Endure everything to face the actuality.

JOCASTA: Which actuality can we face after today?

OEDIPUS: Our unitary being . . . our united family . . . our loving hearts . . . our souls filled with affection and strengthened by compassion. Who would be able to destroy this edifice? What power could demolish this tower built of love, affection, and compassion?

JOCASTA: Oedipus! . . . My . . . I don't know what to call you.

OEDIPUS: Call me anything you like, for you are Jocasta whom I love. Nothing will change what is in my heart . . . So let me be your husband or your son . . . Names or epithets cannot change the love and affection rooted in the heart. Let Antigone and the others be my children or siblings. These terms cannot change the affection and love I harbor for them in my soul. I will confess to you, Jocasta, that when I received the blow I almost collapsed under it . . . But that was not in any way able to make me change my feelings for you a single moment . . . For you will always be Jocasta. No matter what I hear of your being my mother or sister, this will never change the actuality at all . . . For you are always Jocasta to me!

JOCASTA: Oedipus! You whom I cherish more than myself. Don't try to lighten the effect of the catastrophe on me . . . The actuality is as you described it, but the truth, Oedipus . . . What shall we do with the screaming voice of truth?

OEDIPUS: The truth? . . . I have never feared its face a day . . . nor been alarmed by its voice.

JOCASTA *(as though addressing herself):* For how long have I cautioned you against that . . . I have worried about it for you . . . you who have spent your best days chasing after it . . . from city to city in order to grasp its veil . . . until she turned on you at last, bared a little of her terrible face, and screamed in her resounding voice. It devastated the palace of our happiness and brought us to the state you see . . . the wreckage of a family to which no family term applies and for which there is no human description.

OEDIPUS: It was necessary for me, Jocasta, to know the truth.

JOCASTA: Now that you know it . . . do you feel relieved?

OEDIPUS: I truly wish I didn't know it . . . Could I have imagined it would be so terrible? . . . Did it occur to me that it could destroy my bliss? I have realized that only now . . . after it has taken revenge on me for playing with its veil.

JOCASTA: It took revenge on all of us, Oedipus, with a vengeance from which we can never recover.

OEDIPUS: Don't say that, Jocasta. We are capable of recovering. Rise with me . . . Let's put our fingers in our ears and live in actuality . . . with the life which throbs in our hearts overflowing with love and compassion.

JOCASTA: I can't, Oedipus! I can't remain with you . . . Your love for your family has blinded you . . . You are not thinking of people. What would they say if we were to continue this abnormal life after today . . . I am no longer fit to stay. Darling, there is only one solution: for me to go.

OEDIPUS: You will not go! I will compel you to live. I will guard you night and day. I will not permit anything to destroy our happiness and demolish our family. I will abandon the kingship and the palace. We will travel together with our young ones outside this country.

JOCASTA: Travel together? . . . Certainly not. Rather, I will travel alone.

OEDIPUS: Jocasta! Take care you don't proceed with a matter which will bring despair to my heart . . . You know I can't bear to be parted from you. Take heart and rise to meet life with me . . . Rest assured that so long as we have hearts, we are fit to remain.

JOCASTA: We are no longer fit to remain together . . .

OEDIPUS: What is this force which is to separate us?

JOCASTA: You can't overcome it, Oedipus . . . not even with that heroism of yours that vanquished Father Terror.

OEDIPUS *(as though addressing himself):* What a destiny! I am a hero because I killed a beast they claimed had wings. I am a criminal because I killed a man they showed to be my true father . . . I am neither a hero nor a criminal . . . I am just another individual upon whom the people have cast their fictions and heaven its decrees. Must I suffocate under the burden of these cloaks that have been thrown over me? . . . This heart of mine still throbs. I am alive. I want to live. I want to live, Jocasta, and want you to live with me. What is this chasm which separates us now? What hidden enemy and concealed foe rises between us like a giant? . . . Truth? What power does this truth have? If it were a savage lion with sharp claws and teeth, I would kill it and throw it far from our path. But it is something found only in our minds. It is a figment of the imagination, a ghost. My blow does not penetrate its vitals. My hand does not seize its being. It truly is a winged beast, lurking in the air. We can't reach it with our weapons. It kills our happiness with its riddles . . . Jocasta! You are trembling at a ghost, Jocasta. The actuality in which we now live must endure. We must not allow anything we can't see to destroy it. Free yourself from the truth we heard, Darling! Listen to the throbbing of your heart right now. What is it saying to you? Is it telling you that something has changed? Has your love for your young ones changed? Has your love for Oedipus changed?

JOCASTA: No . . . This love will never change . . . Never, never. But . . .

OEDIPUS: What are these tears in your eyes? Say you want to live for our sake.

JOCASTA: Oedipus!

OEDIPUS: Why are you looking at me this way as though I were your child . . .

JOCASTA: Oedipus!

OEDIPUS: What's come over you, Dear Jocasta? . . . You feel sorry for me. My tenacity for our lost bliss fills you with sorrow. I see pain and torment in your face. Give vent to your pain a little . . . rather plunge into the pain, for the greatest forces have collaborated to destroy this happy family. All the powers! . . . Man's rebellious thought, god's ironic planning, the people's traditions, and human fictions . . . Everything conspires to torment us. Even my intellect which spent years searching for my destruction . . . until I brought out into the open for us that ghost which firmly established itself in empty space . . . to disrupt our smiling life, rock our lovely actuality, and prevent us from communing in a nest we have built from the feathers of our mutual regard over a long period of time . . . Jocasta! Let's accept the pain of the blow of the disaster which has overcome us. Our souls were both oppressed by it when it neared . . . Don't you remember? But let's not surrender to what has befallen us. Everything will pass so long as we protect our home. The heart's warmth will melt away all sins, even the intellect's sins and errors. I believe in the purity of your heart and mine, for we did not sin deliberately. We did not will any of this evil the consequence of which we suffer. There is no way anyone can reproach us. No power has the right to request an exorbitant price from us for crimes we made no effort to commit. If we must pay a price, let it be this glory, sovereignty, and wealth . . . But you, Jocasta, and our children . . . No, no, no.

JOCASTA *(whispering):* Our children! . . . Our children . . .

OEDIPUS: What are you whispering?

JOCASTA: Nothing . . .

OEDIPUS: I see something in your eyes . . . I am afraid, Jocasta.

JOCASTA: Have no fear . . . It's just a little fatigue . . . Leave me now.

OEDIPUS: I think you are worn out.

JOCASTA: Yes.

OEDIPUS: If you would sleep a little . . . If you sank into a long slumber, Darling . . .

JOCASTA: This is my resolve.

OEDIPUS: But I won't leave you now until you promise me we will travel together from this country to a distant place . . .

JOCASTA *(as though speaking to herself):* To a distant place . . . Yes, I promise you!

OEDIPUS: I will request that at once from the people and from Creon. Have a rest now and don't think about anything until I return.

JOCASTA: Go along . . . Oedipus!

OEDIPUS *(looking at her for a time):* I won't leave you alone. I'll call the children to remain by your side till I return. *(He calls.)* Antigone! . . . Antigone!

(Antigone appears at the threshold.)

ANTIGONE: Father!

OEDIPUS: Come in with the other children. Look after your mother. Cheer her up until I return.

(He puts his hand on the necks of his children. Jocasta gazes at them while they are joined in this fashion. Oedipus leads them to their mother.)

ANTIGONE: Father, you are the only one who can cheer up Mother. All you have to do is to tell her the story of Father Terror. Mother, as you know, always loves to hear it from you.

OEDIPUS: The people are waiting for me, Antigone. You take care of this for me. You do a better job of telling the story than I do. I entrust your mother's care to you until I come back. Take care not to leave her at the mercy of her thoughts.

(Oedipus goes out followed by the distraught glances of Jocasta.)

JOCASTA *(whispering):* My husband! . . . My son!

ANTIGONE: Mother! You truly seem to be thinking about something sad.

JOCASTA: That won't last long, Daughter.

ANTIGONE: Why are you looking at me this way?

JOCASTA: You love your father a great deal, Antigone. I am sure you will always be at his side . . . if I were fated to go one day to a distant place . .

ANTIGONE: Mother, are you going to a distant place?

JOCASTA: That may happen one day.

ANTIGONE: What distant place do you mean?

JOCASTA: A distant place . . . where the heart lives free . . . like a peaceful dove. That bird with wings and claws which preys on love does not fly in the sky there.

ANTIGONE: I don't understand what you are saying, Mother.

JOCASTA: Never mind. Don't try to understand now. All I ask of you is to take care of your father if one day you see him all alone . . . I leave him to your care, Antigone. For he deserves all our love. If one day you see his tears flowing from his eyes, then with your pure little hands, wipe away those tears.

ANTIGONE: Why are you saying this to me, Mother?

JOCASTA: Because I don't want your father to suffer. He must live bright-eyed and find solace in you for everything.

ANTIGONE: Are you weeping, Mother?

JOCASTA: I entrust him to you, Antigone! I entrust him to you!

(She embraces her daughter for a long time.)

Scene Two

In the square in front of the palace . . . The chorus is assembled as before. The priest and Creon have taken their places in the crowd.

CHORUS: Who would have imagined that these alarming things would be disclosed? Who would have thought that Oedipus would fail to know these things about his reality? This hero who has persevered in his research and was proficient at solving riddles was blind to his situation. He did not notice which woman was in his bed, which child he fathered, or which man he killed . . . It seems that this man who grasped more of what is secret than was necessary for him missed the minimum a person ought to know. He dared to attack even Father Terror to wrest away his secret and shrank from knowing what was hidden in his own house and in his past. How miserable is this man who began to drill into the depths, for nothing burst up at him except the spring of his sorrows . . . What do you suppose he is doing now? What has become of Jocasta? Has she regained consciousness? What do you suppose they can do now? This palace encompasses them in its belly like an animal with unclean and decaying matter in its intestines . . . We don't know whether to pity Oedipus or be angry at him . . . In spite of everything, he is more our king and hero than he is one who has sinned against his own truth and that of his relatives.

PRIEST: That's enough talk from you, People, concerning Oedipus. Leave his suffering now and busy yourselves with yours.

CHORUS: What stratagem do we have at our disposal? Ask Oedipus. He's the one who always sees what must be done for us.

PRIEST: You haven't stopped putting Oedipus up where you raised him. You still imagine him with the same qualities you knew from him. You are not able to get free quickly from the enchantment of an idea you have grown accustomed to nor to make any sudden change in it. For that requires an ability for quick perception . . . How stolid your thought is, People. How slow your hand is to put the statue where it belongs. But I draw to your attention that Oedipus now has sufficient concerns of his own. He has an affliction which saps, a trial submerging him, and work which turns him away from having time for you.

CHORUS *(looking at the palace gate):* Here is Oedipus! He has appeared.

OEDIPUS: It is difficult for me to show myself to your eyes after disgrace has covered me and dishonor has enveloped me. But I have come to receive the verdict of the citizens on me, People. Have a little mercy for me, if your verdict delivered just now in my absence is harsher than I can bear.

PRIEST: They have not delivered judgment on you, Oedipus. Don't expect them to, but remember that you promised to deliver your verdict on the killer of Laius . . . So do not go back on your promise.

OEDIPUS: I will not go back on my promise, Priest. What punishment did I decree for you when I accused you and Creon.

PRIEST: Death or banishment!

OEDIPUS: I am not brave enough for death now, because I love my family . . . so let it be the latter, Priest. Allow me to travel with my family from this land . . . not to return!

CREON: Oedipus, you ask too much! What is your family but mine? How can we allow you to wander off with this family to foreign parts . . . to take them never to return?

OEDIPUS: And can this land support us after today?

CREON: No one here has the right, Oedipus, to authorize this departure for you . . . We are not able to issue any ruling for it before we ask god's guidance.

OEDIPUS: What's this you say, Creon? Aren't you the one who brought the oracle from the temple at Delphi? Didn't it tell you to cleanse this land of the person who defiled it with pollution.

CREON: What you request, Oedipus, is too serious for me to grant without permission . . . The oracle is sometimes obscure for us. There must be some hesitation in your case. It is not easy to have the family of Laius leave its place of origin . . . It's an outcome over which there can be no haste or speed.

CHORUS (turning): Here is Teiresias approaching . . . Perhaps he has an opinion. He is able to understand the oracles.

OEDIPUS: Come here, Teiresias, and settle our disagreement. You know the events which have taken place and the calamities which have landed on my head. Here I am proposing to give up this kingship which is plunged in mud and blood. I wish to flee from this land with my family, but these people refuse to shorten my torment and humiliation.

TEIRESIAS (pushing his boy away from him): Get away from me, Boy. I see my path now. God has struck my eye and I can see.

OEDIPUS: Teiresias! . . . Listen to me.

TEIRESIAS: Who is this calling me? Is it a human being or a god?

OEDIPUS: I'm Oedipus.

TEIRESIAS: Oedipus? . . . Who is Oedipus?

OEDIPUS: Don't you know now who Oedipus is? Allow me to remind you of him. He is the one on whom you brought down all these misfortunes . You are the person so stupid that he wished to interfere in something beyond his power . . . You are the blind man who thought he could see better for people than heaven could. You are the one who willed, and your will was a curse on the innocent. Had you allowed matters to run the course intended for them according to the designated laws, I would not be a criminal today . . . You wished to challenge heaven. You banished young Oedipus from the kingship and placed on the throne a man of your making. But this man you put up is the very same Oedipus you banished. For a long time you have prided yourself on your free will . . . Yes, you truly had a free will. I have witnessed its effects. But it was always operating, without your knowing or sensing it, within the framework of heaven's will.

CHORUS: We don't understand anything of this strange speech Oedipus is uttering.

PRIEST: Allow Oedipus to say whatever he wishes, for he would like to appear in the garb of the innocent and throw the crime on the shoulder of this blind old man. This old man was simply the bearer of a divine oracle . . . and the prophecy has been borne out.

OEDIPUS: Yes! It was correct. This is something causing amazement. It amazes him in his soul . . . this old man who was the bearer of the prophecy. When I uttered that statement just now I did not wish to appear innocent. I have never defended myself before you. It's a statement only Teiresias understands. It is of no significance for you. If you learned, People, what I mean, you would be filled with amazement . And you, Priest . . . Who knows? Perhaps you were, unconsciously, for Creon what Teiresias was for me . . . Man is man. He must act, will, and proceed according to the motivation of his aptitudes and conceit. His shortsightedness does not distinguish between his will and god's.

TEIRESIAS: What is this clamor around me? I hardly hear anything people say. My ear is filled with laughter coming from above.

OEDIPUS: Yes! Heaven wished to make a laughingstock of you . . . You who thought to wage war and tried to make your will a sword. You selected this palace with its peaceful residents as the battlefield! You struck your blow, but god had only to mock you and strike your blind eye. Then you saw your stupidity and conceit . . . The palace, however, has been razed to the ground with its inhabitants by your stupid blow and heaven's irony . . . Although it would have been more chivalrous, Teiresias, to think a little about the victims. Speak and give the judgment you think just . . . I ask only to depart with my family from this land, carrying away our disgrace. Perhaps in another land we will succeed in restoring our fortunes.

TEIRESIAS: Boy! . . . What is buzzing from the depths of silence? The drone of an insect deep in the mud?

OEDIPUS: It's a creature which killed its father, married its mother, and fathered children who were its siblings. Insects deep in the mud do that, because they're blind. I did that, because since I came into existence a blind man has wished to guide my destiny . . . You are the true criminal. If your blood were pure, I would shed it and wash my wounds with it. But it was fated that you live respected and deceive people, while I pay the price of your errors and wear the ignominy of your crimes.

PRIEST: Have pity on the old man, Oedipus! Have pity on the old man!

CHORUS: Bear your destiny alone, Oedipus, as befits a hero!

OEDIPUS: You're right, People. It's foolish to dispute the destinies allotted us. Perhaps some of it is of our own making. Do you hear, Teiresias? Your closed eye could not see god's hand in this existence . . . This system ordained for things is so straight a path that everyone who strays from it finds pits to fall into. You have a path you can proceed down according to your will, or you can stop. But you are not to challenge or deviate. You did, Teiresias, and you fell. But you swept us along with you. The fall affected you only in your pride. God used it to put you back in your place. We, however, were hit in our hearts. No one can give us assistance now. Not even you . . . You keep silent except to prate and babble. No hope remains for us save the people's hearts. We ask them to have some mercy on us . . . Now get away from me, Old Man. From now on you are good for nothing, in my opinion. Take him far away, Boy.

TEIRESIAS (to the boy): Take me to god so I can ask him when he prepared and planned his mockery—before creating us . . . or after our deliberation? Take me up to heaven, Boy. Bring me to god. I would know whether he truly is laughing at me just now . . . or whether he does not know me or care about me . . . Has he laughed in advance, since the beginning of creation . . . since he created this jest and shot it off into time to strike anyone who opposes it? It envelopes anyone who challenges it and clings to anyone who stands in its way . . . Take me up to heaven, Boy, so I may know. If I find god laughing at me, I too will laugh in his presence . . . like this . . . and this . . . (He pushes the boy in front of him. While he laughs, they depart.)

CHORUS (watching Teiresias leave): What has happened to noble Teiresias today? It seems the events have made him oblivious to us and have unbalanced him.

PRIEST: Let him go. I think he's out of sorts today.

(A scream resounds from inside the palace. Everyone turns towards the portal. Then Antigone appears screaming.)

ANTIGONE: Father! Father!

OEDIPUS: What's happened? What's happened?

ANTIGONE: Mother . . . Hurry to Mother!

(Oedipus leaps up the steps and enters the palace, terrified, with his daughter behind him. The crowd stares at them, motionless from alarm, like statues.)

CREON (recovering from the surprise and beginning to move): What's happened to my sister? (He starts to go to the palace.)

PRIEST (catching and restraining him): Stay, Creon! Your place now is with these people who have been left by their guardians. Their protectors are too preoccupied to care for them . . . We can guess the pain you suffer and the sentiment filling you . . . For you are a branch of this ruling tree and a member of this unhappy family. You are shaken by the tempests and losses which toss it . . . Your loyalty to Oedipus and your sister inspires us to request you to put your hand to the tiller of this ship before it sinks with all of us. So rise before this anxious and apprehensive people. Fasten their vessel to a safe shore.

CREON: Who grants me this sovereignty?

PRIEST: The encompassing circumstances and the tyranny of events give you the right to look after the people's welfare. In the same way, waves washing over a ship give the resolute sailor the right to hoist the burden and establish tranquility, stability, and safety when the captain is down.

CREON: Didn't you see how I was accused of desiring the throne?

PRIEST: That accusation against you was dropped, because the truth was on your side. Never listen to any voice except that of your duty.

CREON (shouting into his ear): Hush!

(Screams ring out from inside the palace.)

CHORUS: What are the frightening sounds coming from inside the palace?

PRIEST (turning towards the palace): What has happened? I think matters are becoming increasingly bad.

CREON (starting to go): Allow me to go see what has happened.

PRIEST (restraining him): Not so fast. Here is a servant coming to us from the palace.

CHORUS: Look at this person coming from the palace. His eyes show signs of alarm.

SERVANT: People of Thebes! . . . Queen Jocasta is dead.

CHORUS: Dead?

CREON: O Sister! (He rushes into the palace.)

SERVANT: Dead in such a way that the terror of it chills the marrow. Here's what happened . . . if it concerns you to know . . .

CHORUS: Speak . . . speak. Tell us what happened!

SERVANT: We did not see anything at first, but we heard Antigone screaming, "Where's Father? Where's my father?" When we asked her what was the matter with her, she said that her mother had risen from her bed and kissed her and the other children. She pretended that she was overcome by fatigue and that she wished to sleep for a long time. She drew them outside her room. Then she entered it and blocked the door from the inside. Her eyes flashed in a way to arouse fear and awaken anxiety . . . After that, the young ones heard through the cracks of the door only suppressed cries and choking moans . . . Then there was a dreadful, pervasive silence . . . and Antigone rushed outside to you as you saw to tell her father . . . Then Oedipus hastened after her to the locked room, banging on the door as though crazed. There was no answer. He bellowed like a frightening animal and attacked the door with his shoulder until he knocked it down. And here we saw a sight which froze the blood in our veins . . . Queen Jocasta hanged by her neck from a rope. She was dangling in the air with everything around her quiet as a tomb. Oedipus had scarcely seen her in this state when he rushed to the rope and pulled it down. Then the queen's corpse fell cold to the floor . . . At that time, our eyes saw the most hideous sight observed by the human eye. Oedipus became quite crazed. He bent over Jocasta's body rubbing his cheeks against her and wiping his head against her feet. He shouted: "Give me a sword . . . a sword! I have endured this miserable life only for your sake, O my wife and mother!" When we froze in our place and were oblivious to his call, he roared like a wounded lion and shouted: "They are slow to bring me a weapon of death too . . . I have no need for the sword. Here's something more hideous than death, more violent and painful!" He stretched out his hand like a hawk's talon to the breast of the royal robe which Jocasta wore. He tore off its gold brooches and plunged them violently into his eyes, saying: "I will weep for you only with tears of blood!" He proceeded to tear his eyelids and rip his eyelashes with the brooches. Blood flowed from his eyes in streams, dyeing with its dark color the surface of his cheek like black lines from the judgment of a stern fate.

CHORUS *(including women's voices):* Enough! Enough!

PRIEST: Where is this wretched king now?

SERVANT: He is stumbling about inside the palace writhing from his pain.

PRIEST: Hasn't anyone been quick to attend to him?

SERVANT: Of what use would an attempt to care for him be now? . . . Look. I see his arms beating the air, groping for the way out of the palace. *(Oedipus appears, blinded, with blood on his face and clothes.)*

CHORUS *(shouting in alarm):* Woe!

OEDIPUS *(stumbling while he advances):* Where have my feet led me?

CHORUS: Why did you do this to yourself, Oedipus? It hurts to look at it.

OEDIPUS: This is you, Generous People. I seek your pardon and forgiveness for me . . . I did not wish to hurt your eyes with a distasteful sight. But I am searching for the only path left to me.

CHORUS: What path is this, Oedipus?

OEDIPUS: The path of death . . . There beyond the walls of Thebes. I will wander aimlessly through the countryside until I encounter a beast to devour me. Then the birds will land to feed off the remains of my body.

PRIEST: We won't allow you to go to your destruction.

OEDIPUS: Have mercy on me. Don't bar the way before me any longer. You refused us exile until it was too late . . . Nothing remains for me but to meet death.

PRIEST: You will not walk to meet it.

OEDIPUS: Who will prevent me?

PRIEST: God . . . if he thinks your time has not yet come.

OEDIPUS: What interest does god have in drawing out my torment? Hasn't he fully exercised his right to punish me yet?

PRIEST: Perhaps he wishes you well . . .

OEDIPUS: What good can happen to me after today? The light around me has been extinguished . . . all light in my eye and in my heart. An eternal darkness has blotted out my life. It seems a cloak of mourning which will never be lifted from me.

PRIEST: If you wish to draw near to god and light a lamp to him in your soul, it will give you light on your darkest nights. But you have preferred to light candles in your intellect which have all gone out in the first gust of wind.

OEDIPUS: Don't scold me, Priest, and don't take revenge on me. I truly lit these candles to search for Truth. Teiresias cautioned me one day against letting my fingers touch its face and come close to its eyes. It does not like anyone to look at it more than is necessary. Yes, these fingers have come closer to it than they ought, until I have put out my eyes . . . It has taken revenge on me, so don't you be hard on me, Priest. I need your pity and compassion.

PRIEST: What good will my compassion be to you when all these mishaps have befallen you? But I will ask heaven's mercy for you.

CHORUS: Here's Creon coming pale-browed out of the palace . . .

OEDIPUS: Creon is coming? Ask him to help me and to lighten my pains.

CREON *(when he has appeared):* Why did you do this to yourself, Oedipus? What do you wish from me to alleviate your pains?

OEDIPUS: Allow me to go far away from Thebes. Expel me from your land like a curse!

CREON: Don't ask that of me, Oedipus.

OEDIPUS: I shall not ask you, Creon, to take my family with me . . . as I requested at first. The circumstances have changed now, as you know. I shall go alone, leaving my children with you. You take care of them; you are an excellent father for them. I entreat you to take good care of the two girls, Creon . . . and Antigone in particular . . . She has been very attached to me. She will have greater need for your affection . . . So you can see the matter is easy for you to consent to, for I have committed to you my family and yours, that is what remains of it. So far as I'm concerned, it is of no use for me to remain. I am no longer fit to remain . . . Dear Jocasta was right. I vainly encouraged her to live. She resisted as I did, but something stronger and more violent was victorious. With the departure of Jocasta, I perceived the power of that thing which compelled her death. I understood that my life as well was completely futile. Then I immediately wrapped it in darkness.

CREON: Do you have a last request, Oedipus?

OEDIPUS: Yes! . . . Don't forget to have the appropriate funeral rites performed for the burial of that one who lies shrouded in her chamber. She is your sister, and I am confident that you will do your duty well . . . I have no request beyond that except to commend my children to you once more . . . And I appeal to your generosity, Creon, and ask you to send for them now so that I can touch them with my hand.

CREON (gesturing to the servant near the palace gate): I had thought to spare them these painful sights . . .

OEDIPUS: For a time which may be the last . . . if you allow it, Compassionate Creon, I would touch their innocent faces with my fingers. I would imagine their features and contemplate their images in my head . . . What's this I hear? That is the sound of their little feet and that the sobbing of Antigone which I know. They are coming. I wonder whether you have had mercy on me, Creon, and sent to fetch them?

(Antigone comes out of the palace leading the other children.)

CREON: I ordered them brought to you, Oedipus, for I know how much you love them. Here they are, close to you!

OEDIPUS (stretching his hand out in the air): Thank you, Creon! Where are you, my children? I don't see you. My eyes will never see you again.

ANTIGONE (holding back her tears): Never mind, Father. So long as I have eyes, they are yours. You shall never be alone. I will be by your side wherever you are . . .

OEDIPUS: Antigone, my daughter! My heart is not pleased to drag you with me down the road of suffering. Your place is here beside your uncle with the other children.

ANTIGONE: The only place for me is next to you, Father. I will see for you. Don't you remember that I aspired one day to see things with your eyes . . . to see them as you see them. I will try to observe things the way you would. I will not let you feel for a day that you have lost your sight.

OEDIPUS: To the contrary, I was the one who aspired to see existence, pure and clean, through your eyes, but I am no longer worthy of that. Stay far from me, Daughter. Your radiant youth is yours, not mine. I will not take it from you and thereby commit another crime . . . Live life, my children. Keep your hands clean of me. For I am nothing to you but a blot. I am nothing but a burden on you. My ill-omened shadow which will attend you on the morrow will be enough of me for you to bear. You will be a proverbial example, a tidbit for mouths and toy for tongues. So long as people need fictions to fill the emptiness of their days, you will be a legend for people. The only hope for you is your uncle Creon. Make him your father. You will find affection and sympathy in his care. He has pledged to care for you. Here I extend my hand to you to confirm the pact . . . Where is your hand, Friend?

(Creon takes Oedipus' hand and presses it without speaking.)

OEDIPUS: Young Ones, make Creon your example and model . . . This

man is even tempered and pure hearted, with a believing soul. Take care
. . . take care not to make your father a model. Rather, take a lesson
from his fate.

(Antigone's tears fall on Oedipus' hand with no sob or sound.)

OEDIPUS: What are these tears on my hand? Whose tears are these?

ANTIGONE *(exploding):* Don't say that, Father! I will never take anyone
for a model besides you . . . Never . . . You are the hero of Thebes!

OEDIPUS: This is you, Dear Antigone . . . You still believe your father
a hero? *(He weeps.)* No. I am no longer that today, Daughter. Indeed, I
never was a hero at all.

(Antigone brushes away Oedipus' tears with her hands.)

ANTIGONE: Father! You have never been the hero you are today!

Shahrazad

"I am everything that was, is, or will be. No man has yet lifted my veil."

Isis

For the Clear-eyed One

Characters

MAGICIAN
MAIDEN, the Magician's daughter Zahida
SERF
EXECUTIONER
KING SHAHRIYAR
THE VIZIER QAMAR
SHAHRAZAD
ABU MAYSUR, a tavern keeper
PALACE SERVANTS

Scene One

A desolate road . . . an isolated house with a lamp at its door which gives light. The strains of distant music are carried by the breeze throughout this dark night.

MAGICIAN *(leading a maiden to the house):* What did this scavenger say to you?

MAIDEN: He asked me why the city is so merry. I told him: it's a festival the maidens hold in honor of Queen Shahrazad.

MAGICIAN: Why do you tremble?

MAIDEN *(whispering):* I don't know.

MAGICIAN: Haven't I cautioned you not to get near this old serf? His eyes have a wicked look.

MAIDEN *(whispering):* He's not old . . .

MAGICIAN: Why are you whispering like someone with a touch of insanity? Give me your hand and we'll go in. Perhaps the ugliness of this man has frightened you.

MAIDEN *(whispering):* He's not ugly . . .

(They enter the house. The serf appears. He follows the maiden with his eyes.)

SERF: How beautiful this virgin is! What a fine refuge her body would be!

VOICE *(from behind him):* Refuge? For Satan . . . or for the sword?

SERF *(turning):* Is that you?

EXECUTIONER *(appearing):* You recognized me?

SERF: Where's your sword, Executioner?

EXECUTIONER: With its price I've tasted dreams.

SERF: I understand.

EXECUTIONER: What do you understand?

SERF: The secret of your glory yesterday in Abu Maysur's tavern. The fragrant smoke of cannabis testified to what I received through your grace and generosity.

EXECUTIONER: It's only the due of foreign guests.

SERF: What might you be doing about your master's due?

EXECUTIONER: I'm no longer the King's executioner . . .

SERF: I understand.

EXECUTIONER: What do you understand?

SERF: Isn't today the virgins' festival?

EXECUTIONER: Yes . . . The king has no further need for an executioner.

SERF *(in admiration):* What a body Shahrazad has!

EXECUTIONER: Not at all . . . It is not for love of Shahrazad that the king turns away now from slaughtering maidens.

SERF *(listening intently):* Listen . . . What beautiful singing and how strange! Whose house is this?

EXECUTIONER *(as though confiding a secret):* The magician's. The King comes secretly to this house to meet privately with the magician.

SERF: The magician? . . . The maiden's father?

EXECUTIONER: So they say . . .

SERF *(listening to the singing and smiling):* A song sparrow that escaped your knife!

EXECUTIONER *(starting to depart):* What has departed from my hand has entered Satan's realm.

SERF: Stay a bit . . . I don't think you have work to rush off to . . .

EXECUTIONER: Yes, actually . . . a vision tells me of something red.

SERF *(in jest):* No, it's black. Your vision got the color wrong.

(Suddenly from a window of the house comes a long, strange sigh or moan.)

EXECUTIONER *(whispering):* Did you hear?

SERF: What?

EXECUTIONER: A sound like the hooting of an owl.

SERF *(looking carefully around him):* An owl! . . . Where? I don't see an owl . . . Don't fill the world with ill omens, you unemployed executioner!

EXECUTIONER *(starting to depart):* Then delight in deafness so you won't hear.

SERF: Where are you going? Stay another moment . . . Come tell me about beautiful Shahrazad.

EXECUTIONER: What more do you want to know about Shahrazad that you didn't learn yesterday? . . . I would almost say she's the only reason you came to town . . .

SERF *(shouting suddenly and pointing to a far-off spot):* Executioner, look! What's this light bursting forth there like a fountain . . .

EXECUTIONER *(looking in the direction of the light):* That's the King's chamber.

SERF: And the Queen's?

EXECUTIONER: No . . . The Queen has her room on the other side of the castle.

SERF: How strange! Does the King then no longer need the Queen to tell him stories until morning comes and she ceases the entertainment?

EXECUTIONER *(in a confidential voice):* The King has been afflicted by insanity.

SERF: From love of her?

EXECUTIONER: No, by real insanity.

SERF: How do you know?

EXECUTIONER: They say so . . . but come look!

SERF: What?

EXECUTIONER *(leading the serf a few steps):* Look carefully at the darkened balcony there . . . What do you see?

SERF: Nothing.

EXECUTIONER: Look at the left-hand corner of the balcony.

SERF: Yes . . . yes. I see a motionless figure there like the column of a building.

EXECUTIONER: That's the King.

SERF *(taking a long look):* What's his reason for contemplating the sky for so long, like the star worshippers?

EXECUTIONER: That's what he does at this time every night. And sometimes he spends all night awake and motionless, as you see . . .

SERF: Amazing! What is the secret of that?

EXECUTIONER: Who knows?

SERF: No one knows?

EXECUTIONER: No one knows.

SERF: When was he afflicted by this?

EXECUTIONER: I don't know . . . I don't think he has been afflicted by anything like this before now . . . not even in his most difficult hours. When, one day, he surprised his first wife in the arms of a vile slave all he did was to kill the two of them. He swore that each night he would have a virgin and enjoy her body as he wished and then slaughter her in the morning . . .

SERF: What more than that would you have wanted him to do?

EXECUTIONER: At least he wasn't afflicted by insanity or a mental disturbance . . .

SERF: You're right . . . Then what's the secret of this affair?

EXECUTIONER: Look! . . . He's disappeared from the balcony!

SERF: Yes . . . yes. And the lights have been extinguished!

EXECUTIONER: Perhaps he's coming to the magician.

SERF: Coming here? . . . Now?

(The serf disappears with the speed of lightning.)

EXECUTIONER *(looking for him):* Where did he go?

MAGICIAN *(coming out of his house cautiously and unexpectedly):* Who?

EXECUTIONER: The serf.

MAGICIAN *(extinguishing the lamp illuminating the doorway of his house):* Shame on him . . . This wicked beggar should keep far away from us.

EXECUTIONER: Why are you putting out the lamp?

MAGICIAN: What business of yours is this? . . . And you—what's keeping you too . . . in this place?

EXECUTIONER: You're right . . . I'm just leaving.

(The executioner departs. The magician follows him with his eyes until he is sure he has gone. Then he closes the door of his house and quickly disappears in a different direction from that of the executioner.)

SERF *(appearing):* Alas for anyone forced to walk in darkness!

VOICE *(a long sigh coming from the house's window):* Oh . . .

SERF *(with a start):* Who's this?

VOICE *(from the window):* A person who sees you; who sees the glint of your eyes . . .

SERF: And who knows me?

VOICE: And knows you came before your appointed time, desiring to see the light of the sun.

SERF: And hasn't the time come for me to see her?

VOICE: If you desire to live, then flee in the darkness. Don't let morning catch sight of you.

SERF: Why, Virgin?

VOICE: The man is still a child. He hasn't learned yet not to kill a slave when he sees him.

SERF: My life is in danger.

MAGICIAN: Go before the King's eye falls on you. The King still remembers that he saw a slave in the arms of his wife one day. Save yourself! Disappear, Slave. Return to the darkness.

SERF: One word, Maiden?

MAGICIAN: Be quick.

SERF: I want to see her.

MAGICIAN: Did you come because of her?

SERF: Yes, I want to know who she is.

MAGICIAN: She is everything. Nothing is known of her.

SERF: And you? . . . Don't you know?

MAIDEN: I don't know. They ask me about her frequently. They entreat me to answer, but I don't know. Let them ask my head after it is cut off. It might answer . . . Go.

SERF: Another word!

MAIDEN: No, go away! I told you to go.

SERF: Are you alone in this house?

MAIDEN: I have with me a person who has spent forty days in a pot filled with sesame oil. The magician has fed him only figs and nuts till his flesh has all gone. Nothing remains of him but his veins and mental faculties. Tonight the magician will take him out of the jug of oil and let him dry in the air.

SERF: Why did he do this to him?

MAIDEN: So afterwards he can answer whatever he is asked.

SERF: Answer whom?

MAIDEN: The King.

SERF: What does the King want to know?

MAIDEN: Go, Serf! Get away from this place. They are coming to extinguish the lamp.

SERF *(in anxiety and fear):* The lamp? Didn't your father extinguish it? *(He points to the house's lamp.)*

MAIDEN *(uttering a final moan):* Oh . . .

SERF *(flinching):* Why do you repeat this horrid sound?

MAIDEN: If a green cloud circles round you in the darkness remember crazy Zahida . . .

SERF: Zahida? . . . Is your name Zahida?

MAIDEN: Go.

SERF *(making out a figure approaching and then whispering):* Who's coming?

(The serf quickly hides in an opening . . . The figures of two men . . .)

MAGICIAN: Your Majesty has an anxious soul and uneasy mind tonight. Calm yourself, your Majesty . . . This time we will achieve what escaped us before.

KING: Didn't anyone notice us on our way out?

MAGICIAN: I fear no one but the vizier, your Majesty.

KING: Qamar? Did Qamar notice us? Did Qamar see us?

MAGICIAN *(fearfully):* Your majesty . . .

KING: What's the harm? It won't harm us if Qamar knows and tells her. Let him tell her what he wishes! . . . Who is she? Have you found out or not?

MAGICIAN: Please be calm, your Majesty.

KING: Show me the way.

(They enter the house. The door is closed behind them. The executioner appears from one direction and the serf from another. They meet suddenly in the darkness.)

EXECUTIONER: You startled me . . . Is this you?

SERF: Why did you return?

EXECUTIONER: I returned to look for you so we could go together to Abu Maysur's tavern . . . Do you think I can do without your company? I invite you again tonight.

SERF: And if the King asks you about your sword?

EXECUTIONER: He won't ask me . . .

SERF: Listen, Executioner . . . Your vision has come true.

EXECUTIONER: What vision?

SERF: Didn't it tell you something of red? . . . Tonight a head will fall.

EXECUTIONER: Whose head?

SERF: The vizier's . . .

EXECUTIONER: Qamar? . . . No head is safer or more secure than that of the vizier Qamar.

SERF *(in amazement):* How is that?

EXECUTIONER: The King would dare do anything . . . except harm his vizier.

SERF: Amazing . . .

EXECUTIONER: Let's go savor the scent of the fragrant smoke! Skip the talk of swords and heads! What mortal executioner would chop off a head in the darkness!

VOICE *(the strange, faint, frightening, long moan seeming to come from the depths of a tomb):* Oh . . .

SERF *(in alarm):* Did you hear?

EXECUTIONER: What?

SERF: Didn't you hear?

EXECUTIONER *(in a trembling voice):* This is no doubt the voice of a sleeper awakening from a dream . . . Was darkness created for any reason except for dreams to be seen? Let's go!

SERF *(staring into the darkness):* No, wait.

EXECUTIONER *(apprehensively):* What's the matter with you, Slave?

SERF *(pointing with his finger):* I see something . . . something else . . . in the darkness . . .

EXECUTIONER *(with a shudder):* What do you see?

SERF *(pointing and whispering):* I see . . . there . . . Look.

EXECUTIONER *(alarmed):* What . . .

SERF *(fearfully):* A green cloud . . .circling there . . .

EXECUTIONER *(whispering):* Oh Lord . . .

SERF *(in a whisper):* Did you see?

EXECUTIONER *(with a shudder):* Let's leave this place.

Scene Two

In the palace . . . a hall with a marble basin in its center.

VIZIER: Your Majesty! . . . You are not listening to my words . . .

SHAHRAZAD *(looking at the water in the basin):* Oh yes . . .

VIZIER: It's as though you were saying to me: idle words.

SHAHRAZAD *(smiling):* No . . .

VIZIER: This smile confirms my suspicion . . . But it is an enigmatic smile . . .
I don't know whether it is mocking or sad . . .

SHAHRAZAD *(looking at him):* You are mistaken.

VIZIER: Then this cryptic look . . . Your Majesty! Won't you permit me to
go insane too?

SHAHRAZAD *(laughing):* Why?

VIZIER *(in embarrassment):* Because I . . .

SHAHRAZAD *(smiling seductively):* I understand what you desire.

VIZIER *(upset):* No . . . no. I don't desire this . . .

SHAHRAZAD *(in a magical voice like a whisper):* Yes . . .

VIZIER: I swear to you, your Majesty.

SHAHRAZAD: Why are you upset?

VIZIER: All I want is to know who you are.

SHAHRAZAD: You too?

VIZIER: Yes.

SHAHRAZAD: I would have thought you were above that . . .

VIZIER: My mind is not capable of understanding what you are doing . . .
Why have you let the King go to the magician's residence when you
know he is going to destroy a soul . . . Have you forgotten, your
Majesty, that today is the festival of the virgins? They hold this festival
to honor your secret which saved their blood and resurrected this man
from among their corpses?

SHAHRAZAD *(stretching):* My body is beautiful . . . Don't I have a
beautiful body?

VIZIER *(lowering his eyes in confusion):* No . . . no.

SHAHRAZAD: Don't you think I have a beautiful body?

VIZIER: Yes, your Majesty . . . but . . . I entreat you . . .

(The vizier starts to depart.)

SHAHRAZAD: Where are you going?

VIZIER: To my bed . . . with your permission. The night is half over.

SHAHRAZAD (with coquetry): And leave me alone?

VIZIER (looking at the ground): I'll call the ladies-in-waiting.

SHAHRAZAD: You never pay much attention to me . . .

VIZIER (moving without looking at her): Have a good night, your Majesty.

SHAHRAZAD: Stay a moment! . . . It seems to me you don't want to have the King see you here when he returns . . .

VIZIER: You know I expose myself to his wrath more than I ought.

SHAHRAZAD: For my sake?

VIZIER: And for his too.

SHAHRAZAD: Do you see how much you love him.

VIZIER: And you too, your Majesty.

SHAHRAZAD: Me too? Is what you say true? Me too?

VIZIER (in embarrassment): I mean you too love him.

SHAHRAZAD: Do you think so?

VIZIER (in a peremptory tone): Yes.

SHAHRAZAD: What makes you think I love Shahriyar?

VIZIER (with a slight trace of bitterness): Can love be hidden?

SHAHRAZAD: Amazing! . . . Are you acquainted with love?

VIZIER: Your Majesty . . .

SHAHRAZAD: Answer!

VIZIER: I ask your Majesty's permission to depart.

SHAHRAZAD: Never mind . . . We'll return to our previous subject . . . Why do you think I love Shahriyar? Have you ever seen me kiss him . . .

VIZIER (forcefully and not without sharpness): You did more than that: you resurrected him.

SHAHRAZAD (smiling): Was he dead?

VIZIER: He was worse than dead . . . He was a body without a heart, matter without spirit.

SHAHRAZAD (smiling): What do you think I have made of him?

VIZIER (with conviction): You created him afresh.

SHAHRAZAD (joking): In seven days!

VIZIER (seriously): In a thousand and one nights.

SHAHRAZAD (joking): That was a lot.

VIZIER: Didn't the stories of Shahrazad do to this barbarian what the books of the prophets did for the first generations of mankind?

(Shahrazad smiles questioningly.)

VIZIER: You're smiling? Are you making fun of me? . . . Never mind.

SHAHRAZAD *(craftily)*: I think, Qamar, you praise me too much and denigrate the stature of your friend . . .

VIZIER: I don't denigrate his stature.

SHAHRAZAD *(craftily)*: It seems to me you have forgotten the amazing affection between you . . .

VIZIER *(sharply)*: I haven't forgotten anything.

SHAHRAZAD *(wickedly)*: Oh yes!

VIZIER *(in a blind rage)*: I have forgotten nothing. I am merely showing you why you love him with the most sublime love. So don't claim to me another time that you don't. I am not deceived . . . not deceived . . . I am not deceived!

SHAHRAZAD *(calmly)*: Qamar! What's come over you?

VIZIER *(returning to his senses)*: Your Majesty! . . . Forgive me . . . I . . .

SHAHRAZAD: Sometimes you lose control of yourself.

VIZIER: I . . . wanted to say that you changed him . . . He has become a new man since he has known you.

SHAHRAZAD: He has never known me.

VIZIER: I have told you before today that by virtue of you the King has also become a closed riddle to me. It is as though another, infinite horizon has been revealed to his inner eye. For he always goes about thinking, searching for something, looking for something unknown. He laughs at me whenever I wish to restrain him out of compassion for his overworked head.

SHAHRAZAD: Do you call this a virtue, Qamar?

VIZIER: And what a virtue, your Majesty! The virtue of one who transported the child from the level of playing with things to that of thinking about things.

SHAHRAZAD: How skillful you are in manipulating words!

VIZIER: What do you want, your Majesty? I wish I could understand at times what you want.

SHAHRAZAD: It would be best for you not to try . . .

VIZIER: I'm not trying anything. I would simply like to celebrate your love for the King.

SHAHRAZAD: This too?

VIZIER: Yes.

SHAHRAZAD: Are you still determined to accuse me of loving him?

VIZIER: I'm not accusing . . .

SHAHRAZAD: How simple your mind is, Qamar! Do you think I did what I did out of love for the King?

VIZIER *(with quiet anger):* For whom besides him then?

SHAHRAZAD *(smiling):* For myself.

VIZIER: For yourself? . . . What do you mean?

SHAHRAZAD: I mean that all I did was to contrive to live.

VIZIER: You mean you turned the King's mind away from killing people only to save yourself?

SHAHRAZAD *(smiling):* That's it.

VIZIER *(after some thought):* I won't believe it . . . Was this planned by you? Was all this premeditated by you? No . . . It's just that you're a great heart.

SHAHRAZAD *(smiling):* You see me in the mirror of your soul.

VIZIER: I see the reality.

SHAHRAZAD *(in a mysterious tone and with a strange smile):* Reality!

VIZIER: You smile?

SHAHRAZAD: Then why have I allowed him to go tonight to the magician's house to cut off the head of the virgin Zahida?

VIZIER: I don't know . . . and nonetheless, I don't believe that you are not concerned about the head of this poor girl . . . I don't understand your wisdom, and sometimes I don't know what ideas and secrets these two eyes, as clear as this water, contain.

(Shahrazad laughs questioningly.)

VIZIER: What makes you laugh?

SHAHRAZAD: Ideas and secrets! . . . Bravo to Shahriyar! . . . I see he has taught you many of his expressions.

VIZIER: Yes, I have stolen his words and many of his ideas . . . during the long days he has been alone with me speaking to me of you.

SHAHRAZAD: What does he say of me, Qamar?

VIZIER: I don't understand most of what he says.

SHAHRAZAD *(rising):* Go, Little Fox.

VIZIER: Is your Majesty going to bed?

SHAHRAZAD: I won't turn in until Shahriyar returns . . .

VIZIER *(bitterly):* Do you see how your eyes stay open till he comes back . . . to greet the King with this lovely affection.

SHAHRAZAD *(with a smile):* Qamar, you poor dear.

VIZIER *(listening carefully):* I hear the grating of a key . . .

SHAHRAZAD: Perhaps it is the door of his underground passage . . . Go and bring him to me. Beware of allowing him to go to bed before I see him.

VIZIER: I will do this for you, your Majesty.

(The vizier departs quickly.)

SHAHRAZAD *(at the door):* Start playing, Girls! . . . I want to see Shahriyar's eyes. Will I detect in them failure and defeat . . . Tonight Shahriyar returns to me powerless, exhausted, despairing, sensing annihilation, like a force at its end.

(Music is heard from outside the chamber.)

SHAHRIYAR *(shouting from outside):* Woe to me—what a headache! Who gave you permission for this hubbub at this hour, Fallen Women . . .

SHAHRAZAD *(with mild sarcasm):* Don't let anger get hold of you, Shahriyar . . . Anger is a mark of weakness.

SHAHRIYAR *(appearing):* I didn't come for you to make fun of me. Here I am . . . What do you want from me?

SHAHRAZAD: I want you to make fun of me . . . to announce your triumph to me.

SHAHRIYAR: Can't one of us meet the other for any reason other than to make fun of him . . .

SHAHRAZAD *(laughing):* This is a new statement which I haven't heard from you before tonight. Shahriyar, do you know why I invited you? I wish to read your eyes . . . Come close to me, Shahriyar!

SHAHRIYAR *(drawing near her):* What is making you laugh . . .

SHAHRAZAD: Obedience and submission I am unaccustomed to in you.

SHAHRIYAR *(drawing away from her):* Sorry! . . . I will never obey a woman.

SHAHRAZAD: That too!

SHAHRIYAR: You were created only for me . . . I am everything, and you are nothing.

SHAHRAZAD: I had thought you had progressed beyond the stage of childhood . . .

SHAHRIYAR: I am at the pinnacle of intellect and knowledge.

SHAHRAZAD: You're the Shahriyar of before the thousand and one nights . . . You haven't progressed or changed.

SHAHRIYAR: No, I've changed.

SHAHRAZAD: At that time you were shedding blood, and here you are doing it again today too . . .

SHAHRIYAR: I used to kill for amusement . . . Today I kill in order to know . . .

SHAHRAZAD: It's all the same . . . Nevertheless, what have you learned? What did the decapitated head of Zahida tell you? And what did the inhabitant of the oil jar confide to you? . . . Have magic and learning revealed to you a single secret of those you are burning to understand?

SHAHRIYAR: Shahrazad . . . be quiet.

SHAHRAZAD: I'm hard on you.

SHAHRIYAR *(in a tired voice):* I entreat you to leave me alone at this time.

SHAHRAZAD: Do you see how you have lost your way by resorting to magicians and diviners . . .

SHAHRIYAR: What do you want me to do? I've despaired of you . . .

SHAHRAZAD: Do you still desire me to disclose something to you?

SHAHRIYAR: Shahrazad?

SHAHRAZAD: Why do you look at me this way?

SHAHRIYAR: Don't mock me!

SHAHRAZAD *(whispering while looking at him carefully):* You're not even fit to mock . . .

SHAHRIYAR: What are you saying?

SHAHRAZAD: What do you want to know from me?

SHAHRIYAR: You are not unaware of what I want.

SHAHRAZAD: You want to know who I am?

SHAHRIYAR: Yes.

SHAHRAZAD *(smiling):* I'm a beautiful body . . . am I anything but a beautiful body?

SHAHRIYAR *(shouting):* To hell with the beautiful body!

SHAHRAZAD: I'm a great heart . . . Am I anything but a great heart?

SHAHRIYAR: To hell with the great heart!

SHAHRAZAD: Do you deny you were crazy about my body once and that you loved me with your heart once . . .

SHAHRIYAR: This has all passed . . . passed . . . *(as though addressing himself)* I am today a miserable man . . .

SHAHRAZAD *(approaching him):* Don't despair, Darling!

SHAHRIYAR: Get away from me, Liar! You love nothing but yourself.

SHAHRAZAD: Do you think so?

SHAHRIYAR: Deceitful Woman!

SHAHRAZAD *(smiling):* Why do you put up with me then?

SHAHRIYAR *(as though speaking to himself):* What devil brought me here now . . .

SHAHRAZAD: You spare me, because you don't know who I am.

SHAHRIYAR *(wearily turning his face away):* I am no longer concerned with you or anything.

SHAHRAZAD: You turn your face away, Blind Man . . . What if you looked a little?

SHAHRIYAR: I have looked more than I need to . . .

SHAHRAZAD: You are not observant, Shahriyar.

SHAHRIYAR *(wearily):* I seek just one thing.

SHAHRAZAD: What is it?

SHAHRIYAR: To die.

SHAHRAZAD: Why? . . . What's wrong with you?

SHAHRIYAR: There's nothing new to life . . . I've exhausted everything.

SHAHRAZAD: All of nature contains no pleasure which tempts you to stay?

SHAHRIYAR: All of nature is nothing but a silent jailer which is tightening its grip around my neck.

SHAHRAZAD: I swear you've gone insane . . . You've strained your mind till it has become disturbed . . . What secret do you seek from it, Simpleton? Don't you see that you are wasting the remainder of your life in a deceptive love of discovery?

SHAHRIYAR: What value does my remaining life have? . . . I've had enjoyment and abstain from everything.

SHAHRAZAD: Do you think that is the way to what you seek? How do you know that what you seek exists? Do you see anything in the water of this basin? Aren't my eyes too as clear as this water? Do you read in them any secret . . .

SHAHRIYAR: Down with clarity and everything clear! How much this clear water frightens me! Woe to anyone who plunges into clear water . . .

SHAHRAZAD: Woe to you, Shahriyar!

SHAHRIYAR: Clarity! . . . Clarity is her veil.

SHAHRAZAD: Whose veil?

SHAHRIYAR: Her veil . . . hers, hers . . . hers.

SHAHRAZAD: I fear for you, Shahriyar.

SHAHRIYAR: Her veil is woven from this clarity . . . The clear sky . . . clear eyes . . . clear water . . . the air . . . space . . . everything that is clear. What is beyond the clarity? The thick veils are of the most diaphanous clarity.

SHAHRAZAD: The affliction is, Shahriyar, simply that you are a miserable king who has lost his humanity and his heart.

SHAHRIYAR: I am free of humanity . . . free from the heart. I don't want to feel. I want to know.

SHAHRAZAD: To know what? . . . There isn't anything worth knowing.

SHAHRIYAR: A lie and a deceit. Give the answer then to what I ask you . . . This is all I seek in life.

SHAHRAZAD: Ask what you will.

SHAHRIYAR: Who are you?

SHAHRAZAD (smiling): I'm Shahrazad.

SHAHRIYAR: Stop beating around the bush . . . I know your name is Shahrazad . . . But who is Shahrazad?

SHAHRAZAD: The daughter of the former vizier.

SHAHRIYAR: I know likewise that my former vizier was the father of Shahrazad, just as I know that God created nature. Thus it cannot be said that Shahrazad is a foundling. Thus it cannot be said that nature is the offspring of coincidence. But you know that I am not one to be convinced by these lineages.

SHAHRAZAD: Why? Why don't you want to see me a woman like any other with a father, a mother, and a known past.

SHAHRIYAR: You are not a woman like the others.

SHAHRAZAD: Are you praising me or finding fault?

SHAHRIYAR: I don't know . . . Indeed, it may be that you are not a woman.

SHAHRAZAD: Do you see how far insanity has taken hold of you . . .

SHAHRIYAR: She may not be a woman . . . Who is she? I ask you who she is. She is a prisoner in her boudoir all her life, yet she knows everything on earth, as though she were the earth. She has never left her bosk, yet she knows Egypt, India and China. She is a virgin, yet she knows men like a woman who lived among men for a thousand years. She perceives man's qualities both lofty and low . . . Although she is young, knowledge of the earth is not enough for her. She ascends to the heavens and discourses on its design and secrets as though she were a foster daughter of the angels. She descended to the depths of the earth to speak of its demons, devils, and amazing underground kingdoms as though she were a daughter of the jinn. Who could that one be who had lived fewer than twenty years which she spent like her contemporaries in a room with the curtains drawn? What is her secret? Is she twenty years old? Or is she ageless? Was she confined to one place or did she exist every place? My mind boils over in its pot wanting to know . . . Is she a woman when her nature seems nature itself?

SHAHRAZAD: Shahriyar! . . . Abandon this. Your hands are trembling. There's a terrible fatigue apparent on your face.

SHAHRIYAR: Yes. I feel tired. My mind will never rest until I know.

SHAHRAZAD: I've told you to abandon this. Don't think about it.

SHAHRIYAR: You are my wife whom I love . . . Aren't you my wife? . . . Do you think I will endure for long this veil hanging between me and you?

SHAHRAZAD (as though speaking to herself): Do you think you could endure living with me a moment if this veil vanished?

SHAHRIYAR: What are you saying?

SHAHRAZAD: Nothing . . .

SHAHRIYAR: I swear to you that I need to know more about you than I do.

SHAHRAZAD: Go to your bed now . . . You need rest.

SHAHRIYAR *(screaming):* I won't go . . . I want to know now. I have been patient a long time.

SHAHRAZAD: Don't be childish, Shahriyar! You know that even if you insist for twenty centuries you won't win a word from me.

SHAHRIYAR: Why?

SHAHRAZAD: Because I don't possess what you want. You seek the unattainable . . . You are a man with a sick head.

SHAHRIYAR: You know . . . You know everything . . . You are an amazing being who does nothing and does not utter a word except by design, not from passion or chance. You proceed in everything with the utmost calculation not deviating by so much as a hair, like the calculation of the sun, the moon, and the stars . . . What are you but a great intellect . . .

SHAHRAZAD *(smiling):* You, Shahriyar, see me in the mirror of your soul.

SHAHRIYAR: I see reality.

SHAHRAZAD *(mocking and mysterious):* Always reality!

SHAHRIYAR: Won't you say?

SHAHRAZAD: It would be best for you to go sleep and rest, or return to your sapping thought, or to your magicians and diviners.

SHAHRIYAR *(looking at her and whispering):* God's curse . . .

SHAHRAZAD: Why are you looking at me this way?

SHAHRIYAR: Come!

SHAHRAZAD *(approaching):* What do you want?

SHAHRIYAR: To kiss you. *(He takes her head in his hands, lifts her black hair, and withdraws his dagger from its scabbard.)*

SHAHRAZAD *(shouting at him):* Woe to you . . . What are you doing?

SHAHRIYAR *(in a strange voice):* I see a white hair like the thread of dawn in this night.

SHAHRAZAD *(freeing herself from his hand and looking at her reflection in the basin):* Where is it? *(She plucks out the white hair.)*

SHAHRIYAR: Why do you pluck it out?

SHAHRAZAD *(returning to him):* How could it occur to you to do this? I've begun to believe in the danger of your insanity . . . Would you have been able to bear my loss, Shahriyar?

(She rearranges her clothing and displays the beauties of her body. Shahriyar scrutinizes her.)

SHAHRAZAD: Why are you looking at me this way? It's as though you had never seen me before.

SHAHRIYAR *(turning away his face):* No . . . I don't want to see you this way.

SHAHRAZAD: Why?

SHAHRIYAR: She does this too . . . She reveals her beauty with abandon and veils her secret from us.

SHAHRAZAD: Who?

SHAHRIYAR *(as though addressing himself):* Nature.

SHAHRAZAD *(in an affectionate tone):* You poor dear . . .

SHAHRIYAR: You deceiver . . .

SHAHRAZAD *(taking his head in her hands):* Alas for this sick, overworked head, for this pale brow, and for these contracted lips . . .

SHAHRIYAR: My face is pale like the faces of the dead?

SHAHRAZAD: Don't say this.

SHAHRIYAR: Yes, Shahrazad . . . I will die.

SHAHRAZAD: Have fatigue and despair affected you this much? . . . No, Shahriyar. You will live.

SHAHRIYAR: I don't want to . . . I no longer desire anything.

SHAHRAZAD: You say this today . . . but tomorrow, Shahriyar . . .

SHAHRIYAR: I'm not concerned with tomorrow.

SHAHRAZAD *(caressing his hair with her fingertips):* You are not old, Shahriyar . . . Your hair is still the color of night.

SHAHRIYAR: Play with my hair as you like . . . Let me hear your tender voice . . . I didn't know you were this beautiful! Is this your mouth, Shahrazad . . . It's a cup of pearls! Is this your hair, Shahrazad . . . It's a cluster of grapes!

SHAHRAZAD: Come . . . Rest your body a little.

SHAHRIYAR: Let me pillow my head on your lap as though I were your child or your husband . . . Am I truly your husband? . . . I don't believe myself if I say this is true . . . Put your arms around my neck . . . Your arms are of silver, Shahrazad! I want to know whether these treasures are mine . . . Why don't you tell me of your love, if you do love me a little? . . . But you bear no love for me.

SHAHRAZAD *(with veiled sarcasm):* I see you've returned to the heart and love . . .

SHAHRIYAR *(in a sleepy voice);* Shahrazad! I feel now as though I were happy . . . but I have a desire to know my place in your heart. Anxiety grips me at times and it seems to me you are great . . . so great you couldn't descend to the love of one like me . . .

SHAHRAZAD *(cunningly):* Do you no longer desire to know who I am?

SHAHRIYAR: I desire to kiss your lovely, silver body.

SHAHRAZAD: I see you've returned to the body!

SHAHRIYAR *(fighting drowsiness):* I want you to recite poetry to me. Shahrazad! Tell me one of your stories.

SHAHRAZAD *(turning to the door):* Play your instruments and sing, Girls.

(Gentle music and a soft singing are heard from outside the chamber.)

SHAHRIYAR *(drowsily):* Sing me a song.

SHAHRAZAD *(in a voice like a whisper):* Shahriyar . . .

(Shahriyar, asleep, does not answer.)

SHAHRAZAD *(smiling and whispering):* Do you want a song?

(Shahriyar does not respond.)

SHAHRAZAD *(as though talking to herself):* Sleep . . . sleep . . . sleep, Child, tired by play.

Scene Three

The King's Hall . . . Faint music from outside . . . The morning sun fills the whole area.

THE VIZIER QAMAR *(speaking to one of the servants):* Have you gotten the camels ready?

MAGICIAN *(appearing):* Is the news true then?

QAMAR: What brings you, Magician? . . . Don't you know the King is not pleased to see you now?

MAGICIAN: God preserve his Majesty! . . . I heard a rumor going about town that the King intends to travel . . .

QAMAR: What business of yours is this?

MAGICIAN: Perhaps the King will need me.

QAMAR: The King will not be accompanied by anyone on his trip.

MAGICIAN: Strange! . . . What induces him to do this?

QAMAR *(looking towards the door and whispering):* Hush . . . the King . . .

SHAHRIYAR *(in a strange agitation, appearing and seeing the magician, then shouting at him):* What are you doing here, Fellow? Were I not certain that your life is not worth a dirham I would take it from you . . . Weird one, return to your mates . . . you great worms created only to eat your young . . .

MAGICIAN *(whispering as he departs):* You're no different, King. Wouldn't your young eat you?

SHAHRIYAR: What did this man say . . .

QAMAR: Nothing, your Majesty . . . He was asking the King's forgiveness.

SHAHRIYAR *(listening to the music coming from outside):* What's this music? It is imprisoning and restricting my soul . . . Silence it, Qamar! Or have its tunes ring out . . . ring out . . . limitlessly.

(Qamar motions to one of the servants to silence the music.)

SHAHRIYAR: Have you prepared the necessities for the trip?

QAMAR: Yes, but . . .

SHAHRIYAR: But what, Qamar?

QAMAR: Will you really travel?

SHAHRIYAR: Yes . . . and do you still oppose my idea?

QAMAR: I don't see what prompts you to travel.

SHAHRIYAR: What prompts me to stay?

QAMAR: Does your Majesty think that if he tours the length and breadth of the world he will know more than he knows when in this hall of his?

SHAHRIYAR: Free yourself from imagination, Qamar. No one has ever harvested anything from imagination and thought. That naive age has passed. Today we want realities, Qamar . . . We want facts. We want to see with our own eyes and hear with our ears.

QAMAR: This isn't what we live for, your Majesty.

SHAHRIYAR: If we don't live to learn, then what do we live for, Qamar?

QAMAR: To worship what in existence is beautiful.

SHAHRIYAR: And what is the most beautiful thing in existence?

QAMAR: A woman's eyes.

SHAHRIYAR: You poor man . . . a woman's eyes! According to you, Handsome Youth, this is all there is in existence . . . You ought to have a virgin every night so your eyes could look then.

QAMAR: Don't scoff . . . Rest assured that a man who possesses a beautiful woman in his room possesses the whole world there.

SHAHRIYAR (smiling): You will remain with her then in one castle.

QAMAR: With whom?

SHAHRIYAR: The woman with the beautiful eyes!

QAMAR (frowning): What do you mean?

SHAHRIYAR: You and Shahrazad stay here. You will guard her and look out for her until I return from my long voyage.

QAMAR (protesting): You are dreaming . . .

SHAHRIYAR: What do you say?

QAMAR (sharply and forcefully): I say you're dreaming.

SHAHRIYAR: Do you defy my command?

QAMAR: In this . . . Yes. A thousand times yes.

SHAHRIYAR: I won't take you along with me.

QAMAR: Then let the Queen be your companion.

SHAHRIYAR: Her? What's the point of the trip then?

QAMAR: Do you think yourself deliberately parting from your wife?

SHAHRIYAR: And parting from you too.

QAMAR: You flee those who love you!

SHAHRIYAR: And from myself too.

QAMAR: God's mercy!

SHAHRIYAR: I want to forget this wormy flesh . . . to burst forth . . . ring out.

QAMAR: To where?

SHAHRIYAR: To where there are no limits.

QAMAR: I don't understand the meaning of what you say.

SHAHRIYAR: Yes. You won't understand now the meaning of what I say.

QAMAR: Your soul is no doubt unsettled.

SHAHRIYAR: And my body will be also, shortly . . .

QAMAR: Can you bear parting with the Queen?

SHAHRIYAR: The same way she bears parting with me.

QAMAR: And me?

SHAHRIYAR: You, Qamar, are a moon which does not shine without the sun. So stay to derive your life from her light.

QAMAR: Your Majesty!

SHAHRIYAR: Don't be upset, Qamar. By staying here you do me a favor, added to the many others.

QAMAR: And if I refuse . . .

SHAHRIYAR: You won't. I trust no one but you with Shahrazad. Here she is coming in a gown—I've never seen her in one like it. Look Qamar! How beautiful she is.

(Qamar bows his head.)

SHAHRIYAR: Won't you look? Don't you worship beauty . . . All right, Shahrazad! You have come no doubt to bid me farewell.

SHAHRAZAD *(appearing):* Yes, I have come to see you before your departure for . . . Where are you going, Shahriyar . . .

SHAHRIYAR: Where am I going?

SHAHRAZAD: Yes, where are you travelling to?

SHAHRIYAR: Waq al-Waq.

SHAHRAZAD: Are you joking?

SHAHRIYAR: Do you think this land exists only in your fictions of which you are the beautiful inventor . . .

SHAHRAZAD: And when do you intend to return?

SHAHRIYAR: From the first trip?

SHAHRAZAD: Are there to be other trips?

SHAHRIYAR: Have you forgotten Sindbad, Shahrazad? Didn't Sindbad make seven consecutive voyages?

SHAHRAZAD: Yes . . . the travel disease.

SHAHRIYAR: You're right. It's the travel disease, as you call it. Once a person is able to free his body from the hobbles of a place he is afflicted by the travel disease. He never stops touring the earth until he dies.

SHAHRAZAD: That finishes the matter. You've become Sindbad.

SHAHRIYAR: Are you sad to lose me?

SHAHRAZAD: Had I known you would shoot off one day like a stray thought, I would not have told you those stories.

SHAHRIYAR: It's not those stories that are making me shoot off . . .

SHAHRAZAD: Oh yes.

SHAHRIYAR: Rather, it's the constriction of your arms tightening their grip around my neck.

SHAHRAZAD *(smiling):* My silver arms! . . . Good for me. Do you hate me this much today?

SHAHRIYAR: Who is there who hates Shahrazad? . . . Do you believe that? Is it my fault that I feel in my human soul a dissolution of the spatial attribute?

SHAHRAZAD *(whispering):* A human soul deserving forgiveness . . .

SHAHRIYAR: In spite of that, what does Shahrazad care? . . . She is the last person who would be conscious of this.

SHAHRAZAD: And you, Qamar. What do you say about that? Do you agree with your friend about it?

QAMAR: We ought to have expected this, your Majesty . . . What should we look for from a man who had a virgin every night . . .

SHAHRIYAR: You mean I've lost my desire for women?

QAMAR: A man without a heart.

SHAHRIYAR: Qamar is angry with me. Woe to me! Qamar's anger is vehement only over one thing: it seems to him I don't adore Shahrazad as much as I should.

SHAHRAZAD: Qamar is a man.

SHAHRIYAR: Qamar is still a child.

SHAHRAZAD: You're the child, Shahriyar.

SHAHRIYAR: That's what I always am to you . . . Never mind! Let the man stay to serve you then, so the child can tour the world in order to return a youth with discernment.

SHAHRAZAD: The young one's travels will be of no use to him so long as he has no heart.

SHAHRIYAR *(sarcastically):* What is the heart's occupation . . . love?

SHAHRAZAD: Who knows . . .

SHAHRIYAR: Love! . . . Where did this word come from? . . . It is doubtless an ancient word, a remnant from the distant past.

SHAHRAZAD: No, a remnant from last night.

SHAHRIYAR: As recently as last night? You exaggerate! How then have you forgotten its purport so quickly . . . I would believe you if you said it has the same meaning for me as that tender music . . . the language of the emotions which I don't understand now because I don't understand the emotions now . . . Silence it, Qamar! Didn't I tell you to silence it? It confines my being to the limits of place.

SHAHRAZAD: Despite all this, there is a step between you and childhood.

SHAHRIYAR: That's all right. I will not return to your beautiful body. I will not be intoxicated by the nectar of your mouth, the fragrance of your hair, and the embraces of your arms . . . I've had my fill of bodies. I've had enough of bodies. I'm fed up with bodies!

SHAHRAZAD: You no longer feel . . .

SHAHRIYAR: I don't want to feel. Before, I was feeling and not aware . . . Today I am aware and not feeling . . . like the spirit.

SHAHRAZAD: The spirit? . . . How remote you are from the spirit! . . . Come, Qamar! . . . This poor man thinks that words are everything.

SHAHRIYAR *(suddenly):* Shahrazad! . . . The hour of departure has come. Don't you hear? Stunning music calls me to depart.

SHAHRAZAD *(whispering to Qamar):* You stay, Qamar.

SHAHRIYAR: What are you saying to him?

SHAHRAZAD: I'm telling him to remain . . . But you can travel as much as you wish.

SHAHRIYAR: What do you mean?

SHAHRAZAD: It is said a man may achieve with his heart what another does not with his intellect.

SHAHRIYAR *(his eyes searching for Qamar who has slipped out):* Will you confide in him?

SHAHRAZAD: I don't know.

SHAHRIYAR *(anxiously):* Shahrazad . . .

SHAHRAZAD: Go!

SHAHRIYAR: Deceit and cunning . . . I know you better than you do yourself . . . In any case, Qamar won't hide anything from me . . . Your talk no longer tempts me. Farewell, Queen! . . . No, come. I have forgotten to kiss you.
(He kisses her quickly, but she detains him and kisses him warmly. He stands shaken . . . Shahrazad leaves him silently.)

SHAHRIYAR *(trembling):* Shahrazad . . .

SHAHRAZAD *(turning to him):* What's wrong with you? . . . You're trembling.

SHAHRIYAR: No . . . this is . . .

SHAHRAZAD: This is from the effect of the separation, Shahriyar.

SHAHRIYAR *(moving resolutely):* Where's Qamar? . . . Where are you, Qamar? The journey . . . the journey . . . journey . . . *(He goes out quickly.)*

SHAHRAZAD *(to herself):* This poor man! If he knew how I pity him . . .

Scene Four

(A wilderness ... an open space at sunset ... The sun plunges beyond the sand at the far horizon.

QAMAR *(with bitter sarcasm):* What is behind this silence and despondency? Do you think all this is sadness at the setting of the sun?

SHAHRIYAR: What concern of yours is it?

QAMAR: We are roaming through limitless space . . . travelling through wastelands, without encountering a living creature, without hearing in its expanses anything but the echo of our lost voices . . . Are you happy with this? . . . Your soul rejoices so far as I can see . . .

SHAHRIYAR: Who gave you permission to accompany me?

QAMAR: Amazing! . . . Have you just become aware of my presence?

SHAHRIYAR: Your presence!

QAMAR: Your Majesty?

SHAHRIYAR *(vexed):* What do you want from me? . . . What do you want from me?

QAMAR: What a good humor you're in today!

SHAHRIYAR: It's no business of yours whether I am in a good humor or vexed . . . Leave me and my affairs alone, Man.

QAMAR *(after a moment):* Will you accept some advice from me?
(Shahriyar does not move.)

QAMAR: Let's head back and return.

SHAHRIYAR *(raising his head):* Where to?

QAMAR: To where we were.

SHAHRIYAR *(shouting):* To where Shahrazad is? . . . You poor man! Your weakness has appeared before a day of our journey has passed.

QAMAR: My weakness?

SHAHRIYAR *(rising resignedly and forcefully):* Get up. Let's explore the place . . . It is no doubt the desolation of the desert . . . You're not accustomed yet to travel, since you haven't travelled before, Qamar.

QAMAR: You haven't either.

SHAHRIYAR: Oh yes . . . I've travelled before now . . .

QAMAR: Much?

SHAHRIYAR *(as though speaking to himself):* But . . . not like this time . . .

QAMAR *(with satisfaction):* Here, you've confessed.

SHAHRIYAR: What have I confessed?

QAMAR: Your pain.

SHAHRIYAR *(pretending to be calm):* You're a greenhorn, Qamar. I'm not pained by parting from her. No, it's another man you know better than I . . .

QAMAR *(with anxiety and anger):* What do you mean?

SHAHRIYAR *(with satisfaction):* Nothing . . . Don't be angry, and don't attach any importance to these words, Young Man.
(Qamar bows his head and suppresses his anger.)

SHAHRIYAR *(looking suddenly at the sun as it vanishes):* Look, Qamar! The sun's parting is truly saddening.
(Qamar raises his head and contemplates the sunset silently.)

SHAHRIYAR *(after a moment of contemplation):* Like every parting . . .
(Qamar does not reply.)

SHAHRIYAR: Perhaps she too is sad . . . Don't you see the weakness of her rays and her sickly color? But it is a moment's sadness . . . only at the moment of separation . . .

QAMAR *(in a faint voice):* Here she has descended beyond the sand . . .

SHAHRIYAR: Yes . . . and her sorrow has gone. If you were able to see her at this moment in her new location you would be amazed by her fresh, artistic rays.

QAMAR: With this speed?

SHAHRIYAR: What more than this do you desire of her? She does not know the heart and imagination like you.

QAMAR: Like me?

SHAHRIYAR *(continuing):* Since she has a body, she is naturally affected by the separation . . . but only at the moment of separation. Anything beyond that would be idle talk and not part of her nature.
(Qamar looks at the King silently.)

SHAHRIYAR *(moving suddenly with force and enthusiasm):* And we too are like her. Let's go, Qamar! Let's keep on marching, marching, marching.

QAMAR *(looking at him and repeating the words bitterly):* Marching . . . marching . . . marching.

SHAHRIYAR *(stopping):* Why are you looking at me this way?

QAMAR *(mockingly as though angered):* You amaze me!

SHAHRIYAR: Why?

QAMAR: Because you think you can silence your heart with idle talk . . .

Scene Five

In the King's Hall on a gloomy, dark night. Shahrazad is stretched out thinking. The serf climbs in through the window.

SHAHRAZAD *(with a start):* Who's this?

SERF *(advancing while whispering):* Don't be afraid! It's me.

SHAHRAZAD: Who told you I'm here?

SERF *(approaching her):* Your radiating fragrance and this window informed me that behind there was a body awaiting love.

SHAHRAZAD: Don't touch me! Go away.

SERF *(contemplating her):* How beautiful you are! You're nothing but a beautiful body.

SHAHRAZAD *(smiling):* Even you see me in the mirror of your soul as well.

SERF: I see the reality.

SHAHRAZAD: Leave the reality quietly in its place . . . Go away.

SERF: Why have you deserted your chamber this evening and come here? Why this frowning face tonight? Are you sad at being separated from him?

SHAHRAZAD: I can't stay with you in this hall.

SERF: What do you fear?

SHAHRAZAD: I'm not afraid for myself . . .

SERF: You know he's now on his way to Egypt or India . . . Anyway, what do you think he would do if he came upon us now?

SHAHRAZAD: Don't say that.

SERF: Haven't you taught him yet not to kill a slave when he sees one?

SHAHRAZAD: Certainly not.

SERF: Because you don't want to, you traitor.

SHAHRAZAD: I wouldn't want him to spare you if he saw us together? Do you believe that, my darling?

SERF: I'm not your darling, Faithless Woman.

SHAHRAZAD: Who are you then?

SERF: A wretch you will betray.

SHAHRAZAD: Do you think so? Had I wanted to betray you, I wouldn't have invited you.

SERF: I sense you're preparing a trap for me.

SHAHRAZAD: Your feeling is mistaken.

SERF: Is it possible for someone like you to desire a base serf like me?

SHAHRAZAD: Isn't that what Shahriyar's first wife did?

SERF (*pointing first to her body and then to his*): This silver delicacy . . . and this tawny roughness . . .

SHAHRAZAD (*smiling*): The delicate, silver flower grows from the rough, tawny earth.

SERF: What of my ugliness and humble origin . . .

SHAHRAZAD: It's necessary for you to be a serf, of humble origin, and ugly . . . These are your immortal qualities which I love.

SERF: Those are the qualities of passion.

SHAHRAZAD: Come closer . . .

SERF: It seems to me you're a woman unlike all the rest. You can't love anyone.

SHAHRAZAD: My heart is no concern of yours.

SERF: You're only playing with me . . . I fear you.

SHAHRAZAD: You're imagining things.

SERF: And your husband?

SHAHRAZAD: What's he to you?

SERF: Why did you come to this hall tonight? You were thinking of him.

SHAHRAZAD: Yes . . . I want him to return.

SERF: You see?

SHAHRAZAD: No, I want him to return so I won't tire of you.

SERF: I don't understand.

SHAHRAZAD: If Shahriyar returns, I will see you only after dark when people are sleeping.

SERF: After dark?

SHAHRAZAD: Yes, Darling. If you wish to live you will speed through the darkness like a snake. Take care not to let morning catch you so you get killed.

SERF: If the King sees me?

SHAHRAZAD: No, I . . . My love for you lives only in the dark.

SERF: I understand . . . What a miserable infatuation yours is, Woman! Openness and publicity kill desire in you the way sunshine kills germs.

SHAHRAZAD (*pushing him away since he is shaking her angrily*): Don't shake me this way!

SERF: I feel my end is not far off. You're my assassin.

SHAHRAZAD: Where do you get these notions?

SERF: Aren't you the one who never told her husband a story about a slave in a woman's boudoir without decreeing that the slave be killed like a snake found in the folds of the body?

SHAHRAZAD: Yes . . . I decreed that, but to this day has a man been able to destroy a slave?

SERF: How's that?

SHAHRAZAD: Do you know how a slave is destroyed?

SERF: How?

SHAHRAZAD: By emancipating him. *(The serf laughs without replying.)* You laugh . . .

SERF: How clever you are!

SHAHRAZAD: I'm neither clever nor sarcastic.

SERF: You really meant this then.

SHAHRAZAD: Yes . . . but the man is a child. He does not yet know how to kill a slave. Do you know how the priests in India kill snakes? . . . By letting them speed around the temple grounds.

SERF: Why doesn't the King know that then?

SHAHRAZAD: I think he doesn't need to know it now.

SERF: Isn't he the one who slaughtered his first wife and her . . . lover in bed?

SHAHRAZAD: That was the first Shahriyar . . . Shahriyar is a different person now . . . He was a man who spent a long life in a castle of flesh and blood. Every night he was presented a virgin, and every morning this wife was slaughtered for him. He was a human being who had exhausted all meaning from the words 'body' and 'matter'. He has now changed into a person who wants to flee from everything material and bodily.

SERF *(in astonishment):* Where does he want to flee to?

SHAHRAZAD: He doesn't know where. This is the secret of this poor man's torment.

SERF: Where is he now?

SHAHRAZAD: He has left the earth and hasn't reached the sky. He is suspended between earth and sky . . .

Scene Six

Abu Maysur's tavern . . .

ABU MAYSUR *(addressing the executioner who is stretched out on a comfortable cushion):* Get up, Insolent Executioner! This isn't your place. There are two wealthy merchants of Basra at the door. Get up and vacate the space!

EXECUTIONER *(without moving):* Who says I'm here?

ABU MAYSUR: Aren't you here?

EXECUTIONER: Oh no.

ABU MAYSUR: I thought you were. *(He goes out and returns with the two merchants. They are Shahriyar and Qamar.)* Make way for the fine gentlemen!

QAMAR *(whispering to the King):* Did we need to come to this hole after those long travels?

SHAHRIYAR: Follow me silently!

QAMAR: Is it right for people like us to be found in this house?

SHAHRIYAR: What compelled you to accompany me that day . . .

ABU MAYSUR *(leading them around the edge of a carpet):* Walk slowly . . .

QAMAR: See what he is doing, your Majesty!

ABU MAYSUR: Be careful to stay close to the shore so you don't get your feet wet.

QAMAR *(whispering):* Strange! . . . He thinks the carpet is a sea.

SHAHRIYAR: Hush, Qamar, and obey, for he sees more than you do.

QAMAR: Are you joking?

SHAHRIYAR: Seat us, Tavern Keeper!

ABU MAYSUR *(pointing to the soft cushions):* Please be seated here.

SHAHRIYAR *(noticing the executioner):* Who is this man here?

ABU MAYSUR: A man? . . . where?

SHAHRIYAR: On the cushion. Don't you see him?

ABU MAYSUR: A man? . . . How could there be a man on our cushion when it is the very cleanest?

SHAHRIYAR *(pointing to the room's window):* Perhaps he came in with the wind through this window.

(Abu Maysur removes his sandal but does not answer.)

SHAHRIYAR: What are you doing?

ABU MAYSUR: I'll kill him with my sandal.

SHAHRIYAR: You should rather pick him up and throw him out of the place.

ABU MAYSUR *(stretching his hand towards the executioner):* Amazing!

SHAHRIYAR: What?

ABU MAYSUR: He has a leg like a man's!

SHAHRIYAR: Compare it to yours, Abu Maysur . . . Where did this man come from?

ABU MAYSUR *(examining the executioner's leg):* You're right . . . Then what is this?

EXECUTIONER *(without moving):* Don't touch it when its master is absent.

QAMAR *(whispering):* Your Majesty! . . . This is your old executioner!

SHAHRIYAR: Absent . . . Where? How is it he left his leg here?

EXECUTIONER: He left it planted in the earth. Was the leg created to travel?

SHAHRIYAR: Strange . . . What was the leg created for then?

EXECUTIONER: To remain planted in the earth to carry the trunk, the limbs, and the twigs.

ABU MAYSUR: Where is the master of this fruitless tree now?

EXECUTIONER: I will rise to meet him.

(The executioner rises to his feet and departs.)

ABU MAYSUR *(pointing to the empty cushions):* Come climb on the wings of the bird! *(He also departs.)*

QAMAR: Bird? . . . What bird?

SHAHRIYAR *(sitting on the cushions):* The Roc.

QAMAR: Are you joking? . . . I can't imagine that you come to this place with a serious purpose. Do you like the talk of these half-mad people . . . Look at the other room! Why are they leaning against the house wall like this? By God, truly these human beings resemble nothing more than hollowed out stumps of dead palm trees.[1]

SHAHRIYAR: How excellent are they who have fled their bodies!

QAMAR: Is it for this that we have fled our homes and left our families and wandered through the lands of the earth? So that this could be the conclusion of our journey?

SHAHRIYAR: Our journey? . . . Hush, Fool! We haven't started moving yet.

QAMAR *(looking at him fearfully):* Your Majesty . . .

SHAHRIYAR: Don't be afraid, Qamar. Do you think I'm crazy? No. I'm not insane. *(He points to his legs.)* How can you say we travelled when these pegs have bound us to the earth?

QAMAR *(rising):* By God, stop this talk.

SHAHRIYAR: Sit down.

QAMAR: I can't remain here another moment. I won't follow you this time in this insanity.

SHAHRIYAR: You should say rather that you burn with desire to see her.

QAMAR: What are you saying?

SHAHRIYAR: You can't bear not going to her at once when you have finally returned to where she is.

QAMAR: Me?

SHAHRIYAR: Why deny it, Poor Chap? Your distress is plainly visible. I envy you, Qamar! Shouldn't you have taken me to task for my apathy?

QAMAR: Yes, how dead your heart is!

SHAHRIYAR: Is this all you chide me for?

QAMAR: You're right. This is light censure for a man who knows that he and his wife are in one community after being far apart and separated for a long time and who then comes and loiters in this place.

SHAHRIYAR *(smiling):* Nevertheless, I love her more than you do.
(Qamar trembles but does not answer.)

SHAHRIYAR: What might you say about yourself?

QAMAR *(trying to keep calm):* Your Majesty . . . let's be on our way.

SHAHRIYAR: Qamar . . . didn't I ask you to stay beside her? Why did you flee and run to catch up with me? Why did you prefer to endure with me travels and dangers you weren't made for?

QAMAR: I don't know why you have done this?

SHAHRIYAR: Do you regret it now? . . . Have you perceived that the trip did not produce what you wanted?

QAMAR *(upset):* What did I want?

SHAHRIYAR: Qamar, you poor chap . . . Her shadow followed you through every land. You discovered her everywhere. Don't you remember your cry which astounded everyone in front of the portrait of Isis in Egypt?

QAMAR: More nonsense.

SHAHRIYAR *(his glance having fallen on the wall):* Never mind . . . Look, Qamar, at the wall of this place. What do you see hanging on it? Isn't this my executioner's sword?

QAMAR: Isis?

SHAHRIYAR: Have you forgotten?

QAMAR: You're the one who said to me that Isis resembles her.

SHAHRIYAR: I don't deny this . . . but . . .

QAMAR: Would you have stopped me from expressing my amazement at a resemblance which defies the intellect . . .

SHAHRIYAR: And was Bidpay[2] a woman too like her, so that you should shout out before his portrait in India?

QAMAR: Bidpay? . . . Yes. The eyes of Bidpay had the amazing clarity of hers.

SHAHRIYAR: Do you see? . . . Poor man, everything is Shahrazad to you.

QAMAR (protesting): Your Majesty . . .

SHAHRIYAR: Do you dislike my candor?

QAMAR: Your Majesty . . .

SHAHRIYAR: What is this pale face, Qamar? You're trembling as though you had a fever.

QAMAR (flaring up): Beware of speaking to me this way again! Beware of saying to me what you said again! . . . You don't understand. I think of the Queen the way the Magians do the light of the fire.

SHAHRIYAR (smiling calmly): I know that. Calm yourself, Child. Who told you I meant anything else? Do you see? In truth, you love her the way a handsome man must love a beautiful woman.

QAMAR: Your Majesty . . . your Majesty.

SHAHRIYAR: If only it were this, Stupid . . .

QAMAR: You don't know.

SHAHRIYAR: I know this moth which worships the fire. He doesn't want to see anything but the fire. He continues united to it like part of it, unable to flee or free himself from it until he perishes in it.

QAMAR: Don't make fun of me.

SHAHRIYAR: I'm not making fun of you. Indeed, I love you. Do you know why I will love you forever, Qamar?

(Qamar looks at him for a time in silence.)

SHAHRIYAR (continuing): Because I can love you without embracing you.

QAMAR: What kind of man are you?

SHAHRIYAR (pointing to his body): A man who has fled from this . . .

QAMAR: Nonsense.

SHAHRIYAR: I forgive you everything, because I am no longer a member of your species.

QAMAR (looking carefully at the sword): It seems the sword of fate! . . .

How many bodies has it torn apart! How much blood has streamed out from under its blade!

ABU MAYSUR *(appearing):* Strange! I don't see any smoke or smokers.

SHAHRIYAR: Have you brought us anything?

ABU MAYSUR *(searching about with his eyes):* The devil take the bankrupt executioner. The cursed fellow has gone off with the implements of the prosperous ones.

SHAHRIYAR *(pointing to the suspended sword):* Who brought this sword here, Abu Maysur?

ABU MAYSUR: The executioner sold me this sword against a debt.

QAMAR: How much will you take for it?

SHAHRIYAR: Would you buy it, Qamar? What will you do with it?

(Qamar gives Abu Maysur money and takes the sword in silence.)

SHAHRIYAR: Then what, Abu Maysur! Do you wish us to depart before you bring us what we ordered?

ABU MAYSUR *(shouting angrily):* Executioner . . . by your errant spirit, I have not seen anyone more brazen than you. Are you smoking with the implements of the prosperous ones . . .

EXECUTIONER *(from the other room):* What's the offense since I am one too.

ABU MAYSUR: Who would assert this when you are more impecunious than the dead of India.

EXECUTIONER: Would you like your house to fill with gold?

ABU MAYSUR: When?

EXECUTIONER: Tonight if you wish . . . Bring your containers so I can fill them for you with gold dust purer than the ashes of the dead Indians.

ABU MAYSUR: Where did you get this wealth?

EXECUTIONER: From my friend the slave.

ABU MAYSUR: Your friend the slave! Is he still alive?

EXECUTIONER: He will come shortly.

ABU MAYSUR: Why haven't I heard anything of him since the day the king of the city set forth?

EXECUTIONER: He has been in a silken bed entertaining the queen of the city.

(Qamar, raging and furious, starts to rise.)

SHAHRIYAR *(restraining him):* Qamar . . . have you lost your senses?

ABU MAYSUR *(to the executioner):* Strange! . . . Is this your friend the slave who used to come here sometimes and you would pay for him?

EXECUTIONER: Now he's the pampered lover of Shahrazad.

QAMAR *(jumping up unable to bear what he hears):* You filthy dogs! You animals!

(Abu Maysur turns in alarm.)

SHAHRIYAR *(soothing Qamar's rage and speaking to Abu Maysur):* My comrade has grown impatient with waiting, Abu Maysur.

ABU MAYSUR: Is this his way of speeding things up? I was so frightened that I almost crawled inside my skin.

SHAHRIYAR: We're leaving.

ABU MAYSUR: Have patience a moment till I bring you some other implements with the speed of the jinn. *(He goes off quickly.)*

SHAHRIYAR *(to his vizier):* Qamar . . . What's wrong with you? What has come over you?

(Qamar does not reply.)

SHAHRIYAR: Why has your expression changed?

(Qamar does not reply.)

SHAHRIYAR: Qamar . . . why are you looking at me this way?

QAMAR: You poor man!

SHAHRIYAR: Calm yourself, Qamar, and speak to me without emotion.

QAMAR: I hadn't thought you were wretched to this degree.

SHAHRIYAR *(laughing):* What degree?

QAMAR *(looking at him askance):* You laugh?

SHAHRIYAR: In spite of that I love you, Qamar.

QAMAR: I swear to you by the One who created man that I have never loathed you and held you in such contempt as now.

SHAHRIYAR: It doesn't matter . . .

QAMAR *(furiously):* I know you are pretending to be unmoved, affecting calm, trying to rid yourself of your nature to rise above your human characteristics, and making assertions and imagining fictions . . . but you're a man . . . a despicable man . . . despicable.

SHAHRIYAR: It doesn't matter.

QAMAR *(as tears flow from his eyes without any sobbing):* Your Majesty . . .

SHAHRIYAR: Qamar, why are you weeping?

(Qamar does not reply.)

SHAHRIYAR: My friend Qamar!

QAMAR: Your Majesty.

SHAHRIYAR: Don't grieve.

QAMAR: Could she do this? Would she undertake something like this? . . . This is a lie. It's a slander.

SHAHRIYAR: Dry your tears first. Don't you be a despicable man too . . . Dry your eyes.

QAMAR: Are you making fun of me?

SHAHRIYAR: God forbid. Do you think I'm free to mock a man's heart?

QAMAR (suddenly): Your Majesty! . . . What if what we heard is true?

SHAHRIYAR: Don't say that, Qamar. Can your mind imagine Shahrazad in the arms of a slave? . . . Not a Magian who is a slave to fire but an unclean, filthy serf . . .

QAMAR: Suppose the matter true. You would no doubt do your duty, your Majesty.

SHAHRIYAR: What duty?

QAMAR (pointing to the executioner's sword): As you did for your first wife.

SHAHRIYAR: At that time I was like you.

QAMAR: What do you mean?

QAMAR: Qamar, do you really love her? You're imagining things, Poor Man. You don't love her.

QAMAR: Your Majesty . . .

SHAHRIYAR (pointing to Qamar's body): This is what loves her.

Scene Seven

Shahrazad's boudoir . . .

SHAHRAZAD *(to the serf sitting beside her):* Why are you silent?

SERF: Why did you invite me tonight?

SHAHRAZAD *(smiling):* So that Shahriyar can see you here shortly.

SERF: And kill me like a snake found in the folds of the body.

SHAHRAZAD: Oh no. He won't kill you.

SERF: Woman! Why do you play with me?

SHAHRAZAD: Calm yourself. You're safe.

SERF: My suspicion is confirmed. You've done nothing but prepare to repeat the tragedy for some time.

SHAHRAZAD: Which tragedy?

SERF: The murder of the slave in the boudoir of Shahriyar's wife. It was for this reason you invited me, luring me to this community.

SHAHRAZAD: Yes. I want to see how much Shahriyar has changed.

SERF: It doesn't matter to you that I should become the victim of this experiment?

SHAHRAZAD: And I as well?

SERF: You?

SHAHRAZAD: You fool . . . if he kills, he will kill us both.

SERF: And if he forgives, he will forgive only you.

SHAHRAZAD: He didn't forgive his first wife.

SERF *(after a moment):* Then we're done for.

SHAHRAZAD: If he kills us.

SERF: Do you have any doubt he will do it?

SHAHRAZAD: If he doesn't, he will be among those who perish.

SERF: I don't understand.

SHAHRAZAD *(listening closely):* Hush! . . . Someone is knocking at the door . . .

SERF *(rising quickly):* Here he is . . . The time of death has come.

SHAHRAZAD: Don't be frightened. Hide behind this screen. *(She motions to a black screen in the room.)*

SERF *(looking at the screen startled):* Its color seems an ill omen. Something cries out to me that a head will fall tonight.

SHAHRAZAD: Quickly.

(The serf hides behind the screen. Shahrazad goes to open the door.)

SHAHRAZAD: Who is it? . . . Is it you, Shahriyar?

SHAHRIYAR *(with a trembling voice):* Yes.

SHAHRAZAD: What's wrong with you? Why are you trembling?

SHAHRIYAR: It's . . . the hardship of travel.

SHAHRAZAD *(smiling):* No, this is the effect of the meeting . . . The way it was when we separated. Don't you remember?

SHAHRIYAR *(in despair):* I remember, Shahrazad.

SHAHRAZAD *(leading him to the pillows):* Come.

SHAHRIYAR: This strange calm on your part . . . and this serenity. How impossible it is for me to attain some of this.

SHAHRAZAD: No matter how much you travelled and toured the world?

SHAHRIYAR: I didn't travel. I didn't budge.

SHAHRAZAD: Do you see?

SHAHRIYAR *(casting his eyes around the place):* Here I am in the castle again? Where have I ended up? . . . At the place I began . . . like the ox at the mill with its eyes covered. It goes round . . . and round . . . and round, while thinking it is covering the ground and proceeding in a straight line.

SHAHRAZAD *(after a moment):* And Qamar?

SHAHRIYAR *(turning to the door):* I almost forgot his presence . . . Come in, Qamar . . . Why are you casting your eyes all around the room? Have you found anyone?

QAMAR: Your Majesty . . .

SHAHRIYAR: Here's the room in front of you. Together we have taken her by surprise. Do you see a slave in it?

QAMAR: Your Majesty, I entreat you.

SHAHRIYAR: Let your heart be at peace, Qamar. Shahrazad's body has not been possessed by a slave. Shahrazad is always nobler than an idol and purer than fire. Isn't that so, Shahrazad?

SHAHRAZAD: Shahriyar . . . I forgot to kiss you when you came in.

SHAHRIYAR: You grant me a kiss?

SHAHRAZAD: Yes.

SHAHRIYAR: I donate it to Qamar.

QAMAR *(disapprovingly):* Your Majesty . . . your Majesty.

SHAHRIYAR: Take it, Dolt. Who would refuse a kiss from Shahrazad?

(Qamar exits forthwith.)

SHAHRIYAR: The stupid fellow has fled.

SHAHRAZAD *(looking at her husband for a time):* Shahriyar! You are concealing things from me in your soul.

SHAHRIYAR: I'm not the one who is concealing things.

SHAHRAZAD: Oh, yes. You are frightening now.

SHAHRIYAR: I am calmer now than before. Don't you think so?

SHAHRAZAD *(doubtingly):* Perhaps . . .

SHAHRIYAR: Do you think me less than calm?

SHAHRAZAD: Did you think of me during the trip?

SHAHRIYAR: I thought of you only at the hour of departure and the hour of return. In between, I was living in the hour and place enfolding me.

SHAHRAZAD: You forgot me?

SHAHRIYAR: I forgot everything past and its characteristics—like a dream which never comes true. My life quickly took on the shape of the space and time containing my body.

SHAHRAZAD: Like water taking on the shape of the container.

SHAHRIYAR *(despondently):* And am I different from water, Shahrazad? . . . Always imprisoned like water? . . . Yes, I'm nothing but water. Do I have any true existence outside of the time and space which encompass my body . . . Even travel or locomotion is nothing but changing one container for another . . . and when did a change of containers liberate the water.

SHAHRAZAD: It is not travel, Shahriyar, which will liberate your body.

SHAHRIYAR: You're right.

SHAHRAZAD *(after a moment):* You haven't asked me, Shahriyar, what I did during your absence.

SHAHRIYAR: How does this affair concern me . . .

SHAHRAZAD: Do you no longer desire to know who I am?

SHAHRIYAR: You're a beautiful body.

SHAHRAZAD: Certainly not. You are misrepresenting me.

SHAHRIYAR: You are a great heart.

SHAHRAZAD: Certainly not.

SHAHRIYAR: You are intellect and design.

SHAHRAZAD: Certainly not.

SHAHRIYAR: You are I. You are we. Nothing exists but us. Wherever we go, there is nothing but us, our shadow, our imaginings. We are all of existence. There is nothing save our image in this great mirror which surrounds us on every side. I am weary of this crystal prison.

SHAHRAZAD: What you are doing will not bring deliverance.

SHAHRIYAR: What will?

SHAHRAZAD: I don't know.

SHAHRIYAR: Oh . . . You are still yourself. You haven't changed.

SHAHRAZAD: And you are still yourself. You haven't changed.

SHAHRIYAR (after a silence): Confess, Shahrazad . . . It's you who have brought me to this end.

SHAHRAZAD: No, it is the nature of things.
  (Silence.)

SHAHRIYAR (sighing): Shahrazad . . . I feel a chill creeping through my joints.

SHAHRAZAD: Sit down, Shahriyar!

SHAHRIYAR: Oh no . . . I don't want to sit. I don't like to sit on this earth . . always this earth . . . Nothing but this earth. This turning prison . . . We aren't moving . . . We aren't advancing or retreating. We aren't rising or falling. We're merely going round. Everything is going round. That's eternity . . . What a deception! We ask nature for its secret, and it answers with detours and evasions.

SHAHRAZAD (smiling): Yes, you are going round . . . and now you are at the end of the cycle.

SHAHRIYAR: The end is followed by the beginning according to the law of eternity and of rotation.

SHAHRAZAD: Didn't you know this before?

SHAHRIYAR: I used to think nature more dextrous than this.

SHAHRAZAD (smiling): Are you resentful against nature to this extent?

SHAHRIYAR: It combats me and leaves me powerless, imprisoned, inside a turning ring.

SHAHRAZAD (smiling): I don't think it is combatting you or concerned with you . . . You are nothing but a hair on nature's head.

SHAHRIYAR: Whenever it goes white, she plucks it out.

SHAHRAZAD: She hates old age.

SHAHRIYAR: Yes.

SHAHRAZAD: She plucks it out so it can return anew.

SHAHRIYAR: Young and strong.

SHAHRAZAD: Yes.

SHAHRIYAR: Everything that grows old, she makes young again. Every end she links to a beginning. How long will this cycle with no exit continue?

SHAHRAZAD (after a moment): How far removed you are from Qamar who thinks life is unconfined and nature beautiful.

SHAHRIYAR (letting out a moan): I can't bear this place.

SHAHRAZAD: And me?

SHAHRIYAR *(pointing into space and then to his body)*: This place . . . this body . . . The body which space has formed the way a container gives form to the water . . .

SHAHRAZAD: Shahriyar? . . . How difficult your life is now. Won't you be a little less hard on yourself?

SHAHRIYAR: It's too late.

SHAHRAZAD: Forget what's beyond your life, Shahriyar . . . Contemplate the surface of the cloak. Don't worry about what is inside it, for it is nothing but threads.

SHAHRIYAR: All the cloak is in those threads.

SHAHRAZAD: There is nothing to concern you behind the cloak . . .
    (A silence . . .)

SHAHRIYAR *(looking at the black curtain indifferently)*: There is nothing that concerns me behind the screen.

SHAHRAZAD: This screen? Why do you look this way at this screen?

SHAHRIYAR: Black?

SHAHRAZAD: Yes, black!

SHAHRIYAR: The color of darkness . . . How must I detest its color!

SHAHRAZAD: What prevents you from killing it?

SERF *(emerging suddenly from behind the screen, shouting)*: You traitor! May he kill you with me . . .

SHAHRIYAR *(calmly)*: Don't abuse Shahrazad! I don't like people who abuse Shahrazad.

SERF *(fearfully)*: Your Majesty . . .

SHAHRIYAR *(to the serf)*: Go.

SHAHRAZAD: Won't you kill him and me?

SHAHRIYAR: Certainly not.
    (The serf goes out puzzled but happy with his deliverance.)

SHAHRAZAD: Shahriyar!

SHAHRIYAR: Why are you looking at me this way?

SHAHRAZAD: You are a doomed man.

SHAHRIYAR: Didn't you know that before?
    (All at once, a cry of fright rises from outside. Then there is a call for help. The serf appears retracing his steps in a strange manner. He is terrified.)

SERF: Help . . . Help. The vizier.

SHAHRIYAR: The vizier? Qamar? What about him?

SERF: The executioner's sword! He severed his head from his body with the the executioner's sword . . . when he saw me coming out of the room.

SHAHRIYAR: Qamar's dead!

SHAHRAZAD: Don't mourn, Shahriyar.

SHAHRIYAR: Qamar's life is snuffed out!

SHAHRAZAD: Alas.

SHAHRIYAR *(after a moment):* Qamar ceased drawing life from the sun?

SHAHRAZAD: Because he ceased believing in her.

SHAHRIYAR: Belief!

SHAHRAZAD: He was a man.

SHAHRIYAR: Yes, he was a man.

SHAHRAZAD: But you, Shahriyar . . .

SHAHRIYAR: I . . . Who am I?

SHAHRAZAD: You are a man suspended between earth and sky. Anxiety eats away at you. I have tried to bring you back to earth. The attempt has not succeeded.

SHAHRIYAR: I don't want to return to earth.

SHAHRAZAD: I've told you, Shahriyar . . . There's nothing but the earth.

SHAHRIYAR *(moving away):* Farewell, then, Shahrazad!

SHAHRAZAD: Are you going? Let me try one more time.

(Shahriyar goes out in questioning silence.)

SERF *(following him with his eyes until he disappears):* He has gone.

SHAHRAZAD: This is inevitable for him.

SERF: I swear it is his wives' blood . . . It's the blood of his wives. The time for blood has passed . . . but this is what the man has come to.

SHAHRAZAD *(as though addressing herself):* He has gone round and come to the end of the cycle.

SERF *(moving suddenly):* I can bring him back to you.

SHAHRAZAD: It will be the vision of another Shahriyar which returns . . . born anew, fresh and moist . . . but this one is a white hair which has been plucked out.

Notes

[1]Compare Qur'an 69:7.

[2]The Indian narrator of a book of fables forming the basis of the Arabic literary classic *Kalila and Dimna.*

Princess Sunshine

Characters

SULTAN NU'MAN

VIZIER, in the service of Sultan Nu'man

PRINCESS SUNSHINE, the daughter of Sultan Nu'man

FIRST SUITOR

SECOND SUITOR

MOONLIGHT, the third suitor

INSPECTOR OF THE TREASURY

AIDE to the Inspector

PRINCE HAMDAN

ATTENDANT, in the service of Prince Hamdan

DOORMAN, in the service of Prince Hamdan

TREASURER, in the service of Prince Hamdan

A TREASURY GUARD

A LADY-IN-WAITING

SOLDIERS

A TREASURY SCRIBE

GHOST of an old villager

GHOSTLY VILLAGERS

Act One

Scene One

The Great Hall in the castle of Sultan Nu'man, the Sultan is conversing with his vizier.

SULTAN: I asked you to take care of it for me, Vizier!

VIZIER: God is our Caretaker, your majesty the Sultan.

SULTAN: I've heard you say that twenty times! Of course, God is our caretaker . . . but you are my vizier. I employ you to think with me and to take care of things for me. Do you wish to collect the salary and let God handle the work for you . . .

VIZIER: Have I ever abandoned my work . . .

SULTAN: Frequently. The easy work you undertake yourself and the hard work you abandon to God.

VIZIER: What harm is there if I ask God's assistance?

SULTAN: Why don't I ask him myself, directly, and save the salary?

VIZIER: My salary, in any case, is not an exorbitant sum.

SULTAN: I know that . . . but I am not talking about the official salary!

VIZIER: I'm not the only one, your Majesty.

SULTAN: I know that too. Everyone . . .

VIZIER: The whole kingdom . . . both high and low . . . and you, your Majesty, wanted it that way.

SULTAN: What did I want!

VIZIER: You said: "These are the official salaries . . . and in addition to that each one has his wits."

SULTAN: That everyone can have what his wits bring him doesn't mean . . . Moreover, there has been a big increase in wits.

VIZIER: Today, everyone wants to make a good living.

SULTAN: True . . . except my foolish daughter! And you, Vizier, aren't willing to think of a solution to this problem for me.

VIZIER: You know, your Majesty, the princess' character. Nothing stands in the way of her will.

SULTAN: Is it right to obey such an eccentric will as hers?

VIZIER: What can we do, your Majesty? We have held firm to our position while she has become more insistent on hers.

SULTAN: On what ill-omened night was this daughter born? Years pass and she doesn't wish to get married. Her two sisters have been married in a way fitting the daughters of kings . . . to the pick of the princes and the richest of the sultans. But she . . . is not tempted by wealth or rank. I don't know, then, what in life does attract her.

VIZIER: Princess Sunshine has been this way since she was young, your Majesty. Amazing, unique . . . she has excelled at horseback riding, sword play, reading books, and prolonged meditation and abstinence to an amazing and dazzling extent . . .

SULTAN: All this could be endured except that will of hers . . . except that condition she stipulates for marriage.

VIZIER: I have an idea, your Majesty.

SULTAN: At last! Speak and be quick.

VIZIER: We'll accept the condition.

SULTAN: Is this an idea?

VIZIER: Accept the condition with a change.

SULTAN: What change? The condition is that all the men pass below her window and she can choose from among them without distinction!

VIZIER: We will obey that with one minor proviso. She should allow us to make a preliminary selection. That way we can weed out anyone who is not worthy of her.

SULTAN: You're right. Yes . . . Perhaps we could fake it. We would slip in some princes and restrict the choice to them.

VIZIER: This is my intention.

SULTAN: It's not a bad idea . . . Let's call Sunshine and put this simple stipulation to her.

VIZIER: It's a very simple one.

(The vizier goes to the door where he whispers to one of the ladies-in-waiting. Then he returns to the Sultan.)

VIZIER: The princess is coming . . . but . . . should I remain?

SULTAN: Naturally, it's your idea, and it's your duty to undertake to present it.

VIZIER: Me? . . . I . . .

SULTAN: Do you wish to abandon your work another time . . . Your idea won't be of any value unless you can convince her of it.

VIZIER: Whatever you command, your Majesty.

SULTAN: Here comes Sunshine.

SUNSHINE *(appearing from the door):* Did you send for me, Father?

SULTAN: Yes . . . Do you insist on your condition?

SUNSHINE: Of course I insist.

SULTAN: We have accepted the condition, but . . .

SUNSHINE: But?

SULTAN: No . . . nothing worth mentioning . . . It's merely a simple procedure the vizier suggested. Speak, Vizier!

VIZIER *(clearing his throat):* The idea . . . the topic . . . is merely . . . a simple procedure . . . a very simple one.

SUNSHINE: Very simple?

VIZIER: Very . . . mere formalities . . .

SUNSHINE: The important thing is for the condition to be carried out . . . with great precision.

VIZIER: It will be carried out with great precision, only . . . The question of inviting all the populace . . .

SUNSHINE: This is a necessity.

VIZIER: Of course, naturally . . . This is a necessity . . . only . . . denying access to the hoi polloi.

SUNSHINE: What are you saying, Vizier . . . Indeed, I wish the hoi polloi to come.

VIZIER: I understand . . . I understand. Only to prevent crowding below the window . . .

SUNSHINE: How does crowding disturb you?

VIZIER: No . . . nothing disturbs me personally . . . only . . .

SUNSHINE: Only what? What exactly are you trying to get at?

VIZIER: No . . . I don't wish to infringe on the condition, only . . .

SUNSHINE: So long as this is your intention, then there is no need to speak.

VIZIER: Of course, there is absolutely no need, only . . .

SUNSHINE: You've said 'only' enough. Proceed to the subject, I entreat you, if you have something to say.

SULTAN: She's right.

VIZIER: The subject in brief, Princess, is that there must be some organizing done.

SUNSHINE: Organizing? Why?

VIZIER: Organizing for screening . . . merely organizing.

SUNSHINE: How would this organizing be done?

VIZIER: The matter is very simple: we specify for suitors a certain number and certain qualities.

SUNSHINE: Who will specify that? . . . You?

VIZIER: If you authorize me.

SUNSHINE: I authorize you? Then you would be the one choosing my husband!

VIZIER: In the end, the choice is yours.

SUNSHINE: After you specified the qualities of my husband for me . . .

VIZIER: No, Princess . . . the qualities you specify as you wish. Our only duty is to carry it out.

SUNSHINE: Who told you I could specify these qualities?

VIZIER: Can't you specify them?

SUNSHINE: I can't specify them in advance . . . because I don't know them.

VIZIER: You don't know the qualities you desire in your husband?

SUNSHINE: No, all I know are the qualities I don't want for him.

VIZIER: What are the qualities you don't want?

SUNSHINE: I don't want him to be one of the stupid, lazy princes.

SULTAN: Beware, Sunshine, of allowing any intentional allusion into your speech.

SUNSHINE: I intend no allusion with my words . . . as long as my two sisters are happy and content, they are of no concern to anyone else. I speak only of myself.

VIZIER: The point of your statement then is that you want a poor husband?

SUNSHINE: I told you that I haven't specified the qualities yet.

VIZIER: How will you choose then?

SUNSHINE: I will not choose until after I examine . . .

VIZIER: You examine?

SUNSHINE: For this reason, I have determined and remain determined to have the door opened equally to all men. I will receive each one who comes forward to seek my hand. I will converse with him myself and attempt to test his metal.

SULTAN: You will receive all the men?

SUNSHINE: Yes, here in this Hall . . . with you present, Father, and the vizier.

VIZIER: The question is more complicated than we suspected.

SULTAN: Truly . . . The thought was that she would look out the window and choose the one pleasing her among the passersby.

SUNSHINE: I should choose from the window? Choose what? Choose bodies?

SULTAN: Then you wish to confront and converse with all the men?

SUNSHINE: All those who come forward to request me.

SULTAN: All the men will come forward to request you . . . so long as the door is wide open.

SUNSHINE: The opportunity must be afforded each of the men.

VIZIER: But this will be an oppressive amount of work for you, Princess. Imagine all the citizens . . .

SULTAN: Both serious and frivolous ones . . .

SUNSHINE: I have one small condition.

VIZIER: What is it?

SUNSHINE: Whoever comes forward and fails will receive three lashes.

VIZIER: A reasonable condition to check the flow of jokers.

SUNSHINE: So that only those who are sure of themselves will come forward.

VIZIER: This type of safeguard is necessary.

SUNSHINE: Then we've agreed.

VIZIER: Just as you command, Princess.

SULTAN: Just as she commands! . . . Then you acknowledge your failure, Vizier.

VIZIER: The fact is, your Majesty, that I . . .

SULTAN: The fact is that you weren't able to convince her. This is what I expected. From the first word you uttered. We have wasted our time for naught. The result is still the same . . . after long months. Listen, Daughter, I'll accede to your wish, God help me. All that I have sought has been what is good for you. It's only your welfare that I wish and seek . . . but since you insist on your opinion, it's up to you. Know that from now on you alone are responsible for your fate.

SUNSHINE: This is all I desire, Father . . . that I should be the only one to create my destiny.

SULTAN: I tell you frankly . . . I'm not happy . . .

SUNSHINE: I know that.

SULTAN: I would have desired for you a comfortable life with a guarantee of opulence and ease.

SUNSHINE: Yes . . . the life you created for my two sisters.

SULTAN: We shall see what you create for yourself.

SUNSHINE: If I do it myself, that's enough.

SULTAN: Carry out her request, Vizier!

VIZIER: At once . . . I will send the criers out with the announcement that everyone who comes forward to seek the hand of Princess Sunshine and fails will receive three lashes.

SUNSHINE: No. They must announce, before, that all men of the town without distinction have the right to present themselves to request Sunshine.

Scene Two

The same Great Hall in the castle of Sultan Nu'man. Some soldiers stand in a line. The Sultan is seated. Sunshine is near him, while the vizier looks out the window.

VIZIER: No one.

SULTAN: During the last days, the number has indeed begun to decrease.

VIZIER: Today there's absolutely no one. There's not a sign of any one of the passersby approaching the castle.

SULTAN: How different that is from the first week when the townsfolk crowded in, each trying to get ahead of the other.

VIZIER: Now they all flee.

SULTAN: Yes, for fear of the whip.

VIZIER *(returning from the window):* It's no use. No one will come forward.

SULTAN: Not today or tomorrow . . . since most of the men in the city have been lashed.

VIZIER: They failed the examination.

SULTAN: In spite of that, some of the men were quite acceptable.

VIZIER: In the opinion of the princess, they were entitled to a zero.

SULTAN: You are too strict, Sunshine.

SUNSHINE: Isn't it a fateful question?

SULTAN: Yes, but . . . it has seemed to me at times that you are not serious about choosing.

VIZIER: This also seems to be the men's feeling. I've heard that they have begun whispering to each other that Princess Sunshine does not really intend to marry. She wishes rather to make fun of the men and have them whipped.

SULTAN: If this really is your intention, it is best for you to be frank.

SUNSHINE: Is this what you think of me, Father? Have you known me to be anything but frank?

SULTAN: Actually . . . you are frank.

SUNSHINE: Rest assured that I'm not playing around, being a hypocrite, or temporizing. I am rather examining and discovering.

SULTAN: But you haven't discovered anything yet.

SUNSHINE: This is beyond my control.

SULTAN: It seems the matter will go on for a long time.

SUNSHINE: It will require patience.

SULTAN: My patience is exhausted.

(A soldier enters and whispers into the vizier's ear.)

VIZIER: There's a man at the door who wishes to come forward . . .

SULTAN: Invite him in of course.

VIZIER *(to the soldier):* Bring him in!

SULTAN *(to Sunshine):* Perhaps, maybe . . .

SUNSHINE: We shall see!

SUITOR *(entering):* Greetings to you, your Majesty the Sultan, and your Majesty the Princess.

SULTAN: Greetings to you.

SUITOR: I come from a distant country striving after the loftiest goal: the hand of Princess Sunshine.

SULTAN: Do you know what is awaiting you?

SUITOR: I know . . . and I am ready.

SULTAN: Are you this sure of yourself?

SUITOR: Yes.

SULTAN: Your case is in the hands of the princess.

SUITOR: I am entirely at her disposal.

SUNSHINE: I desire one thing from you. You are to tell me what you will do with me if I become your wife.

SUITOR: I will make you happy. I will obey your every request. Even if what you desire is in the heart of the Roc bird, I will hunt it down for you.

SULTAN: Would you be able?

SUITOR: I would . . . and you will learn that I am capable of much.

SUNSHINE: What besides the Roc bird?

SUITOR: I will adore you. I will erect for you a palace with seven coral columns on the island of Waq al-Waq.[1]

SUNSHINE: Waq al-Waq? . . . This too?

SUITOR: It's an island I possess by this name. It has fruit which tongue and lip crave.

SULTAN: This is magnificent.

VIZIER: Very magnificent.

SUNSHINE: What would I do during the course of a day?

SUITOR: You would command and we would obey. You request and we comply.

SULTAN: God's will be done!

VIZIER: Whatever God wills!

SUNSHINE: God's will be done indeed. This is very lovely. I order and am obeyed. I request and my request is honored.

SUITOR: Whatever the request may be. I have much gold. It will all be spread at your feet. I will make happiness like a pillow under your head. Felicity will waft over you like a fan of ostrich feathers.

SUNSHINE: My goodness!

SULTAN: Really, this is splendid.

VIZIER: Very splendid.

SULTAN: Now . . . what is your decision?

SUNSHINE: Lash him!

SULTAN: What are you saying?

SUNSHINE: I said: lash him.

VIZIER: There is no might or power save God's.

SULTAN: Reconsider a bit, Sunshine.

SUNSHINE: There's no need for that. Carry it out, Vizier!

VIZIER *(looking at the Sultan):* Carry it out?

SULTAN: May God look after us.

VIZIER *(to the suitor):* Please prepare . . . unfortunately.

SUITOR: Did I say anything that merits this lashing?

VIZIER: Are you asking me?

SUITOR: But . . .

VIZIER: Submit to the verdict I entreat you. This was the precondition.

(He hands him over to one of the soldiers who takes him out. The vizier goes back near the Sultan.)

SULTAN *(to his daughter):* How will it all end, Sunshine?

SUNSHINE: What is my offense, Father? Do you like this type of man?

SULTAN: What's wrong with him? A man who adores you . . . who wishes to provide you abundant happiness . . . who will obey your every request.

SUNSHINE: Do you want me to live on the Isle of Waq al-Waq?

SULTAN: So long as he will build a palace there for you with coral columns . . .

SUNSHINE: I beg you, Father . . . Don't make me laugh!

SULTAN: Is this a laughing matter? This calls for rejoicing and pride. Someone who will surround you with all this opulence and luxury comes forward for you.

SUNSHINE: No one wants to understand me.

SULTAN: Indeed . . . I acknowledge my inability to understand you.

SUNSHINE: Then pay no heed to me and my concerns.

SULTAN: This is what I promised you. I am always true to my promise. It's nothing but a few observations which I know will make no difference.

VIZIER: What does her Majesty the Princess command? We have not achieved anything. Are we to continue?

SUNSHINE: Of course we will continue. So long as people continue to present themselves they must be received. The door is always open.

SULTAN: Which door?

SUNSHINE: The door of endeavor.

VIZIER: And the door of lashing.

SUNSHINE: What are you saying?

VIZIER: I'm saying the door of endeavor . . . must remain open to all who . .

SULTAN: Who are foolhardy.

(One of the soldiers comes in and whispers to the vizier.)

VIZIER: Another foolhardy person.

SULTAN: Of course have him come in, bringing his luck with him.

VIZIER *(to the soldier):* Bring him in!

SULTAN: Perhaps . . .

VIZIER: Maybe . . .

SECOND SUITOR *(entering):* Greetings to Sultan Nuʿman and to Princess Sunshine!

SULTAN: Greetings to you.

SECOND SUITOR: I come to you with my hand extended in entreaty, asking that you give me the hand of the sun out of the heart of heaven . . If only you knew what a difficult goal it is . . .

SULTAN: We know.

SECOND SUITOR: I await your command.

SULTAN: The Princess is in charge.

SECOND SUITOR: What does the Princess command?

SUNSHINE: Listen, Fellow. Do you want me to be your wife?

SECOND SUITOR: This is the dream of a lifetime and the hope of the heart.

SUNSHINE: Suppose I became your wife—what would you do with me?

SECOND SUITOR: I'd place you in my eye and guard you with my eyelashes.

SUNSHINE: Do you think your eye is large enough for me or a fit residence for me? Look at me closely. I am not a grain of sand or dust that you can stick in your eye.

SECOND SUITOR: I meant rather . . .

SUNSHINE: Speak to me in clearly defined terms. What will my life with you be?

SECOND SUITOR: Love . . . the happiness of love in a beautiful, comfortable nest, neither too grand nor too small. We will have enough for a life of plenty and more . . . a vast field, a lush garden, and a brook . . . some servants about you to serve you and look after your comfort. We will have a bright and handsome son, with silver and gold hair, and a most beautiful and lovely daughter. When she laughs, the sun rises. If she weeps the rain falls in torrents.

SULTAN: Lovely!

SECOND SUITOR: Yes, your Majesty . . . your grandson by me will be bright and handsome and your granddaughter most beautiful and lovely.

SULTAN: Do you hear this, Daughter?

SUNSHINE: Very lovely!

SULTAN: Isn't it? This is the best a grandfather could hope for.

SUNSHINE: But how can one be certain of that?

SECOND SUITOR: This is certain.

SUNSHINE: How can it be, now?

SECOND SUITOR: I saw that in a dream . . . and my dreams are never wrong.

SUNSHINE: We shall see . . .

SULTAN: Imagine—I will be the grandfather of a bright and handsome boy and a most beautiful and lovely girl. Isn't that splendid?

VIZIER: Most splendid, your Majesty.

SULTAN: The hair of his head alternating between silver and gold.

VIZIER: If the girl laughs the weather is perfect. If she weeps, it is overcast and rainy.

SULTAN: Yes . . . yes. How happy I will be at that . . . as the grandfather.

VIZIER: And the happiness of the Princess as mother, too.

SULTAN: Without doubt . . . no doubt! Now, Daughter, what is your . . . decision?

SUNSHINE: Whip him!

SULTAN: What did she say?

VIZIER: I did not hear well.

SUNSHINE: I said: whip him. Have you heard now?

SULTAN: It's no use . . . no use.

VIZIER: Yes . . . no use.

SULTAN: This decision of yours is final of course.

SUNSHINE: Of course.

VIZIER *(to the second suitor):* This way, please.

SECOND SUITOR: I'm to be whipped?

VIZIER: Don't you believe your ears?

SECOND SUITOR *(imploringly):* O your Majesty the Sultan . . . O Grandfather of my children . . .

VIZIER: How is it that in your dream you saw yourself procreating and didn't see yourself being whipped?

SUNSHINE: You tell him!

VIZIER: Let's go. Don't waste your time. Accept your luck. God assist you and those like you, before and after. *(He hands him over to a soldier who takes him out.)*

SULTAN: Even this man is rejected?

SUNSHINE: Yes.

SULTAN: You exaggerate, Daughter, more than necessary. Not even motherhood tempts you?

SUNSHINE: I must be something before I can be a mother.

SULTAN: These are words I can't understand.

SUNSHINE: I know.

VIZIER: Wouldn't it be good to think once again of closing this door? The results of these examinations can be known in advance.

SULTAN: She has already told you she will meet anyone who comes forward.

VIZIER: Anyone who comes forward, after all this, is crazy.

(A soldier enters and whispers to the Vizier.)

SULTAN: It seems that . . .

VIZIER: Yes . . . the very one.

SULTAN: Who is it?

VIZIER: The crazy man.

SULTAN: Let him in of course.

VIZIER: Of course. So long as there are still those in the land who are infatuated with whipping, what concern is it to us?

THIRD SUITOR *(entering):* Greetings to you all.

SULTAN: Greetings to you.

THIRD SUITOR: Where is the one they call Sunshine?

SUNSHINE: Me of course. Is there any other woman besides me in this Hall?

THIRD SUITOR: One has to be certain.

SUNSHINE: Are you certain now?

THIRD SUITOR: So this is you, then, Sunshine? I had imagined something else!

SUNSHINE: How did you imagine me?

THIRD SUITOR: Something other than this, never mind. What concerns us . . . the important thing is that I've come. What do you want from me?

VIZIER: Strange! Did we invite you?

THIRD SUITOR: Who else? . . . This crier you sent out through the land?

SULTAN: He's right.

THIRD SUITOR: "Everyone in the land without distinction has the right to come forward for the hand of Princess Sunshine." Wasn't this the text of the announcement? "Without distinction" . . . I liked this expression. I said to myself: why not use my right?

SUNSHINE: Then you've come to use your right? Isn't that so?

THIRD SUITOR: Without doubt. I have been a little slow, because I had to raise the price of this suitable cloak.

SULTAN *(with bitter sarcasm):* God's will be done!

VIZIER: God's will be done indeed. Then you didn't even own this simple cloak?

THIRD SUITOR: I own only myself.

VIZIER: We are honored.

SULTAN: And you dare, Man . . .

SUNSHINE: Leave him alone, Father. This is not his fault. We truly said: without restriction or distinction.

SULTAN: This is the result!

THIRD SUITOR: A happy result!

SULTAN *(to his daughter):* What is your decision?

VIZIER: Whipping naturally.

SULTAN: Naturally.

VIZIER: This time it is deserved and merited.

SUNSHINE: Have patience till I question him.

SULTAN: Hurry then . . . our patience is exhausted.

SUNSHINE *(to the man):* Listen, Fellow!

THIRD SUITOR: Fellow? First of all, my name is Moonlight, but you can call me Mr. Moon.

VIZIER: A very lovely thing!

SULTAN: Truly.

SUNSHINE: Is this your real name?

THIRD SUITOR: And you? Sunshine? . . . Is this your real name? If you are the sun of the day, then I am the moon of the age.

VIZIER: Shall we silence him?

SULTAN: The fact is he . . .

SUNSHINE: One moment, I beg you. Listen, Moonlight! Suppose I become your wife—what will you do with me?

MOONLIGHT: What will I do with you? I won't do anything with you. You are the one who will act on yourself and for yourself. What are you good at?

SUNSHINE: What am I good at?

MOONLIGHT: Yes . . . what kinds of work are you good at? Are you good at cooking for example?

SUNSHINE: Cooking?

MOONLIGHT: Making clothes? Mending tears? Getting rid of spots? Repairing sandals? Basket making? Spreading out laundry, kneading dough, baking bread, ladling soup, raising chickens, cleaning glass, filling water jars from wells and pouring it into storage containers, sweeping out the dust, making pickles, and all the other chores and tasks . . .

SUNSHINE: I? . . . The daughter of Sultan Nuʿman?

MOONLIGHT: But you will become the wife of Moonlight.

SUNSHINE: This then is what awaits me with you?

MOONLIGHT: Assuming the best happens.

SUNSHINE: Is there anything worse?

MOONLIGHT: Sometimes . . . for there might not be any clothing to make, dough to knead, or chickens to raise . . . not even any dust to sweep.

SUNSHINE: In a case like this, how would we live?

MOONLIGHT: I have no love for prophecy.

SUNSHINE: And you—what are you good at?

MOONLIGHT: Nothing . . . and everything.

SUNSHINE: I don't understand what you're saying.

MOONLIGHT: If you live with me, you will understand.

SUNSHINE: Do you imagine it possible for me to live with you?

MOONLIGHT: Do you want the truth? . . . I don't imagine that. It's not possible for me to imagine it.

SUNSHINE: Why did you come and present yourself then?

MOONLIGHT: To employ my right. I couldn't resist this temptation . . . to make use of a right I had. So long as I was allowed to enter the contest, why not enter?

SUNSHINE: But you on failing will be whipped.

MOONLIGHT: A whipping? Nothing could be simpler!

SUNSHINE: Suppose you win?

MOONLIGHT: That would be a disaster!

SUNSHINE: Disaster? If you take me, you consider that a disaster!

MOONLIGHT: Certainly.

VIZIER: The impudence of this man has increased. Permit us to whip him at once, your Majesty. At once!

SUNSHINE: Wait!

SULTAN: Wait till when, Daughter? . . . Are we to listen to this talk from a tramp like this?

SUNSHINE: One moment more . . . Listen, Moonlight! Hasn't it occurred to you that if you gain me that I, with my wealth and rank, will be yours?

MOONLIGHT: What will you do with me then?

SUNSHINE: This is my concern.

MOONLIGHT: But it's my concern too.

SUNSHINE: You will be my husband. No one will require you to do anything.

MOONLIGHT: I am not accustomed to living without doing anything.

SUNSHINE: You will do something. We will train you to become a ruler one day.

MOONLIGHT: A ruler?

SUNSHINE: Yes . . . a ruler like my father.

MOONLIGHT: Who said I want to be like your father.

SULTAN: This is insufferable!

VIZIER: We will silence him at once.

SUNSHINE: Patience! Patience, I entreat you. Why don't you, Moonlight, want to be a ruler like my father?

MOONLIGHT: Your father was never one of those ruled.

SUNSHINE: Of course not.

MOONLIGHT: The ruler ought to come from those ruled.

VIZIER: This man is a danger.

SULTAN: Truly.

SUNSHINE (to Moonlight): This however is true of you.

MOONLIGHT: No . . . it's the excellent follower who makes the excellent leader. I have not yet practised and been formed enough to be an excellent follower.

SUNSHINE: Tell me . . . Explain to me: what do you want exactly?

MOONLIGHT: You are the one who wants . . . What do you want from me exactly?

SUNSHINE: The truth is that I'm like you and don't know head from tail.

VIZIER: We'll whip him and be done with it.

SUNSHINE: With a person like this whipping is of no significance.

SULTAN: We must finish this subject!

SUNSHINE: First, I must finish my examination. Tell, Moonlight, if one supposes, I became your wife—can't you have me do anything besides dough, bread, and soup . . .

MOONLIGHT: Why do you always speak about what someone will do with you? Why don't you make something of other people?

SUNSHINE: What are you saying?

MOONLIGHT: I want to ask you in turn: if one supposes that I married you, what would you do with me?

SUNSHINE: The fact is I . . .

MOONLIGHT: That you haven't thought about that, but I want to know now what my fate will be with you?

SUNSHINE: Your fate with me?

MOONLIGHT: I now am not good at anything . . . a clod of earth . . . but in the hand of a master potter I could become a jug. You haven't put your hand in the dirt before. Try . . . perhaps you could make me into something.

SUNSHINE: Make you into something?

MOONLIGHT: Why not? . . . Even you might succeed.

SUNSHINE: Even I? Am I in your opinion . . .

MOONLIGHT: Yes . . . sorry.

SUNSHINE: You are mistaken . . . and I will challenge you!

MOONLIGHT: I accept the challenge.

SUNSHINE: I will prove to you that I can make of you not just a jug . . . but something more important and greater.

MOONLIGHT: What? A large jar? . . . A caldron?

SUNSHINE: A man.

MOONLIGHT: A man? . . . from me? I hope you are successful!

SUNSHINE (to the Sultan and Vizier): Here's my decision.

VIZIER: Whipping.

SUNSHINE: Marriage.

SULTAN: What's this nonsense, Sunshine? You marry this creature?

SUNSHINE: He has succeeded.

VIZIER: Glory to God!

SULTAN: You term impudence and insolence success . . .

SUNSHINE: Yes. I will make something of this clod of impudence and insolence.

SULTAN: But the price is exorbitant!

VIZIER: Truly, your Majesty . . . We could without difficulty get hold of a ready-made man for you.

MOONLIGHT: The important thing is what she does with her hand!

SUNSHINE: This is true.

SULTAN: I am not content with this marriage.

SUNSHINE: You consented to the condition: without distinction or discrimination.

SULTAN: I agreed under compulsion.

SUNSHINE: Then you must be faithful to our pact.

SULTAN: You are wrecking your life.

MOONLIGHT: Perhaps she is building it.

SULTAN: Be quiet, Tramp!

VIZIER: Shut up, Rogue!

MOONLIGHT *(to Sunshine):* Do you like these insults for the substance from which you will make your extraordinary masterpiece?

SUNSHINE: I entreat you . . . Leave him and his affairs alone.

SULTAN: We will leave him and his affairs alone and you and yours too. Do what you want! I am not responsible for you.

SUNSHINE *(to Moonlight):* When do you want to get married?

MOONLIGHT: Marriage? Who told you I want to marry?

SUNSHINE: Strange! Did you think all this a comedy, Fellow?

MOONLIGHT: But I don't have any dowry money with me.

SUNSHINE: We'll loan it to you temporarily.

MOONLIGHT: I don't like marriage on credit.

SUNSHINE: Then what? You put me in a strange position.

SULTAN: In spite of everything, he is a candid man. Is it right to force him into something he doesn't want?

VIZIER: The situation has a simple solution. He is whipped and goes on his way like the others.

SUNSHINE: Why whipped?

VIZIER: He goes without being whipped.

SUNSHINE: But he won.

SULTAN: He refuses the prize.

SUNSHINE: It wasn't a prize, I didn't present myself as a prize. It was rather my condition for marriage . . . and he's the one who has infringed on the condition.

SULTAN: What can we do in this case?

VIZIER *(threateningly to Moonlight):* Listen, Man! Will you be whipped or married?

SUNSHINE: What stupidity is this? He'll say he'd rather be whipped.

MOONLIGHT: Of course. This doesn't cost a dirham.

SUNSHINE: Come, Moonlight! Let's reach an understanding based on logic. Are you ready to submit to the rule of logic?

MOONLIGHT: I'm ready.

SUNSHINE: Answer me then. Didn't you ask me to make something of you?

MOONLIGHT: That happened.

SUNSHINE: If I am to make something of you, isn't it necessary for you to be within reach of my hand?

MOONLIGHT: It's necessary.

SUNSHINE: How can you be in reach of my hand unless I marry you?

MOONLIGHT: Allow me to answer you with logic. Are you ready to submit to the rule of logic?

SUNSHINE: I am ready.

MOONLIGHT: Didn't you agree that I am a clod of earth?

SUNSHINE: It happened.

MOONLIGHT: For this earth to be fit for you, isn't it necessary for you to make a man of it?

SUNSHINE: It's necessary.

MOONLIGHT: How then is it possible for you to marry now the clod of the earth?

SUNSHINE: What talk is this?

MOONLIGHT: Logic.

SULTAN: The fact is that what he says is reasonable.

VIZIER: Very reasonable. How is it possible to marry a lump of earth, of filth.

MOONLIGHT: No please . . . just earth.

SUNSHINE: Then in brief . . . the whole proposal has collapsed.

MOONLIGHT: No, only the idea of marriage is postponed until you make a man of me. This is, if you are able to succeed.

SUNSHINE: I shall succeed.

MOONLIGHT: Do you see such promise in me?

SUNSHINE: No, I see ability and will in myself.

MOONLIGHT: Let's go then with God's blessing.

SUNSHINE: Where to . . .

MOONLIGHT: To life.

SUNSHINE: You want me to go with you.

MOONLIGHT: Of course. You must go where the earth is.

SUNSHINE: How's that?

MOONLIGHT: How did you picture matters then? . . . That you would sit in your castle surrounded by luxury and comfort, while you give orders and the earth is brought to you so you can play with it with your fingers?

SUNSHINE: That means I must leave my castle and wander with you through the countryside.

MOONLIGHT: In the fresh air.

SUNSHINE: The fact is I . . .

MOONLIGHT: Reflect well. This is the way. There is no other.

SULTAN: What way is this, Man? You would take our daughter and go off with her like this without any legal bond?

VIZIER: This is the greatest disaster!

SULTAN: And you, Sunshine? Do you accept this humiliation? Do you accept this stranger . . .

VIZIER: A tramp.

SULTAN: Who comes and wrests you from your castle; who goes off with you without marrying you?

SUNSHINE: Truly . . . this . . .

SULTAN: This is atrocious! Where is your womanly dignity?

VIZIER: What will we tell the people?

SUNSHINE: Indeed, Moonlight. It seems you have forgotten I am a woman.

MOONLIGHT: A woman?

SUNSHINE: Naturally . . . Don't you see that?

MOONLIGHT: I confess I don't.

SUNSHINE: What do you see before you then?

MOONLIGHT: A contest, examination, challenge.

SUNSHINE: You have a right to this view, but in the view of the people I am still . . . a woman.

MOONLIGHT: I'm sorry. I miscalculated.

SUNSHINE: How did you plan to describe the link between us . . . between a man and a woman going through life together like this?

MOONLIGHT: I told you that I didn't think of the sex difference between us.

SUNSHINE: You thought we were two men . . . or two women!

MOONLIGHT: More correctly two men, for I don't imagine myself a woman.

SUNSHINE: You can imagine me a man?

MOONLIGHT: Isn't that better?

SUNSHINE: Your taste doesn't concern me. We are now in circumstances which we must confront. Do you think it acceptable to take me this way?

MOONLIGHT: The right way to put the question is that you are taking me . . . I don't know where . . . in order to make something of me. Have you forgotten that?

SUNSHINE: This does not change anything. Everyone will see us as two people going through life together with no proper bond. One of us is a woman, the other a man. Suppose I am the man, so long as you believe that.

MOONLIGHT: So long as you're the man, the question is solved . . . because the other one—that's me—would be the woman . . . and what fool would look at me and say I'm a woman?

SUNSHINE: Is there another fool who would look at me and say I'm a man?

MOONLIGHT: This fool won't be the only one. You can count on that!

SUNSHINE: What do you mean?

MOONLIGHT: Don't get angry . . . The idea has ripened in my head.

SUNSHINE: What idea?

MOONLIGHT: Inform me first . . . Did you picture us travelling together with me like this and you like that, with your hair and jewelry, dragging the train of your robe?

SUNSHINE: You mean . . .

MOONLIGHT: I mean you must wear a man's clothing.

SUNSHINE: A man's clothing? Yes . . . indeed. I'll wear a man's clothing.

MOONLIGHT: This will simplify everything. First of all, it will stop people from talking. Secondly, it will save me the fatigue of guarding your chastity.

SUNSHINE: Guarding my chastity . . . from whom?

MOONLIGHT: Not from me of course . . . from the others.

SUNSHINE: Fellow, I can guard my chastity by myself. You must learn right now that since childhood I have been excellent at swordplay.

MOONLIGHT: The sword?

SUNSHINE: Yes . . . and at any first hint of treachery or bad manners, my blade will be quicker than my tongue.

MOONLIGHT: Bravo! Excellent! And was it said it was you who had anything to fear in accompanying me?

SUNSHINE: This wasn't the point of the matter.

MOONLIGHT: I understand . . . what would people say.

SUNSHINE: An acceptable pretext has to be created for our relationship . . . for our conduct.

MOONLIGHT: Say . . . say for example that we have become engaged.

SUNSHINE: Engaged? . . . Yes . . . this is the weakest of oaths, but never mind.

MOONLIGHT: A long engagement . . . during which you will examine this unknown man.

SUNSHINE: Going off together? What shall we say of it?

MOONLIGHT: Say that you wished to go out with this man on a trip . . . a trip in the wilds . . . a hunting trip to test his bravery in bagging lions and leopards.

SUNSHINE: This is convincing talk. What's your opinion, Father?

SULTAN: When you go out to hunt and bag you must be accompanied by attendants and soldiers.

VIZIER: It is announced through the land and the drums are beaten.

MOONLIGHT: If everything you do is accompanied by drum and horn, it's best if you sit in your castle and turn your eyes away from the whole subject.

SUNSHINE: Turn away my eyes? Do you wish to flee from my hand?

MOONLIGHT: I never flee. I am accustomed to confronting all adversities.

SUNSHINE: Adversities?

MOONLIGHT: I am a brave man. I indeed do not carry a sword like you, but I am brave. If you are truly brave, advance! Advance so long as you are convinced by the idea. Put your castle behind your back. Travel . . . travel.

SUNSHINE: Yes, I must travel.

SULTAN: My daughter . . . Daughter, don't let this vagrant deceive you with this talk.

SUNSHINE: I shall go with him.

SULTAN: And leave me, Daughter? Leave me, Sunshine?

SUNSHINE: You knew I would leave you one day.

SULTAN: Yes, but not in this fashion.

SUNSHINE: This is the fashion I choose for myself.

SULTAN: Ill have you chosen.

SUNSHINE: Father, you promised to leave me to the destiny I make for myself. Remember your promise!

SULTAN: Yes, but I didn't suspect the affair would be so bad.

SUNSHINE: Cleanse your hand of me then. Pretend I am not related to you.

SULTAN: You really can't be related to me!

SUNSHINE: Allow me to go then, Father.

SULTAN: Go!

VIZIER: Will you allow your daughter, your Majesty, to go like this?

SULTAN: What can we do?

VIZIER: If she must go, can't we at least send someone with her to protect her from this trickster?

SUNSHINE: I refuse.

SULTAN: Here, she has refused. The idea is that they should go off together alone.

VIZIER: What a disaster!

SULTAN: Indeed, it is a disaster which has overcome us. We have been unable to ward it off.

VIZIER: Where are they going to alone?

SULTAN: Ask them!

VIZIER *(to the princess):* In what direction are you travelling, your Majesty?

SUNSHINE: I don't know yet.

VIZIER: And you, Vagabond?

MOONLIGHT: I don't know.

VIZIER: How amazing! You don't know where you are going? You will roam like this without direction or goal . . .

SUNSHINE: The goal is first to leave this castle. After that we shall find our way.

VIZIER: Your Majesty, so long as you insist on this, you can do no less than to take some money to support you on the trip.

MOONLIGHT: I refuse.

VIZIER: What business is it of yours, Rotter?

MOONLIGHT: I am not speaking to you. I am speaking to her. The condition is that we go off together with nothing. Don't carry with you from this castle of yours money, jewelry, or clothing. Even your sword must be an ordinary, cheap sword . . . not precious or inlaid. You must be divested just as I am.

SUNSHINE: Yes.

MOONLIGHT: It would be good if you took the sword of a simple soldier like this one and dressed in his clothing.

SUNSHINE: Good idea! Vizier, bring me . . . *(She motions to the uniform of one of the soldiers lined up. The vizier looks at the Sultan.)*

VIZIER: Your Majesty!

SULTAN: Take care of everything she wants and let her go.

VIZIER: Whatever you command, your Majesty.

(Sunshine goes out with the vizier behind her.)

SULTAN: Listen, Moonlight! I have washed my hand of my daughter's affair. The matter is finished, for I know her willpower and strong resolve. There is no way to oppose what she has decided. She has strange ideas which are beyond my comprehension. Clever stratagems have failed me in her case. So let her go where she wishes . . . But I, despite everything, am a father. For that reason, I ask you to be as attentive to her as you would be to your own sister.

MOONLIGHT: Have confidence, your Majesty!

SULTAN: I don't know anything about you . . . and I tell you frankly that I would not have chosen a man like you for my daughter. I am in no way pleased by what has taken place . . . nor with these arrangements which no one will accept. But in spite of all that, I feel something in my heart that inspires confidence in you.

MOONLIGHT: Always have confidence, your Majesty.

(Princess Sunshine appears in the garb of a simple soldier carrying an ordinary sword. The vizier is behind her.)

SUNSHINE: I'm ready!

MOONLIGHT: Kiss your father!

VIZIER*(to Moonlight):* What business of yours is it, Destitute . . . Are you a member of the family?

MOONLIGHT: I am a refined individual.

SUNSHINE*(kissing her father):* Don't be angry at me, Father!

SULTAN: Go away from me! . . . I'm afraid for you.

SUNSHINE: Farewell, Father . . . Let's go, Moonlight!

MOONLIGHT: Yes . . . Let's be off . . . and begin from scratch.

SUNSHINE: Yes, let's begin at zero!

(They start off.)

Act Two

Scene One

In the countryside . . . near a stream and some trees . . . Moonlight and Sunshine are sitting in the shade of a tree.

SUNSHINE *(rubbing her feet):* Oh . . .

MOONLIGHT: Are you tired, Gallant Soldier? It seems your tender feet are not accustomed to walking over rugged terrain. I see they have become swollen.

SUNSHINE: Be quiet, I beg you.

MOONLIGHT: I would have wanted to carry you part of the way . . . but I was afraid someone would notice and say: what kind of soldier is this to be carried on somebody's back like an infant?

SUNSHINE: Your sarcasm is silly.

MOONLIGHT: Possibly.

SUNSHINE: Instead of talking idly, do something useful.

MOONLIGHT: For example?

SUNSHINE: A meal . . . Don't you feel hungry?

MOONLIGHT: And you?

SUNSHINE: I'm about to die of hunger.

MOONLIGHT: What are you waiting for? Get up and look for something you can eat.

SUNSHINE: I should get up and search?

MOONLIGHT: Who else?

SUNSHINE: You for example.

MOONLIGHT: Get up and search for food for you? Sorry! You have left your castle behind you. There everything is served to you while you sit in your bed. Here you have to make everything for yourself.

SUNSHINE: But I'm tired.

MOONLIGHT: I, like you, am tired. Have you forgotten you are a man like me? Indeed, you excel me since you are a soldier armed to the teeth.

SUNSHINE *(struggling to her feet):* That's the way it will be.

MOONLIGHT *(getting up):* I too will search for my food by myself . . . so I won't be a burden on you.

SUNSHINE: Why don't we cooperate and divide the work between us?

MOONLIGHT: Bravo! Excellent!

SUNSHINE: Then let's discuss first of all what there is to eat in this place.

MOONLIGHT: Before anything else let's begin by exploring our surroundings.

SUNSHINE*(looking):* There's an apple tree!

MOONLIGHT: Then we'll eat apples.

SUNSHINE: Here's a stream with fish in it.

MOONLIGHT: Then we'll have fish first and apples for dessert.

SUNSHINE: Who will pick the apples and who will catch the fish?

MOONLIGHT: Which task is easier?

SUNSHINE: Harvesting the apples of course, because it requires nothing more than shaking the branches.

MOONLIGHT: Then I'll harvest the apples!

SUNSHINE: And leave me the hardest work?

MOONLIGHT: Out of respect for you.

SUNSHINE: Respect for me?

MOONLIGHT: Naturally. It is the greatest man who undertakes the hardest work.

SUNSHINE: Why shouldn't you be the greatest man?

MOONLIGHT: Because I have not yet reached the rank of man.

SUNSHINE: What are you then?

MOONLIGHT: Mere matter . . . raw material . . . earth. You are the one who is to make a man from it. Have you forgotten your mission and challenge?

SUNSHINE: Indeed . . . indeed.

MOONLIGHT: Let's go then. Get busy. Get to work.

SUNSHINE: Fishing?

MOONLIGHT: Yes . . . There's the river in front of you.

SUNSHINE: How do I catch these fish?

MOONLIGHT: Work it out!

SUNSHINE: I don't have a hook or a net!

MOONLIGHT: You have a sword.

SUNSHINE: A sword? Can fish be caught with a sword?

MOONLIGHT: Try!

SUNSHINE: How do I try something like this?

MOONLIGHT: How did our first ancestors try to catch fish without hooks or nets?

SUNSHINE: How?

MOONLIGHT: They would be on the lookout for the fish when it passed, then strike it with something sharp.

SUNSHINE: Did this succeed?

MOONLIGHT: Of course it succeeded . . . because they didn't die of hunger.

SUNSHINE *(drawing her sword):* I will try! *(She goes toward the river with her sword.)*

MOONLIGHT *(in front of the tree):* One apple for me and one for you. No, this is not enough. Two apples for you and two for me. Yes, this is reasonable. I will harvest four apples . . . no more and no less. Shaking the branches is a wasteful approach, for more might fall off than we need. So I must pick them one at a time . . . attentively and carefully . . . Like this . . . and this. *(He gathers four apples from the low-hanging branches with great care and attention. Then the voice of Princess Sunshine is heard shouting. She appears carrying a large fish impaled on her sword.)*

SUNSHINE: Moonlight! Moonlight! I caught a fish! Look! Look! A big fish!

MOONLIGHT: Didn't I tell you . . .

SUNSHINE: Indeed, truly . . . I didn't think the sword would do this!

MOONLIGHT: You thought the sword was only for decapitation.

SUNSHINE *(gazing at the fish):* This is astonishing!

MOONLIGHT: Enough admiration of its qualities! Now you need to clean it and remove the scales and fins. The sword will help you in that as well.

SUNSHINE: This is a job I have never done.

MOONLIGHT: You will do it now.

SUNSHINE: I will try.

MOONLIGHT: Meanwhile I will gather some firewood . . . for you to light a fire.

(He gathers some dry branches from here and there, while she is engrossed in cleaning the fish.)

SUNSHINE: Is lighting the fire my specialty also?

MOONLIGHT: It's always been your specialty.

SUNSHINE: Me?

MOONLIGHT: Of course you . . . Didn't you light fire in hearts?

SUNSHINE: In whose heart . . . for example?

MOONLIGHT: The hearts of the others.

SUNSHINE: Oh . . . the others.

MOONLIGHT *(bringing the wood):* I think this amount of firewood will be enough.

SUNSHINE: I don't know yet.

MOONLIGHT *(sitting down):* In any case, I have finished my tasks . . . in the best possible way. Now I have the right to relax . . . Oh . . . how pleasant rest is after work!

SUNSHINE: Do you call what you did work?

MOONLIGHT: Suited to my ability.

SUNSHINE: Can't I expect any more assistance from you?

MOONLIGHT: Of course.

SUNSHINE: When?

MOONLIGHT: When it's time to eat. I'll help you devour the food.

SUNSHINE: Thanks!

MOONLIGHT: Please hurry a bit. I'm hungry.

SUNSHINE: I've finished cleaning the fish. There is still the question of the fire.

MOONLIGHT: The firewood is in front of you.

SUNSHINE: I know . . . I'm not blind . . . but the fire . . . How do I kindle it?

MOONLIGHT: Haven't you heard of fire that comes from striking two stones together?

SUNSHINE: I've heard something like that . . . but . . .

MOONLIGHT: There are a lot of stones here in front of you.

SUNSHINE *(peevish and sarcastic):* You are very useful!

MOONLIGHT: To the limits of my knowledge.

SUNSHINE: Knowledge alone does not suffice.

MOONLIGHT: Transform it into work.

SUNSHINE: This is what I desire . . . but you must aid me. Show me how this is done. I beg you.

MOONLIGHT *(rising):* I'll show you this time . . . but it won't be repeated. Watch closely! *(He takes two stones and sparks fly into the firewood.)* Like this . . . Now you know.

SUNSHINE: Yes . . . yes. We must practice things with our hands in order to know.

MOONLIGHT *(going back to sit under the tree):* Now cook.

SUNSHINE: The fish of course is going to be grilled.

MOONLIGHT: Who told you I expect it fried in oil and surrounded by rice and shrimp.

SUNSHINE: I only wanted to caution you, because your demands on me are beginning to increase.

MOONLIGHT: By the way, setting the table is within your competence.

SUNSHINE: The table?

MOONLIGHT: Of course. Since there is food, there is a table. So long as there is a table, it must be set. I like work done expertly. The perfect man is the one who does perfect work.

SUNSHINE: How can a table be set here?

MOONLIGHT: Think!

SUNSHINE: I want to know your thinking first.

MOONLIGHT: Haven't you ever seen a table set?

SUNSHINE: Is this a question asked of someone like me? Of course I've seen . . .

MOONLIGHT: In your castle . . . I understand . . . all the tables are set up. You see them when they are already set. Everything is presented to you prepared in advance. But the situation here is different.

SUNSHINE: I know.

MOONLIGHT: You used to see flowers on your tables there . . .

SUNSHINE: A must.

MOONLIGHT: Look at the bank of the stream . . . What do you think of these lovely wild flowers?

SUNSHINE: That's what it will be. Could you watch the fish a little until I return?

MOONLIGHT: I think I could.

SUNSHINE (leaving): Don't burn it!

MOONLIGHT: Never fear!

SUNSHINE (near the bank): They really are lovely flowers. The colors are truly marvelous.

MOONLIGHT (shouting at her): Pick only as many as are needed! No more and no less . . .

SUNSHINE (at the bank): Why do you say that? The flowers here cover the bank.

MOONLIGHT: I know that the flowers cover the bank, indeed they cover the whole world, but beware of bringing a single flower too many.

SUNSHINE (appears carrying the flowers): Look!

MOONLIGHT (looking at a flower): This flower is repetitious. Its presence in the bouquet spoils the arrangement.

SUNSHINE: That's a simple question. We'll throw it away. (She casts it on the ground.)

MOONLIGHT: You're throwing it away? Then you've killed it for nothing.

SUNSHINE: I've killed it?

MOONLIGHT: Naturally . . . it was on its stalk enjoying the sun . . . then you came and plucked away its life without it serving any mission.

SUNSHINE: Mission?

MOONLIGHT: No doubt . . . Don't you know that the flowers are happy to give their lives to delight and cheer us . . . and are miserable if their lives go in vain.

SUNSHINE: Miserable?

MOONLIGHT: Yes . . . for this is death . . . true death, for everything that performs its mission is alive.

SUNSHINE *(taking the flower from the ground):* I won't let it die . . . It shall live in my bosom . . . alone! *(She puts it in her bosom.)*

MOONLIGHT: You have done well! Come now and take charge of your kitchen.

SUNSHINE: One moment till I prepare the table. I brought this green grass with me to spread like this. Then I'll strew the flowers in the center like this. Between them the food will be placed. *(She prepares the table.)*

MOONLIGHT: Very pretty!

SUNSHINE *(near the fire):* Now let's see if it's done. The food has a delicious fragrance . . . It's fully cooked. Can you smell it?

MOONLIGHT *(inhaling):* God! . . . Hurry! . . . Hurry!

SUNSHINE *(carrying the fish on two sticks and placing it on the grass table):* Dinner is ready. Please come.

MOONLIGHT *(approaching the food and reciting):* It matters not to us whether it comes early or late. We appear with the cook at the hour he serves.

(They eat together.)

SUNSHINE: Well! . . . What's your opinion?

MOONLIGHT: Bless your hands, Sunshine! It seems to me I've never tasted fish so good before today.

SUNSHINE: Are you joking?

MOONLIGHT: No, I say it from the depths of my heart . . . and my gullet. I could almost eat my fingers.

SUNSHINE: Me too . . . would you believe it if I told you it is the most delicious food I've ever eaten.

MOONLIGHT: Do you know why?

SUNSHINE: Why?

MOONLIGHT: Because you made it with your own hands. What we make with our own hands is a part of us . . . a part of our life which is revealed to us.

SUNSHINE: Yes, many things are being revealed to me now.

MOONLIGHT: Will you serve the dessert?

SUNSHINE: Have you picked the apples?

MOONLIGHT: Of course . . . there under the tree.

SUNSHINE (*going to bring them*): Only four apples?

MOONLIGHT: Aren't two apples for each of us enough?

SUNSHINE: Why this limit? Look! There is a limitless number of apples on the tree.

MOONLIGHT: I know . . . but the enjoyment is limited.

SUNSHINE: Do you think I couldn't eat three apples by myself?

MOONLIGHT: Who said you couldn't . . . Anyone could . . . but rest assured that most of the pleasure is in the first apple. Some of it for the second is body without spirit.

SUNSHINE: Without spirit?

MOONLIGHT: Gluttony kills the spirit of the enjoyment.

SUNSHINE: I'm not a glutton.

MOONLIGHT: Extravagant . . . wastrel.

SUNSHINE: All this on account of one extra apple?

MOONLIGHT: Extra! Here, you have said it yourself. 'Extra' implies extravagance . . . squandering, squandering the pleasure and squandering the resource. Squandering is part of our human nature.

SUNSHINE: Human nature?

MOONLIGHT: Naturally . . . The perfect man, like anything else that is perfected, does not admit increase or decrease.

SUNSHINE: No . . . permit me . . . I will decline the second apple . . . I will satisfy myself with one. Are you happy?

MOONLIGHT: No . . . you can't now.

SUNSHINE: You perplex me. Why can't I? Don't I have the right to be satisfied with one apple?

MOONLIGHT: And the second? What is to be its fate?

SUNSHINE: What concern of mine is its fate?

MOONLIGHT: Now that it has been picked, it must be of some use.

SUNSHINE: You eat it!

MOONLIGHT: It's your share. You are responsible for it. Preserve it the way you preserved the flower. Eat it at another meal.

SUNSHINE: So be it. Can you relax now?

MOONLIGHT: Yes.

(*They chew on their apples in silence.*)

SUNSHINE: You are a little tiring, my friend. Don't you think so?

MOONLIGHT: Indeed I am tiresome.

SUNSHINE: For yourself . . . and others.

MOONLIGHT: Especially for others. It is not easy for people to check the unruliness of their excessive desires.

SUNSHINE: What harm is there in excessive desires?

MOONLIGHT: Don't you see the harm? They are squandered resources which should be preserved for something more useful.

SUNSHINE: Why are you concerned about people and their resources?

MOONLIGHT: I am a part of them.

SUNSHINE: How is this feeling that you are a part of people possible when you don't know them?

MOONLIGHT *(moving his finger):* This finger doesn't know the rest of the hand, but it feels the pain of the rest. This is a natural thing.

SUNSHINE: But I . . .

MOONLIGHT: You are an anesthetized finger . . . inside a silk glove, anesthetized by the gold, diamond and turquoise rings around it.

SUNSHINE: I'm not anesthetized now.

MOONLIGHT: Then you will feel.

SUNSHINE: Today I truly feel that I am happy. What about you, Moonlight?

MOONLIGHT: Don't be concerned about me. Tell me what has made you happy?

SUNSHINE: I'm happy that I . . . that everything I see around me is something lovely and new . . . as though I were seeing the water and the trees for the first time. Everything has another meaning now.

MOONLIGHT *(leaning back against the trunk of the tree):* Speak!

SUNSHINE: What are you doing? Getting ready to sleep?

MOONLIGHT: No . . . no . . . I'm only resting my back . . . after this delicious food . . . Speak, speak!

SUNSHINE: What shall I say?

MOONLIGHT: You were saying . . . Oh . . . you were saying that the water and the trees . . . You were saying something about the water and the trees . . .

SUNSHINE: Then you weren't paying attention.

MOONLIGHT: No . . . no . . . only I didn't hear the rest of the words clearly . . .

SUNSHINE: I was saying that everything around me now has a new meaning.

MOONLIGHT *(struggling with drowsiness):* Definitely . . .

SUNSHINE *(resuming):* Without any doubt . . . that life in the same key . . . in the same frame . . . with my seeing and knowing only what they present to me wrapped in opulence . . . was a life presented to me ready-made on a golden tray . . . Are you listening?

MOONLIGHT *(out of his sleep):* Yes . . .

SUNSHINE *(continuing):* I was always troubled by a feeling of the triviality of that kind of life . . . because it is sterile . . . false. It does not permit us to discover anything. Indeed it is as you say, Moonlight: an anesthetizing of our deeper feelings . . . perceptions and abilities. Wasn't that what you meant? . . . Moonlight!

MOONLIGHT *(waking up):* Yes . . . yes . . . indeed.

SUNSHINE: Don't sleep, I entreat you. What I'm saying now is very important!

MOONLIGHT: I know.

SUNSHINE: Despite that you were the one who said this important thing a little while ago . . . It truly is important. Do you know what it is?

MOONLIGHT: What?

SUNSHINE: That we must make every part of our lives with our hands. When life is presented to us ready-made we are unable to understand or to transform any of it. We accept it lazily . . . with eyes closed . . . *(Moonlight's eyes are completely closed, and he does not respond.)*

SUNSHINE *(looking at him):* You've closed your eyes and gone to sleep . . and left me talking to myself. Do you hear? . . . Moonlight?

MOONLIGHT: Yes . . . speak.

SUNSHINE: No . . . it's no use to speak to a person like you.

MOONLIGHT: Aren't you going to rest? Sleep! Sleep a little . . . and postpone these words . . . to an appropriate time.

SUNSHINE: I don't feel like sleeping now . . . The desire for this important talk has been awakened in my soul . . . but unfortunately when I find something useful to say I find people who go to sleep around me.

(Moonlight snores in his sleep.)

SUNSHINE: Tuneful snoring . . . music.

MOONLIGHT *(waking up suddenly):* Music? . . . Where?

SUNSHINE: Go to sleep and you will hear it.

MOONLIGHT: I truly did hear sweet singing.

SUNSHINE: No, I beg you. It was not at all sweet . . . Perhaps your words are sweet at times, but your snoring . . .

MOONLIGHT: My snoring? I never snore when I sleep.

SUNSHINE: Never?

MOONLIGHT: Never . . . this is one of my virtues.

SUNSHINE: Glory to God!

(The neighing of horses is heard far away.)

MOONLIGHT: What's this?

SUNSHINE: I believe it is horses whinnying.

MOONLIGHT: I fear someone has come to search for us. Let's hide behind these trees until we see who is coming. Hurry! Quickly!

(They hurry to conceal themselves behind the trees. Then two men appear. One of them carries a money bag. They are the inspector and his aide.)

INSPECTOR *(to his aide):* I think this place is right for us.

AIDE: This tree will do.

INSPECTOR: Yes . . . an apple tree. It's the only one here. That way, it won't be possible for us to go astray or make an error.

AIDE: We'll dig under it and hide the money bag.

INSPECTOR: Yes . . . and be quick about it!

AIDE *(hesitating):* Wouldn't it . . . wouldn't it be better for us to divide it now . . .

INSPECTOR: Now is impossible! Perhaps some of the Prince's soldiers have already set out after us.

AIDE: No one saw us when we left the city.

INSPECTOR: How do you know?

AIDE: I didn't notice anything suspicious.

INSPECTOR: There are many envious people. Each of them is lying in wait for the other.

AIDE: It's true . . . and all it takes is one person to squeal on us.

INSPECTOR: For that reason, we must not prolong our absence lest we arouse suspicions. Afterwards we'll return to settle our accounts without being rushed . . . Be quick . . . Quickly!

(The aide begins to dig at the bottom of the tree while Moonlight and Sunshine watch from their hiding place.)

SUNSHINE *(whispering to Moonlight):* Are they thieves?

MOONLIGHT *(whispering to her):* It seems so.

SUNSHINE: What about us? Shall we keep quiet?

MOONLIGHT: No . . . it's not right for us to keep quiet.

SUNSHINE: What shall we do?

MOONLIGHT: Listen! You are wearing a soldier's uniform. Show yourself and raise your sword. I'll be behind you.

SUNSHINE *(appearing suddenly with the sword):* You're under arrest.

INSPECTOR: The soldiers?

MOONLIGHT *(shouting):* Don't move! The prince's forces are behind us.

INSPECTOR: We haven't done anything.

AIDE: We're innocent.

MOONLIGHT: And this money bag?

INSPECTOR: Our personal possessions.

MOONLIGHT: Why are you hiding it like this?

INSPECTOR: We're free . . . to hide it as we wish.

MOONLIGHT: Where did you get this money?

INSPECTOR: From our salaries . . .

AIDE: Yes . . . from our hard work and sweat.

MOONLIGHT: What are your professons . . . *(to the inspector)* what do you do?

INSPECTOR: I am the inspector of the treasury.

MOONLIGHT: The prince's treasury?

INSPECTOR: Yes.

MOONLIGHT *(to the aide):* And you?

AIDE: His assistant.

MOONLIGHT: How swell . . . the inspector of the treasury and his aide have stolen from the treasury.

INSPECTOR: Hold you tongue, Man. We aren't thieves. God forbid! We told you this wealth comes from our salaries.

AIDE: From our lifetime savings.

SUNSHINE: This bag appears to contain enough gold for a city!

MOONLIGHT: Your salaries in this city must have been as large as the prince's.

INSPECTOR: What concern of yours is that, Man? And what right do you have to interrogate us?

MOONLIGHT: Indeed, we do not have this right . . . all we can do is to hand you over to your prince so that he can take care of you.

INSPECTOR: Hand us over?

MOONLIGHT: And the money bag with you.

INSPECTOR: Listen! Here's something that would be more profitable for you . . . Let us hide the bag and cover up for us. We'll give you a share of it.

SUNSHINE: A share?

INSPECTOR: Yes . . . you can have a quarter of it . . .What do you say?

MOONLIGHT: A quarter?

INSPECTOR: Yes . . . a quarter . . . for you and this soldier with you.

MOONLIGHT: What kind of talk is this, Inspector?

INSPECTOR: Do you think a quarter is too little?

AIDE: Without their doing anything . . .

INSPECTOR: Merely to cover up . . . A quarter! A quarter of the bag of money.

SUNSHINE: What's this they are saying?

MOONLIGHT: How do you dare say this?

INSPECTOR: Then let it be a third.

MOONLIGHT: What third, Man?

INSPECTOR: No . . . more than this is nothing but greed.

AIDE: What would remain for us when we are the ones who have tired ourselves for it . . .

INSPECTOR: This on our part is the limit of generosity.

SUNSHINE: Do you suppose we would accept stolen money.

INSPECTOR: It's not stolen money.

MOONLIGHT: Skip the story of salaries and savings . . . Tell us first where this wealth came from.

INSPECTOR: Do you want the truth?

SUNSHINE: Yes . . . we want the totally candid truth.

INSPECTOR: Frankly, these are profits from merchandise we imported and sold in the city.

MOONLIGHT: And the money for these imported goods?

INSPECTOR: We borrowed it.

MOONLIGHT: From the prince's treasury? . . . Of course!

INSPECTOR: Of course.

MOONLIGHT: With his knowledge?

INSPECTOR: With God's knowledge.

MOONLIGHT: God's will be done!

AIDE: What's wrong with that?

MOONLIGHT: Nothing . . . so long as the prince doesn't know about this loan from his treasury . . . and only God knows. For God, the High and Mighty, calls these loans by another name—embezzlement.

INSPECTOR: Of what importance is the difference in names?

AIDE: Indeed . . . it's merely a difference of names. What's wrong with that?

MOONLIGHT: Nothing . . . a loan . . . embezzlement . . . all the same thing.

INSPECTOR: Do you want the truth? . . . We are not the only ones.

MOONLIGHT: Are there many like you?

INSPECTOR: The whole city!

SUNSHINE: How so?

AIDE: This is what's happening.

INSPECTOR: Loans . . . embezzlement . . . bribes . . . It's all the same thing.

AIDE: Yes . . . it's all the same.

INSPECTOR: Everyone has his hand in someone else's pocket . . . your hand in my pocket and mine in yours. Our pocketbooks are all in the prince's hand, and we have our hand in the prince's pocket. There is perpetual motion.

MOONLIGHT: Perpetual motion?

INSPECTOR: It's not possible to earn a living without cunning.

SUNSHINE: But there must be values.

MOONLIGHT: Values and standards.

INSPECTOR: What does that mean?

SUNSHINE: What goal do people have? What do they believe in?

INSPECTOR: A living . . . a comfortable income . . . luxury . . . ease.

SUNSHINE: But this alone does not make a man.

INSPECTOR: I don't understand what this soldier is saying?

AIDE: I don't either.

INSPECTOR: Your statement in brief? Have we agreed?

SUNSHINE: What is the name of this prince of yours?

INSPECTOR: Prince Hamdan.

MOONLIGHT: I know his land . . .

INSPECTOR: Release us before anyone comes.

MOONLIGHT: What do you say to our all going together to the city. We'll return the purse to the treasury. You will have our oath and pact with God to keep quiet about what happened and to cover up this slip for you as long as we live.

INSPECTOR: We should return the purse to the treasury?

SUNSHINE: Without anyone seeing or hearing.

AIDE: Our effort should go for naught?

INSPECTOR (to his aide): Don't believe them! We have fallen into the hands of men who are haggling.

AIDE: How much more than that can we pay them?

INSPECTOR: Ask them . . . what will satisfy them?

AIDE: How much will satisfy you?

MOONLIGHT: Do you want to know what will satisfy us?

AIDE: Yes, be frank.

MOONLIGHT: Frankly—handing you over to justice.

INSPECTOR *(to his aide):* Do you see how mean?

AIDE: If we leave them half the purse?

SUNSHINE: Not even the entire purse.

INSPECTOR: Nothing would be left but to strip us of our clothes.

SUNSHINE: Not even this.

INSPECTOR: What then are your demands exactly?

MOONLIGHT: We have already told you. Return the money to the treasury. If you refuse, we will turn you and the purse over to justice.

INSPECTOR: What will you get out of this?

SUNSHINE: Nothing.

INSPECTOR: Cut out this chatter. You must covet something greater.

AIDE: Perhaps they desire the prince's reward . . .

INSPECTOR: Then their hopes are in vain . . . All that the prince can do for you is to present each of you a hundred dinars.

AIDE: When your share in the purse is more than a thousand for each of you.

SUNSHINE: We don't covet money.

INSPECTOR: What's your angle then?

MOONLIGHT: We don't have an angle.

INSPECTOR: Is this credible? You want to return the purse to the treasury without there being anything in that for you?

MOONLIGHT: You could say we have a motive . . .

INSPECTOR: What is it?

MOONLIGHT: Duty.

INSPECTOR: What's that? . . . Duty? Who imposed this duty on you?

SUNSHINE: No one.

AIDE: What's this we hear . . .

INSPECTOR: Truly . . . it is something amazing.

MOONLIGHT: This is something natural.

INSPECTOR: Listen, please . . . Say something we can understand. So long as no one charged you to return the purse or to turn us in, what point is there to volunteering to do something which will not benefit you? Rather to the contrary . . . it will deprive you of certain gain and of plunder which will enrich you for life.

AIDE: It will not harm or injure them in any way, for the money is ready here. They do not expose themselves to the dangers of gathering it together.

INSPECTOR: They will take it now and go with no one watching or keeping count.

AIDE: With no one seeing or hearing!

INSPECTOR: This is the reasonable view and understandable statement.

SUNSHINE: What would we do with this wealth!

INSPECTOR: What would you do? Don't you know what to do with it?

MOONLIGHT: We wouldn't relish it, because we wouldn't have gained it by our work.

AIDE: You wouldn't relish it?

INSPECTOR: Listen and marvel!

MOONLIGHT: What about you? Do you relish wealth like this?

INSPECTOR: Is this a question that needs to be asked?

SUNSHINE: Of course you haven't asked yourselves this question before.

INSPECTOR: Of course not . . . For we are not insane!

AIDE: A taste for money? Is this something open to debate?

INSPECTOR: It seems we have fallen into the hands of creatures . . . God knows what they are . . .

AIDE: So long as you have no taste for this money, then leave it to us. We like it.

MOONLIGHT: Leave you what you embezzled . . . after we have learned of the crime?

INSPECTOR: What business of yours is it?

SUNSHINE: We can't cover up a crime.

INSPECTOR: Who requires you to expose it?

SUNSHINE: Duty.

AIDE: We've come back to this cursed thing.

INSPECTOR: What does this duty weigh? . . . Ten carats? . . . Twenty? How much would it bring in the market?

SUNSHINE: It's not found in a market run by people like you.

INSPECTOR: I want to know the price of this thing for the sake of which you sacrifice all this wealth.

SUNSHINE: It has no price!

INSPECTOR: Everything has a price.

SUNSHINE: There are some things that are not for sale.

INSPECTOR: Help me understand this talk, People . . . A bag of gold . . . and two tramps . . . and we can't reach an understanding?

MOONLIGHT: You have no currency suitable for us to reach an understanding.

INSPECTOR *(pointing to the sack):* Isn't all this currency?

MOONLIGHT: We can't do business together except with jewels.

INSPECTOR: Jewels! . . . Oh . . . you say this . . . now we understand.

SUNSHINE: No, you don't understand.

INSPECTOR: How don't I understand? Jewels are something I understand. Doesn't a person like me understand jewels?

SUNSHINE: They aren't the jewels you wear on the outside.

INSPECTOR: What are you saying?

SUNSHINE: They are jewels we carry inside . . .

INSPECTOR: Inside?

AIDE: Are there jewels which are worn inside?

INSPECTOR: Ask them, Brother!

AIDE: This is something no one has heard of . . .

INSPECTOR: What use are these jewels you wear inside and no one sees?

SUNSHINE: Their owner sees them. They light up his soul.

INSPECTOR: Is that all?

SUNSHINE: Those who value them see them, and then their souls are illuminated.

AIDE: All this from the inside?

SUNSHINE: Yes.

INSPECTOR: I want to purchase one of these jewels.

MOONLIGHT: How much will you pay for it?

INSPECTOR: You tell me how much?

MOONLIGHT: All this sack!

AIDE: All of it?

MOONLIGHT: Yes. All of it.

INSPECTOR *(to his aide):* What do you think? Its value may be very great . . . and we would rid ourselves of this heavy bag which gives us away. We would carry something light in weight and high in price.

AIDE: It's an idea . . . we could sell it for a great price.

INSPECTOR *(to Moonlight):* We accept.

MOONLIGHT: Congratulations! With God's blessing. Hand over the sack.

INSPECTOR: And the gem?

MOONLIGHT: I will take the bag first and return it to the treasury.

INSPECTOR: Return it to the treasury?

MOONLIGHT: Of course . . . I'm free.

INSPECTOR: Yes . . . free to do with the money whatever you want . . . to return it or keep it. But the gem?

MOONLIGHT: As soon as this wealth is secure in its place in the treasury building, you will find the jewel.

INSPECTOR: Where?

MOONLIGHT: In your chests.

AIDE: Who will put it there?

MOONLIGHT: No one.

SUNSHINE: It is actually present inside you.

INSPECTOR: Inside us?

SUNSHINE: But smut, filth, and dust have accumulated around it, so it is dull, hidden, and not giving off light.

MOONLIGHT: As soon as you return this money to its place, you will feel the light shining inside you.

INSPECTOR *(to his aide):* Do you like this?

AIDE: We're wasting time with these madmen.

INSPECTOR: What shall we do then?

AIDE: What can we do?

INSPECTOR *(to Moonlight and Sunshine):* So finally? Isn't there a way for us to reach an understanding like others of God's creatures?

MOONLIGHT: We've told you the way. Return the sack to the treasury.

INSPECTOR: Besides this . . .

SUNSHINE: There's no way besides this.

INSPECTOR: You must enjoy harming us.

SUNSHINE: Indeed we find enjoyment . . . but not in harming you or anyone.

INSPECTOR: Where's the enjoyment then?

MOONLIGHT: In performing one's duty.

SUNSHINE: In justice.

MOONLIGHT: In putting everything in its place.

INSPECTOR: Amazing. How amazing that you find pleasure in things like these!

AIDE: It's our unlucky star and ill fortune.

INSPECTOR: With whom are we associating today, Lord?

AIDE: I saw this in my dream last night, by God.

INSPECTOR: What did you see?

AIDE: I saw myself carrying on my head a platter of rice cooked with milk. Then a saker hawk and a kite swooped down and knocked off the platter. They flew away. So they didn't eat it and didn't let me eat it.

MOONLIGHT: A hawk and a kite?

AIDE: Yes, by God!

INSPECTOR: Here, your dream has come true.

AIDE: My dream didn't fall to earth.

INSPECTOR: We're what's fallen to earth.

SUNSHINE: So long as the dream has proven true to this extent . . .

MOONLIGHT: And the bag is the rice cooked with milk . . .

INSPECTOR *(to his aide):* God curse you and your dream!

AIDE: What's my offense?

INSPECTOR: Wasn't it possible for you to drive the hawk and the kite away from your head?

AIDE *(pointing to Moonlight and Sunshine):* Here they are before you. You drive them away any way you want.

INSPECTOR: These two are armed to the teeth . . .

MOONLIGHT: Come on . . . come on. If you won't listen to your conscience, listen at least to the voice of reason.

INSPECTOR: So long as it's no use . . . we trust in God . . . Here's the bag. Let us go on our way.

MOONLIGHT: We want more than that.

AIDE: What else?

SUNSHINE: You are to go with us to the prince.

INSPECTOR: So he can cut our heads off?

SUNSHINE: So that you can confess your guilt, ask forgiveness, and swear to reform.

INSPECTOR: As for this, it's impossible.

AIDE: Are we to walk to our own death?

SUNSHINE: We will defend you.

AIDE: You will defend us . . .

INSPECTOR: You? We are to expect any good of you after what you've done to us?

MOONLIGHT: Have confidence that we will win your freedom.

INSPECTOR: Who will guarantee it to us?

MOONLIGHT: No one can guarantee life or death.

AIDE: You bring such comfort to our hearts!

SUNSHINE: Only one thing can save you.

INSPECTOR: What is it?

SUNSHINE: Be sincere in intention and thought and confront your destiny courageously.

INSPECTOR *(to his aide):* Do you hear these pearls?

AIDE: The jewels!

INSPECTOR: From inside.

SUNSHINE: Yes . . . This is the time for it. A little courage in the soul and you will achieve success.

INSPECTOR: Courage?

AIDE: I'm a coward.

INSPECTOR: Me too.

MOONLIGHT: Then you're lost.

INSPECTOR: Save us . . . we entreat you.

AIDE: We implore you.

INSPECTOR: The money is before you . . . Here it is. Take it! . . . Take it! . . . But let us flee.

SUNSHINE: Where will you flee to? There's no escape.

MOONLIGHT: You won't be able to escape from your selves.

SUNSHINE: The crime is within you.

INSPECTOR: What's to be done?

SUNSHINE: Go with us to the prince. Confess. Cleanse yourselves.

INSPECTOR: And if we refuse this solution?

AIDE: Yes, we refuse this solution categorically.

MOONLIGHT: Categorically? Then we will force you.

INSPECTOR: You will force us?

MOONLIGHT: Yes . . . Would you like to know how?

AIDE: How?

MOONLIGHT: Undo your belt, Soldier . . . and I'll undo mine.

INSPECTOR: Will you beat us?

MOONLIGHT: We will bind your hands and drag you bound to your prince.

INSPECTOR: Then in either case we must go with you . . . whether we are willing or not?

MOONLIGHT: Exactly.

INSPECTOR: Then we will go willingly.

AIDE: Without bonds.

SUNSHINE: This is nobler.

INSPECTOR: Don't take off your belts. Leave us free.

MOONLIGHT: We will let you be free.

INSPECTOR: With your permission then I will consult with my companion.

MOONLIGHT: Go ahead.

INSPECTOR *(whispering to his aide):* We will go along with them and watch for an opportunity to escape.

AIDE *(whispering):* Good man . . . This is the same thing that occurred to me.

INSPECTOR *(whispering to him):* Here's the plan then. *(They whisper together.)*

SUNSHINE *(whispering to Moonlight):* They seem to plotting something untoward.

MOONLIGHT *(whispering):* About fleeing of course.

SUNSHINE: Indeed . . . otherwise they wouldn't need this consultation.

MOONLIGHT: We must keep our eyes open.

INSPECTOR *(out loud):* I agreed with my companion that we will be more obedient to you than your fingers.

MOONLIGHT: Thanks! To you and your companion.

SUNSHINE: We forgot to ask you something.

INSPECTOR: Go ahead.

SUNSHINE: Now you are free and without bonds . . . Who will guarantee to us that you won't flee?

INSPECTOR: Us flee?

SUNSHINE: Why not? Everything is possible . . . What's the guarantee?

INSPECTOR: We swear to you on our honor.

AIDE: Yes, on our honor for ever and ever.

SUNSHINE: Your honor? You swear on your honor to me?

INSPECTOR: Is our honor not to be trusted? Then we swear by your honor!

SUNSHINE: Swear to us by something you hold sacred. What do you hold sacred in life?

MOONLIGHT: There's no need to ask. They hold nothing sacred save this bag.

INSPECTOR *(with regret):* Where is the bag now?

AIDE *(bitterly):* Modified by a 'was'.

SUNSHINE: Then what remains of you as human beings?

INSPECTOR: Nothing remains.

AIDE: If we didn't exist, it would be better.

SUNSHINE: There must be something remaining in you.

INSPECTOR: What remains?

AIDE: Yes . . . what?

SUNSHINE: The better and more eternal things.

MOONLIGHT: They won't understand talk like this.

INSPECTOR: You are right. By God, we don't understand.

AIDE: Aye, by God.

SUNSHINE: Unfortunately!

MOONLIGHT: Are you hungry?

INSPECTOR *(to his aide):* Are you hungry?

AIDE: Of course . . . after all this torment.

INSPECTOR: I am too.

MOONLIGHT *(pointing to the tree):* Here's the tree! Each one of you can have two apples.

INSPECTOR: Two apples!

AIDE: Just two?

MOONLIGHT: That is all. This is the reasonable quantity for the stomach. The stomach is comfortable when the quantity is appropriate.

AIDE: But I'm not comfortable.

MOONLIGHT: Your stomach is more intelligent than you are.

INSPECTOR: There are many apples on the tree.

SUNSHINE: Everything must fit in its place.

INSPECTOR: Like putting the bag in the treasury.

AIDE: And like putting us in prison.

SUNSHINE: Exactly.

AIDE: God help us.

INSPECTOR *(to his aide):* Pick me an apple.

MOONLIGHT: Each person here serves himself.

AIDE: There's nothing wrong with this!

INSPECTOR: Are you listening to their talk?

AIDE: Didn't you say we are more obedient to them now than their fingers?

INSPECTOR: That's so. I will serve myself.

SUNSHINE: You will find enjoyment in that.

INSPECTOR: Spare us your enjoyments.

AIDE *(having plucked an apple and beginning to chew it):* Very tasty . . . Follow my example.

INSPECTOR *(picking an apple):* Isn't it an apple like any other?

AIDE: No . . . This one has a different taste.

INSPECTOR: We have eaten apples all our lives . . .

AIDE: Yes, presented to us on trays . . . But this one I picked myself.

INSPECTOR *(eating his apple eagerly)*: Yes.

AIDE: How is it?

INSPECTOR: I'll pick my other apple.

AIDE: I will too.

INSPECTOR *(to Moonlight and Sunshine)*: Did my stomach speak to you and tell you it wants only two? If it spoke, how is it you heard and I didn't?

AIDE: Good man, by God. This same question occurred to me. My stomach is with me, and I haven't heard it say anything.

MOONLIGHT: You hear it only if it screams.

SUNSHINE: It won't scream unless it is tired.

INSPECTOR: Now that we have eaten the appropriate quantity, shall we let our horses go hungry?

AIDE: True . . . our horses are tied there. They have no fodder with them.

MOONLIGHT: What are you waiting for? There is an ample supply of grass and plants in front of you. Each one of you should gather enough for his steed.

INSPECTOR *(to the aide)*: Let's go.

MOONLIGHT: Don't go more than two steps from us.

SUNSHINE: Otherwise, it's the fetters.

AIDE: No . . . no need for fetters.

MOONLIGHT: We want to be able to hear your voices all the time you are working . . . Speak.

INSPECTOR *(pulling up grass with his hands)*: You speak, Aide.

AIDE: You speak first, Treasury Inspector.

INSPECTOR: Don't remind me of the treasury.

AIDE: You're right. It's gone from us.

INSPECTOR: Our hands are getting coarse from this labor.

AIDE: Hands which have touched only gold dinars for their entire lives . . .

INSPECTOR: We're now performing a groom's work.

AIDE: For the first time our steeds will eat from our hands.

MOONLIGHT: For that reason, they will eat with appetite today.

SUNSHINE: They will feel love for you for the first time.

INSPECTOR: This is the bare necessity.

SUNSHINE: Isn't it worth something . . . that you perform useful work and are loved?

AIDE: By animals?

SUNSHINE: This is even more touching and beautiful . . . for they don't speak and don't dissemble. They feel and appreciate in silence.

AIDE: The fact is that today we are in the greatest need of their love and assistance.

INSPECTOR *(to his aide):* Enough chatter!

AIDE: Did I say something? We are speaking of love and appreciation . . . in general . . . in general.

INSPECTOR: We have gathered more than is necessary . . . Let's go.

AIDE: Let's go . . . Each of us carries his share.

INSPECTOR: Of course, each of us will carry the product of his effort.

AIDE: In any case . . . the work was pleasant.

INSPECTOR: Pleasant . . . In what respect?

AIDE: I don't know exactly . . . but the fatigue itself . . .

INSPECTOR: Let's speak of our feelings later . . . Now to the hungry mounts. Let's go . . . Let's . . .

MOONLIGHT: Where to?

INSPECTOR: To feed the horses of course . . . with the fodder we have tired ourselves to gather.

MOONLIGHT: You're going together like this?

AIDE: Each one of us is going to his horse.

MOONLIGHT: And jumping on it and racing the wind.

INSPECTOR: Would it be right for us to do this?

AIDE: Are we capable of that?

MOONLIGHT: No . . . sorry.

SUNSHINE: Sometimes . . . though not always . . . suspicion is the better part of wisdom.

MOONLIGHT: Listen! One of you stay here while the other goes in the custody of the soldier with his weapon drawn.

INSPECTOR: Which of us will go first?

MOONLIGHT: Choose between yourselves.

AIDE: I or he . . . it no longer matters.

SUNSHINE: Tell us . . . is the city far from here?

INSPECTOR: It's behind these mountains.

AIDE: It takes a quarter of a day.

MOONLIGHT: Then if we set out from here after feeding the horses, we would arrive there shortly before nightfall?

AIDE: Perhaps a little after that.

MOONLIGHT *(to Sunshine):* This is better than our staying here and being forced to take turns guarding them all night.

SUNSHINE: Truly . . . this is an idea.

MOONLIGHT: So let's all go together now to the horses. We'll feed them and go.

INSPECTOR: You'll go riding our horses?

MOONLIGHT: You and your companion on one horse . . . my comrade the soldier on the other one.

SUNSHINE: And you?

MOONLIGHT: I'll tie the horses together and lead them on foot.

SUNSHINE: You'll go on foot?

MOONLIGHT: Why not?

INSPECTOR: Why not ride with your comrade?

MOONLIGHT: This is my business.

AIDE: He's right. It's his business. He wants to tire his feet. He's free. The important thing is that we will ride.

SUNSHINE *(to Moonlight):* If you walk, I will walk too.

MOONLIGHT: And leave the horse without a rider?

INSPECTOR: Why without a rider? . . . I'm here.

AIDE: That's true . . . If each of us rides his horse, the problem is solved.

MOONLIGHT: And we'll run behind you . . .

AIDE: So long as you are enamored of using your feet.

SUNSHINE: Listen, Moonlight! You ride with me on the horse.

MOONLIGHT: What's this talk? How is it possible?

INSPECTOR: The same way my companion and I will ride.

MOONLIGHT: No . . . it's not possible.

AIDE: What is this abundance of manners between them?

SUNSHINE: Don't be stubborn, Moonlight. We'll ride on the horse together. I'll be behind you.

MOONLIGHT: Behind me . . .

SUNSHINE: Yes . . . This is what I want. Let's go. Don't waste time. All of you follow me . . . to the horses.

(She departs, and they all follow.)

Act Three

Scene One

The palace of Prince Hamdan. The prince is seated talking with an attendant.

ATTENDANT: What are your orders for me, your Majesty the Prince, today?

PRINCE: Today is like any other day . . . What could today provide that would be new?

ATTENDANT: Doesn't your Majesty request, for example, something special to eat?

PRINCE: What else is there besides meat, fowl, fish, greens, vegetables, fruits, pastry, and sweets . . . with the exception of salt-cured, pickled, and iced foods . . . et cetera . . . et cetera.

ATTENDANT: There is of course nothing else, your Majesty. These things don't change, but we could change the cook.

PRINCE: We have changed cooks more than a hundred times. You know that.

ATTENDANT: It's true, your Majesty.

PRINCE: Every cook was splendid and inventive his first day. Then his zeal would flag. He became remiss. Everything became the same.

ATTENDANT: Although we raised their salaries.

PRINCE: What more could we do?

ATTENDANT: Truly . . . we can't plant the love of excellence in someone lacking it.

PRINCE: How then can you wish me to find enjoyment in a repast when its maker found no enjoyment in making it?

ATTENDANT: The fact is, your Majesty, that it is a situation . . .

PRINCE: A situation which has become widespread. Even the entertainment you provide no longer amuses or diverts me.

ATTENDANT: We've brought you the best dancers, singers and comedians.

PRINCE: The same gestures, tunes, and jokes!

ATTENDANT: Even though we gave them all the money they asked for.

PRINCE: Yes . . . money, money, money.

ATTENDANT: Life has become hard . . .

PRINCE: Money fills my treasuries . . . and life is hard for me too.

ATTENDANT: Why, your Majesty?

PRINCE: I don't know . . . I have a strange feeling. I feel like an orange placed in a vast basket.

ATTENDANT: Would you permit me an opinion?

PRINCE: Speak!

ATTENDANT: Get married, your Majesty?

PRINCE: I, get married?

ATTENDANT: To prevent the orange in the vast basket from being anxious another orange is put with it. It is not long before there are numerous oranges . . .

PRINCE: Is this the solution?

ATTENDANT: It's merely an opinion . . .

PRINCE: Are you happy in your basket crammed with oranges?

ATTENDANT: I wouldn't say I'm happy, but there's no emptiness to disturb me.

PRINCE: How many oranges are there in your basket exactly?

ATTENDANT: Your Majesty knows—my wife, my five daughters, my three sons . . . and any additions.

PRINCE: You are tightly packed.

ATTENDANT: At times I almost suffocate.

PRINCE: From them?

ATTENDANT: And from their requests.

PRINCE: Do you complain of that?

ATTENDANT: And how! Imagine, your Majesty, that each of these has his own special requests and desires. He thinks he is the only one on earth and insists on his request. He's not concerned about where it will come from or how much it will cost.

PRINCE: However, you draw a fine salary, not to mention . . . well, you and I understand . . .

ATTENDANT: Any sum of money, your Majesty, no matter how large, dissolves like a lump of sugar in the depths of this basket.

PRINCE: Your mind is constantly occupied by this.

ATTENDANT: Speaking candidly . . . yes.

PRINCE: This is regrettable . . . Why you precisely?

ATTENDANT: It's not just me. There are many like me. Life has become hard.

PRINCE: Because the demands on it have increased, so it seems.

ATTENDANT: Demands for its delights in particular. For food isn't the only thing that delights me now.

PRINCE: What's the harm? Work, collect the salary, and spend.

ATTENDANT: The requests outstrip the salaries.

PRINCE: Yes, this race is what . . .

ATTENDANT: What does not allow time . . .

PRINCE: To do something properly.

ATTENDANT: I didn't want to burden your Majesty with my problems . . .

PRINCE: The strange thing is that you wish to solve my problem with another.

ATTENDANT: No, your Majesty. Your marriage will of course not cause you problems of this kind.

PRINCE: Perhaps of another kind?

ATTENDANT: Perhaps it will do nothing but good.

PRINCE: Who do you think is fit for me to marry?

ATTENDANT: We'll search . . .

PRINCE: How much time will your search take when your mind is busy with other things?

ATTENDANT: I'm not too busy for you, your Majesty.

PRINCE: There's no need to search. The woman I want is found.

ATTENDANT: Found?

PRINCE: Yes . . . in another land.

ATTENDANT: You have, then, your Majesty, only to command.

PRINCE: She cannot be obtained by a command. It is this that has kept me from her . . . and turned me away from thinking of marriage at all.

ATTENDANT: Who is she, your Majesty?

PRINCE: Princess Sunshine.

ATTENDANT: The daughter of Sultan Nu'man?

PRINCE: Yes.

ATTENDANT: That woman who flogs the men . . .

PRINCE: Who fail.

ATTENDANT: They've all failed.

PRINCE: Yes . . . it seems that no one has succeeded yet.

ATTENDANT: But your Majesty . . . the question of the flogging . . .

PRINCE: This is what has made me hesitate . . . and has also made me persevere.

ATTENDANT: Persevere for what, your Majesty?

PRINCE: For her in particular.

ATTENDANT: If it weren't for this condition . . .

PRINCE: If it weren't for the thorn of the rose . . .

ATTENDANT: I prefer a rose without a thorn.

PRINCE: But the drop of blood that flows for its sake makes us desire it all the more.

ATTENDANT: It makes me stanch the blood and curse the rose.

PRINCE: But you don't retreat from it.

ATTENDANT: So that my bleeding won't have been in vain.

PRINCE: The fear with this rose of ours is that our blood might flow in vain. We might be whipped without any result.

ATTENDANT: If we were whipped and married, the affair would be easier.

PRINCE: Of course . . . but the one who is whipped is the one who won't marry her. He who marries her won't be whipped.

ATTENDANT: Is there no woman besides this one?

PRINCE: I told you I seek her alone.

ATTENDANT: This is a risky business, your Majesty.

PRINCE: That is clear.

ATTENDANT: How are we to avert these perils?

PRINCE: This is what I've been thinking about . . .

ATTENDANT: We must find a way.

PRINCE: Think with me, although I know you don't like to think.

ATTENDANT: For your sake, your Majesty, I will do anything.

PRINCE: I know . . . you are my loyal attendant. I can bounce my thought off you like a ball off a wall. When it returns to me I grasp it with my hand.

ATTENDANT: The important thing, your Majesty, is for your hand to grasp.

PRINCE: The ball?

ATTENDANT: The wife.

PRINCE: Oh, you were thinking of the wife.

ATTENDANT: Didn't you say for me to think with you?

PRINCE: Indeed . . . Listen. Let's think together step by step. Tell me first of all, by your estimation, what can attract a woman?

ATTENDANT: With reference to you, your Majesty?

PRINCE: In general terms.

ATTENDANT: In general . . . general terms?

PRINCE: Yes . . . with reference to anyone . . . with reference to you for example.

ATTENDANT: Me?

PRINCE: Yes, you. What was it that attracted your wife? What did she like about you, for example?

ATTENDANT: She liked my appearance.

PRINCE: Your appearance? . . . I take refuge in God!

ATTENDANT: It's a question of tastes, your Majesty.

PRINCE: You're right . . . and here's the difficulty.

ATTENDANT: With regard to you, your Majesty, the matter is much simpler.

PRINCE: How so?

ATTENDANT: No woman could resist the temptation of your wealth.

PRINCE: My wealth?

ATTENDANT: Your coffers filled with gold, your Majesty . . . and your castle filled with works of art and jewels . . .

PRINCE: Do you think that Princess Sunshine has not had throngs of princes and wealthy men seeking her?

ATTENDANT: That must have happened.

PRINCE: So search for another trait!

ATTENDANT: Your youth, your Majesty.

PRINCE: My youth?

ATTENDANT: It's a strong point.

PRINCE: Do you think, Stupid, that all the men who have sought the princess have been old?

ATTENDANT: True . . . that's not possible.

PRINCE: Search for a trait peculiar to me.

ATTENDANT: Your qualities are numerous, your Majesty. It is difficult to choose.

PRINCE: I want to appear with something no one else has brought.

ATTENDANT: Wealth . . . rank . . . youth. What more than that does a woman want?

PRINCE: Princess Sunshine is not like other women!

ATTENDANT: What does she have the others don't?

PRINCE: It's that she seeks some quality in men, but we don't yet know what it is.

ATTENDANT: This is bewildering.

PRINCE: Completely bewildering!

(The doorman enters to make an announcement.)

DOORMAN: There are two men at the door, your Majesty, who seek an audience with you.

PRINCE: Who are they?

DOORMAN: They are foreigners carrying a bag of money.

PRINCE: Perhaps it is a gift from one of the princes or kings. Show them in.

(The doorman exits and returns with Moonlight and Sunshine. They carry the money bag.)

MOONLIGHT: Greetings to you, O Prince.

(Sunshine salutes the prince and his attendant.)

PRINCE: Greetings to you.

MOONLIGHT: We have come, Prince, to bring you this bag filled with gold.

PRINCE: Thank you. Whose gift is it?

MOONLIGHT: It is not a gift . . . It is your property being returned to you.

PRINCE: My property?

MOONLIGHT: Yes . . . money that was embezzled from your coffers.

PRINCE: Who is the embezzler?

MOONLIGHT: The Treasury Inspector and his aide.

PRINCE: I know nothing of this.

ATTENDANT: I haven't heard anything.

PRINCE: Bring us the Treasurer.

(The attendant motions to the doorman and whispers the prince's request to him.)

SUNSHINE: We captured the embezzlers . . .

PRINCE: That too?

SUNSHINE: But unfortunately . . . they caught us off guard on the way and fled at a mountain curve. They hid among the ravines and caves.

PRINCE: In any case, you did even more than your duty.

(The treasurer appears.)

TREASURER: Your Majesty sent for me?

PRINCE: Yes . . . Tell me, Treasurer, has anything been stolen from the treasury?

TREASURER: No, your Majesty. Absolutely not.

PRINCE: You are certain.

TREASURER: Totally certain.

PRINCE: Everything in the coffers is in place?

TREASURER: Not a dinar is missing.

PRINCE: Amazing! Whose money bag is this then?

TREASURER: This money bag?

PRINCE: It seems you know nothing of the wealth under your control.

TREASURER: Everything is balanced in the ledgers, your Majesty.

PRINCE: In whose hand are the ledgers?

TREASURER: In the Inspector's hand.

PRINCE: Where is the Inspector?

TREASURER: He has gone on holiday.

PRINCE: Who is taking his place?

TREASURER: His assistant.

PRINCE: Where is his assistant?

TREASURER: He must be here.

PRINCE: He is not here.

TREASURER: The Inspector would know that.

PRINCE: When will we know that?

TREASURER: We'll ask the Inspector when he returns.

PRINCE: He won't return.

TREASURER: He won't return?

PRINCE: Neither he nor his assistant . . . because they are the ones who stole from the treasury.

TREASURER: What is it I hear, your Majesty?

PRINCE: You hear the truth that you don't know anything about . . . or perhaps you did know as well . . . How do I know what goes on behind my back!

TREASURER: I will carry out an investigation into the matter at once.

PRINCE: I will take charge of the investigation myself. Bring me the ledgers and the scribe and guard who look after them.

PRINCE: I hear and obey.

(He goes out quickly.)

ATTENDANT: Why tire yourself with these matters, your Majesty? Of what consequence is something like this . . . All this money—whether it leaves the treasury through theft, salaries, or expenditures—returns to you once again.

PRINCE: What are you saying?

ATTENDANT: Where will this stolen money go? It will be spent of course. It will be used to purchase goods and merchandise you control. Afterwards, the obligatory sales and excise taxes will be forced from everyone. So what departed from one side returns to you from the other.

PRINCE: This is true.

ATTENDANT: You yourself said one day that not a dirham leaves the treasury that does not return to it in one form or another.

PRINCE: True.

ATTENDANT: It's a mill . . . Your Majesty, let the mill move. The movement brings blessings.

PRINCE: In fact . . . my treasury will not have lost anything in the final analysis. They won't actually eat the dinars, and so long as no one eats the dinars . . . and so long as all of them are spent . . .

ATTENDANT: Then all of them will go into your pocket.

PRINCE: This is certain.

ATTENDANT: There's no harm done then to anything.

SUNSHINE: To morality . . .

PRINCE: What is this soldier saying?

SUNSHINE: I'm saying, your Majesty, that your coffers may actually not have suffered any loss, but your subjects . . . Are you pleased to see this dissipation?

PRINCE: Who are you?

SUNSHINE: A simple soldier, as you see.

PRINCE: But you're making a big statement.

MOONLIGHT: It is rather the simple talk of a simple man. We have returned the purse to you, not because you need money, but because there is always a need for justice, probity, and purity.

PRINCE *(to his attendant):* Do you hear?

ATTENDANT: Our country is fine . . . Our country is the best in the world.

PRINCE: Do you think so?

ATTENDANT: It's certain. There is absolutely no need for a commotion against us or the reputation of our country.

PRINCE: It's your opinion then that we should keep quiet and dissemble.

ATTENDANT: This is the best idea.

PRINCE: Then . . .

SUNSHINE: Then . . . if the best idea you have is to cover up corruption, this is your business. We have done our duty in any case. So permit us now to leave.

PRINCE: Indeed . . . you have certainly performed your duty to me.

SUNSHINE: Not to you whom we do not know . . . It was the duty to what ought to be.

PRINCE: However the matter may be, I owe you a reward.

SUNSHINE: We have already had our reward in full.

PRINCE: From whom?

SUNSHINE: From ourselves.

PRINCE: How so?

SUNSHINE: When we did what was right, that gave us a feeling inside which is priceless.

PRINCE *(to his attendant):* Have you heard anything like this here?

(The treasurer enters with a scribe behind him carrying the ledgers followed by a guard.)

TREASURER: Here are the ledgers, your Majesty . . . They are all correct.

PRINCE: Correct?

TREASURER: Yes, your Majesty.

PRINCE: And this correct bag?

TREASURER: We don't know, your Majesty . . . but the figures in the ledgers are correct. All the sums are accounted for.

PRINCE: On paper, yes . . . but the coffers?

TREASURER: The coffers are secure. The keys are with me.

PRINCE: With you?

TREASURER: With me personally.

PRINCE: How did this bag get out?

TREASURER: I don't know . . . The guard may be asked.

PRINCE *(to the guard):* Come here, Guard. Tell me: what do you guard?

GUARD: The door, your Majesty.

PRINCE: Which door?

GUARD: The door of the treasury.

PRINCE: Only the door?

GUARD: The door.

PRINCE: That is, what is behind the door is no concern of yours?

GUARD: Yes . . . only the door. It has locks on it.

PRINCE: Are these locks strong?

GUARD: They were falling apart, and we brought a locksmith to repair them.

PRINCE: He repaired them?

GUARD: He said he had repaired them, took his pay, and left.

PRINCE: And afterwards?

GUARD: God knows best.

PRINCE: You mean he did not repair them well.

GUARD: This, your Majesty, is beyond my competence.

PRINCE: In brief, it is possible to open and close the door while it has these faulty locks?

GUARD: It's possible.

PRINCE: You knew this was possible?

GUARD: Of course.

PRINCE: You didn't report it?

GUARD: Why should I report it? My speciality is guarding the door. The locks are not part of my job.

PRINCE: How lovely . . . And you, Treasurer . . . who accepted from the locksmith his defective work?

TREASURER: I don't know . . . It must have been one of the employees . . . I wouldn't know who it was. This is beyond my competence.

PRINCE: Remarkable . . . Doesn't anyone undertake a regular inventory of the contents of the coffers?

TREASURER: Someone is supposed to undertake this.

PRINCE: Then no one does this either.

TREASURER: The persons responsible may be asked.

PRINCE: Who are these persons responsible?

TREASURER: There are many . . . I don't know them personally.

PRINCE: You only have the keys with you . . . personally?

TREASURER: Yes.

PRINCE: Beyond that you are not concerned by what happens?

TREASURER: Your Majesty, I work to the extent . . .

PRINCE: The extent of the salary?

TREASURER: The extent of my powers.

PRINCE: Thanks for the effort! . . . Simple Soldier, what do you think of all this? You who together with your companion undertook a task without being asked and with no interest for a payment or reward . . . What is your verdict on these men? Issue your verdict, and I'll carry it out.

TREASURER: If it is a death sentence, I would like to point out to your Majesty that the execution cannot be by hanging.

PRINCE: Why not?

TREASURER: Because there is no rope.

PRINCE: What has become of the gallows' rope?

TREASURER: Stolen, your Majesty.

PRINCE: Stolen?

TREASURER: And sold secretly to some of the merchants.

PRINCE: Who would steal something like this rope?

TREASURER: Many people . . . Anyone whose hand touches something snatches it.

PRINCE *(to the attendant):* Did you know that?

ATTENDANT: That's not all, your Majesty . . . The street lamps . . . we rarely find a lamp which hands have not fiddled with . . .

PRINCE: What a game!

ATTENDANT: Horseshoes are removed when horses stand outside, despite the surveillance of the owners. Saddles are stripped off them. Anything that has a price . . . but who would have thought that the iron horseshoe would not escape . . .

PRINCE: This is a plague.

ATTENDANT: This violation of trust and looking the other way . . . have become the norm.

PRINCE: The norm?

ATTENDANT: Yes, your Majesty . . . something normal . . . and there's no need to trouble your mind so long as everything continues to progress as one might hope.

PRINCE: As one might hope?

ATTENDANT: We are progressing at any rate. The important thing is progress.

SUNSHINE: And a code of conduct?

PRINCE: What are you saying, Soldier?

SUNSHINE: Nothing . . . it seems it is possible here to progress without a code of conduct.

PRINCE: This is not something that builds confidence.

ATTENDANT: No, be confident, your Majesty.

PRINCE: What's your opinion, Soldier?

SUNSHINE: So long as these people around you are progressing confidently through the muck, what am I to say?

PRINCE *(to the attendant):* Do you hear? If you haven't heard, I have. If you haven't understood, I have. It's not possible for me to keep quiet, no matter what the situation may be. This is something it is not possible to keep quiet about. There must be a speedy trial. What do you say now, Frank Youth?

SUNSHINE: A trial and punishment won't reform much.

PRINCE: Didn't you say just now that justice, probity, and purity are obligatory?

SUNSHINE: Obligatory, yes . . . But they alone are no longer sufficient. The question is deeper than that. It's something inside.

PRINCE: Inside?

SUNSHINE *(pointing to her heart):* Yes . . . here.

(The doorman enters with an announcement.)

DOORMAN: The Treasury Inspector and his aide request an audience.

PRINCE: The two thieves! They captured them?

DOORMAN: They are not under arrest, your Majesty. They are by themselves.

PRINCE: Send them in!

(The doorman brings in the two men.)

INSPECTOR *(falling to his knees):* Your Majesty, we have come of our own free will.

AIDE *(also kneeling):* Your Majesty, we have come to request . . .

PRINCE: To request forgiveness, of course.

INSPECTOR: No, we have come to request punishment.

PRINCE: Punishment?

INSPECTOR: What you think appropriate for us.

AIDE: We will be content and happy with it.

PRINCE: Why did you flee?

INSPECTOR: An instinctive reflex.

AIDE: A love for life.

INSPECTOR: They had us ride one horse, the two of us by ourselves. They tied it behind their horse. When night came and the opportunity arose, we jumped off the horse and rolled to the bottom of the mountain. We saved ourselves and found ourselves alone.

AIDE: We began to think about our destiny . . . Yes, we were saved . . . but from what?

INSPECTOR: The crime was inside our souls.

AIDE: Wherever we would go we would still be criminals, at least to our own eyes.

INSPECTOR: We felt as though we were in a prison.

AIDE: A mobile prison.

INSPECTOR: Following us at every step.

AIDE: We became a prison, jailer, and prisoner all in one body.

INSPECTOR: Finally we saw that our deliverance lay through punishment.

AIDE: In surrendering ourselves to justice.

PRINCE *(to Sunshine):* What then is your verdict for these two?

SUNSHINE: This verdict for them is easy to give. Since they feel the prison existing inside them, there's no need for another prison of stone. Their inner prison of self is stronger and harsher.

PRINCE: What do you recommend then?

SUNSHINE: Pardon . . . on condition that they not return to their previous employment.

INSPECTOR: We don't want our previous jobs.

AIDE: We want work that will coarsen our hands and purify our souls.

INSPECTOR: Make us grooms for the horses.

AIDE: Yes, this is work we know and like.

SUNSHINE: Did you truly like it?

INSPECTOR: We remembered it afterwards as good.

AIDE: And we can still taste the two apples.

PRINCE: Where was all this?

SUNSHINE: When we seized them in the wilderness.

INSPECTOR: The food was tasty notwithstanding the small quantity.

AIDE: And the work with our hands was enjoyable despite its roughness.

PRINCE: Then . . . you will work in the stables.

INSPECTOR: Anything other than flight in the mountains . . . Thank you, your Majesty!

AIDE: From the depths of our hearts. All this is better than wandering without money.

PRINCE *(looking at the treasurer, guard and scribe):* As for these men . . . what shall we do with them? Shall we put them in a prison of stone?

ATTENDANT: Give them a chance, your Majesty. Are we to free the embezzler and imprison the negligent?

PRINCE: You understand nothing of what has taken place in front of you!

ATTENDANT: I understand only that you have a compassionate heart.

PRINCE: Yes . . . but we must set an example for people . . . Didn't you hear this soldier just now talking about moral standards?

ATTENDANT: But he did not urge that these men be imprisoned.

PRINCE: What can we think of for them besides that?

ATTENDANT: Give them other work too.

PRINCE: Another job? Where?

AIDE *(shouting):* In the stables with us, your Majesty. We will train them!

PRINCE: It's an idea.

SUNSHINE: Indeed, your Majesty. The one who has learned will teach the others.

PRINCE: You all go then to your new jobs.

INSPECTOR: Long live justice!

AIDE: Long live honesty!

(They all go out.)

MOONLIGHT: Your Majesty, permit us to depart also.

PRINCE: Wait a moment! I want to know exactly who you are. From what country?

MOONLIGHT: We are from a distant land.

PRINCE: And this soldier . . .

SUNSHINE: Like my companion, your Majesty.

PRINCE: But you are a soldier . . . in the service of a prince or sultan no doubt.

SUNSHINE: Yes, I am a soldier with Sultan Nu'man.

PRINCE: Sultan Nu'man? The father of Princess Sunshine?

SUNSHINE: Yes, your Majesty!

PRINCE: What good luck! . . . Have you seen Princess Sunshine?

SUNSHINE: I work in her palace . . .

PRINCE: Then you've seen her with your own eyes?

SUNSHINE: Of course.

PRINCE: What is she like? Describe her to me.

SUNSHINE: She's an ordinary woman.

PRINCE: Ordinary? So you're blind and cannot see.

SUNSHINE: How would you have her?

PRINCE: She is surely the wonder of the age.

SUNSHINE: I've never seen anything wonderful about her.

PRINCE: Who are you, Naive Youth?

SUNSHINE: I'm nothing, of course . . . but I speak my personal opinion candidly.

PRINCE: Your personal opinion? . . . Till now I've found your opinions to be wise and correct.

ATTENDANT: Perhaps he is correct, your Majesty. Didn't I say to you not long ago that she might be a woman like any other . . .

PRINCE: You be quiet.

SUNSHINE: Opinions differ in any case.

PRINCE: Does your companion have the same opinion?

MOONLIGHT: No, in my opinion, Sunshine is not an ordinary woman.

PRINCE: Do you see, Soldier? This companion of yours is a man who understands.

SUNSHINE: He believes, your Majesty, that she isn't a woman at all.

PRINCE: What does he mean by this?

SUNSHINE: I don't know . . . Ask him.

PRINCE *(to Moonlight):* Explain!

MOONLIGHT: This companion of mine wishes to embarrass me, your Majesty.

SUNSHINE: I only wanted your true feeling towards her to appear.

MOONLIGHT: My feeling towards her?

SUNSHINE: Yes . . . ask him, your Majesty. If Sunshine were presented to him, would he love her?

PRINCE: What kind of question is this? Is there anyone who would hesitate.

SUNSHINE: He would.

PRINCE: I don't believe it . . . It's just a question of his not wanting to build on hypotheses and fantasies . . . But if he saw her, drew near her, sat with her, and conversed with her, he wouldn't be able to control his feelings.

SUNSHINE: That is your opinion, your Majesty, but it isn't his.

PRINCE *(to Moonlight):* Is this really so? . . . Don't you share my opinion?

MOONLIGHT: Your opinion is respected, your Majesty.

SUNSHINE: Do you see, your Majesty, how he flees from giving a frank answer?

PRINCE: This is strange! This companion of yours is strange. And you are stranger. Is this your opinion of Sunshine to whom each day princes and grandees hasten from every realm, who answers no one and is pleased with no one . . .

SUNSHINE: Why are you, your Majesty, so enthusiastic about Sunshine?

PRINCE: I'm like everyone else . . . How many princes have gone to her despite the threat of flogging.

ATTENDANT: And have in fact been flogged. They are flogged every day.

PRINCE: Yes . . . they are whipped every day.

ATTENDANT: In spite of that, your Majesty . . .

PRINCE: Be quiet.

ATTENDANT: Rest assured, your Majesty, that I . . .

PRINCE: What harm is there in speaking now . . . Let's speak openly.

ATTENDANT: We should speak?

PRINCE: Yes, let's present the matter to this soldier. Perhaps we can benefit from his information. I . . . You speak first.

ATTENDANT: Indeed, since he has been near Sunshine he must know a lot about her.

PRINCE: Get to the point.

ATTENDANT: The point is that he . . . that the time has come for his Majesty to marry . . . He has thought of Princess Sunshine . . .

SUNSHINE *(in astonishment):* Sunshine?

ATTENDANT: His Majesty wishes no one else.

MOONLIGHT *(shouting):* But . . . but this . . .

SUNSHINE *(to Moonlight quickly):* Keep quiet now.

PRINCE: Yes, I desire no one but her . . . but there is that obstacle before me . . .

ATTENDANT: The flogging question!

PRINCE: It is not the flogging itself . . . but the defeat.

ATTENDANT: One leads to the other. The defeat to the flogging and the flogging to the defeat.

PRINCE: But I have now made my decision and resolved to proceed no matter the cost.

MOONLIGHT: But the problem is, your Majesty, that . . .

SUNSHINE *(to Moonlight):* Wait, I entreat you.

PRINCE: We have heard that no one has been victorious yet . . .

MOONLIGHT: But now, your Majesty, what has happened . . .

SUNSHINE *(giving Moonlight a big wink):* Be quiet . . . Be quiet.

PRINCE: All I ask now is guidance to a course by which I can be victorious.

ATTENDANT: Are you able, Soldier, to enlighten us a little on the means?

SUNSHINE: The fact is that the road to victory is strewn with boulders.

PRINCE: I know . . . I know the matter is not easy . . . but what I want to know is what Sunshine is seeking? If she wants me to pave the road to her with roses or gold, I'll do it.

SUNSHINE: I don't think that roses or gold would tempt her or satisfy her.

PRINCE: I know that too. She wants something more significant than all that no doubt . . . something weightier and greater.

SUNSHINE: Truly . . .

PRINCE: What is it? . . . Do you have any idea?

SUNSHINE: I think she would prefer to have you go to her on a road . . .

PRINCE: Strewn with what?

SUNSHINE: Not strewn with anything . . . an ordinary road.

ATTENDANT: Ordinary? . . . Then she wants a procession.

SUNSHINE: Absolutely no procession either.

ATTENDANT: No procession? How is the prince to travel to her then?

SUNSHINE: Alone.

ATTENDANT: On his magnificent charger?

SUNSHINE: On foot.

ATTENDANT: What's this? Does she wish to humiliate him then?

SUNSHINE: Perhaps she wants to see the man he is without the trappings.

PRINCE: I have begun to understand.

ATTENDANT: For me, to the contrary, your Majesty, matters are becoming confused.

PRINCE: It's enough if I understand., This soldier seems to know her very well. This will help me greatly. Listen, Soldier . . . What's your name, first of all.

SUNSHINE *(taken by surprise):* My name . . . my name . . . My companion's name is Moonlight.

PRINCE: I'm asking you your name, not your companion's.

SUNSHINE: My name . . . is Moonbeam . . . Yes, he's Moonlight and I'm Moonbeam.

PRINCE: Moonbeam? . . . Listen, Moonbeam. You talk about Sunshine's propensities like someone close to her . . . How do you know that?

SUNSHINE: Didn't I say I was guard at the palace . . .

PRINCE: Guarding her?

SUNSHINE: Yes.

PRINCE: Yes, she chose you then to be near her . . . This budding youth of yours . . . and your grace . . . as though you were a beardless youth. It was a good choice.

SUNSHINE: No . . . she did not choose me at all. She never spoke a word to me. She has perhaps never sensed my existence. I was only a guard like the others . . .

PRINCE: Are you sure you never caught her eye?

SUNSHINE: Quite sure. She doesn't like my type of man.

PRINCE: What type of man does she like?

SUNSHINE: It's not easy to say.

PRINCE: Of course . . . of course . . . in any case, Moonbeam, we'll discuss all this extensively between us . . . Now I would like to inform you that I have appointed you as of this moment my bodyguard, charged with my chamber, clothes and bath.

MOONLIGHT *(exploding in a whisper):* What a disaster!

SUNSHINE *(whispering to him):* What's come over you?

MOONLIGHT *(whispering):* His bath?

SUNSHINE *(whispering):* Be quiet . . . Be quiet!

MOONLIGHT *(disputing in a whisper):* How can I be quiet about this? His bath? . . . Impossible! . . . Impossible.

PRINCE: What's it all about, Moonbeam?

SUNSHINE: Nothing . . . It's nothing, your Majesty.

PRINCE: It seems your companion isn't happy.

MOONLIGHT *(in a muffled voice):* Happy?

PRINCE: What does he say?

SUNSHINE: Nothing . . . It's just that he was expecting to be appointed to a post too.

PRINCE: This is a simple matter. He needs only to select the work which best suits him.

SUNSHINE *(to Moonlight):* Do you hear? You have only to select a suitable post for yourself.

MOONLIGHT: I choose then to take care of the prince's bath.

PRINCE: My bath? But I have chosen Moonbeam to perform this work.

MOONLIGHT: This is what I want to perform myself.

PRINCE: But I'm the one who chooses who is to bathe me, not the other way around.

MOONLIGHT: This is all I'm good at.

PRINCE: If you want to bathe someone, you can have my attendant.

ATTENDANT *(protesting):* Bathe me? What need is there? I have my wife.

PRINCE: The important thing is for you to look for something that pleases him.

ATTENDANT: We'll look into it for him.

MOONLIGHT: What would please me would be to honor my companion and to keep him from demeaning work.

PRINCE: Demeaning? What is this man saying? Do you call work at my side demeaning?

ATTENDANT: It's an honor . . . What an honor . . .

PRINCE *(to Sunshine):* Moonbeam, do you like this pronouncement by your companion?

SUNSHINE: Of course not, your Majesty . . . but it is jealousy.

MOONLIGHT: Jealousy?

SUNSHINE: Of my winning this honor, your Majesty.

PRINCE: Indeed, this is natural between colleagues.

SUNSHINE *(to Moonlight):* Listen, Moonlight! Cease this childish behavior and let me act for myself.

MOONLIGHT: If the result is bad?

PRINCE: What result will be bad?

SUNSHINE: Don't listen to what he says, your Majesty. He sometimes says things that are meaningless.

MOONLIGHT: Meaningless?

SUNSHINE: And useless.

MOONLIGHT: Am I to relinquish everything then?

PRINCE: This companion of yours, Moonbeam, gives himself more authority over you than is right.

SUNSHINE: By virtue of companionship and friendship. Nothing more and nothing less . . .

MOONLIGHT: No more and no less?

SUNSHINE: Of course, merely an ordinary companionship. Nothing binds one of us to the other.

MOONLIGHT: There's no bond at all?

SUNSHINE: At all.

MOONLIGHT: Is this your opinion now?

SUNSHINE: Yes.

MOONLIGHT: But this isn't my opinion.

SUNSHINE: Since when?

MOONLIGHT: Since now.

SUNSHINE: This is something new then?

MOONLIGHT: New or old it doesn't matter.

SUNSHINE: You are free to your opinions and feelings from this moment.

MOONLIGHT: So?

SUNSHINE: Yes . . . so.

MOONLIGHT: But . . . wouldn't it be good to think a little?

PRINCE (shouting): And finally?

SUNSHINE: Forgive us, your Majesty.

PRINCE: This private conversation between you has become a bit drawn out.

SUNSHINE: I'm at your service.

PRINCE: Shall we go, Moonbeam?

SUNSHINE: Where to?

PRINCE: To my chamber . . . We'll talk over in detail the matter of going and appearing before Sunshine. My attendant will undertake everything for the comfort of this companion of yours.

SUNSHINE: We hear and obey.

PRINCE *(rising and pointing to his cloak on a chair beside him):* Carry my cloak, Moonbeam, and follow me.

SUNSHINE: Carry it yourself, your Majesty.

PRINCE *(astonished):* What did you say?

SUNSHINE: I said you should carry your cloak yourself.

PRINCE: Do you say this to me, Moonbeam?

ATTENDANT: Did he say this to his Majesty the Prince?

SUNSHINE: Yes, because I want the prince to be a perfect man.

PRINCE: How's that? What's this talk?

SUNSHINE: A person who takes care of himself is more perfect. A person who requires another to do what he can is lacking.

PRINCE: Reasonable talk . . . but . . .

SUNSHINE: So long as it is reasonable, why don't you act on it?

PRINCE: Carry my cloak myself?

SUNSHINE: Why not?

PRINCE: This is something I'm not accustomed to . . .

SUNSHINE: Learn how!

PRINCE *(picking up the cloak):* The cloak is light in any case, but this will set a precedent for other things.

SUNSHINE: Of course. If you say to me: "Give me a drink!" . . .

PRINCE: You will say to me: "Get up and pour it yourself."

SUNSHINE: Exactly.

PRINCE: If I say to you, "Help me put my clothes on" . . .

SUNSHINE: I'll tell you, "Put them on yourself!"

PRINCE: And my bath too, naturally.

SUNSHINE: Certainly.

PRINCE: Why did I take you into my service then?

SUNSHINE: To perfect your defects . . . but if you become a complete man, you won't need me.

PRINCE: In any case I need you for a matter for which you are necessary: reaching Sunshine.

SUNSHINE: Sunshine does not want a defective man.

PRINCE: You know her best . . . for that reason I obey you, for her sake.

SUNSHINE: I don't want you to obey me unwillingly, grudgingly . . .

PRINCE: I will carry out everything you suggest. That's enough!

SUNSHINE: Inside your soul?

PRINCE: Are you concerned with the inside of my soul?

SUNSHINE: You must have an inner conviction.

PRINCE: Your commands are becoming numerous, Moonbeam.

SUNSHINE: One who seeks something difficult must endure . . .

PRINCE: I am enduring it as you can see.

ATTENDANT: His Majesty the Prince has never previously suffered anyone the way he has suffered you, Fellow.

PRINCE (to his attendant): Perhaps he will bear witness one day to Sunshine about what I have endured for her sake.

SUNSHINE: You haven't endured anything yet. You are still at the beginning of the road.

PRINCE: So be it. I have determined to travel to the end.

SUNSHINE: Without flagging or complaining!

PRINCE: Rest assured . . . You need only direct me to what is necessary.

SUNSHINE: The matter will be hard on you.

PRINCE: I'm ready.

SUNSHINE: Let's begin now then.

PRINCE: Let's begin . . . Let's go to my room and consider the details.

SUNSHINE: To your room?

PRINCE: Of course. I can't stay here all the time . . . Our conversation may take a long time.

SUNSHINE: But . . .

PRINCE: What is your hesitation about?

SUNSHINE: No . . . nothing. Let's go, your Majesty.

MOONLIGHT (shouting): To his room! To his room? This can't be . . . It cannot be.

PRINCE: Who is this madman? This companion of yours must have lost his mind.

SUNSHINE: Pay no attention, your Majesty.

MOONLIGHT: Not possible . . . impossible.

ATTENDANT (grasping him and restraining him): Stay in your place.

PRINCE: Let's go, Moonbeam.

SUNSHINE (looking behind her at Moonlight while they hold him, smiling, and then following the prince): After you, your Majesty.

Scene Two

A road in the wilds beside a small hill or rise of earth . . . The space is empty . . . then Sunshine appears with the prince and Moonlight behind her.

SUNSHINE *(to the prince):* If you wish to rest a little, here's a suitable place.

PRINCE *(sitting down weakly):* Indeed . . . ugh.

SUNSHINE: You're not used to travelling on foot.

MOONLIGHT: He was limping on the way and tried to conceal it.

PRINCE: You be quiet!

MOONLIGHT: Don't speak to me in this tone of command. You're not prince here, and we aren't your subjects. That was the condition. We are all equal . . . travelling companions.

PRINCE: I know that. I did not address you on the assumption I was a prince and you a subject . . . rather on the grounds that you are a travelling companion . . . a bad companion I am fated to endure.

MOONLIGHT: You aren't the only one to suffer such a fate.

SUNSHINE: Will it end? Will we continue in this state all the way? Isn't it possible for one of you to bear the other for a single moment?

PRINCE: Moonbeam, you are a charming person. For your sake I bear every calamity.

MOONLIGHT: Calamity?

SUNSHINE: Patience, Moonlight . . . Patience, I beg you.

MOONLIGHT: I will be patient.

SUNSHINE: And you, Hamdan. Control yourself . . . not for my sake, but for the sake of the goal you are striving for.

PRINCE: Yes . . . Sunshine. If only she knew what I am doing for her sake.

SUNSHINE: In any case, we are perhaps at the end of the journey. Her city may be behind this hill. Get up, Hamdan, and find out.

PRINCE *(rising):* Yes . . . at once.

SUNSHINE: I am pleased, Hamdan, that you have not complained about any task throughout the trip.

PRINCE: Why should I complain? Whatever you have imposed on me, Moonbeam, has been profitable and useful.

SUNSHINE: Do you really feel that way?

PRINCE: Be confident that I speak from the depths of my heart.

MOONLIGHT: The depths of his heart?

PRINCE: I'm on my way. *(He heads toward the hill.)*

SUNSHINE: You will climb the hill of course?

PRINCE: Of course. *(He raises his eyes.)* But . . . what's this on top of the hill? It seems to be a village. Yes, it is a village, but it's dead. There's no movement in it. Look. They seem to be immobile ghosts, like idols. It's like the enchanted City of Brass.

SUNSHINE *(looking):* Yes, an enchanted village like the City of Brass.

PRINCE: But is it truly under a spell?

SUNSHINE: You can break the spell if you wish.

PRINCE: How?

SUNSHINE: Go up to these ghosts. I'll tell you then what to do.

PRINCE: Up I go. *(He ascends the rise.)*

SUNSHINE: What have you found?

PRINCE: They really are dead, but they stand in their places . . . ghosts with bodies . . . their eyes are open, but their lashes don't move. Their hands are outstretched, but they seem frozen.

SUNSHINE: Is there any bread in your knapsack?

PRINCE *(searching his bag):* Yes.

SUNSHINE: Take it out and put it in those hands.

PRINCE: But . . .

SUNSHINE: Do as I tell you.

PRINCE *(following her instructions):* Here, I'm doing it.

SUNSHINE: Watch what happens now.

PRINCE: Amazing . . . amazing. They've begun to move. The hands have begun to put the bread in the mouths. They are eating. They're eating. They're moving. The spell really has been broken. The spell has been lifted from the village.

SUNSHINE: Do you see?

PRINCE: Indeed. This is amazing.

SUNSHINE: Now ask one of them the way to the city of Sultan Nuʻman, father of the Princess Sunshine.

PRINCE *(asking one of the ghosts who are moving and have begun to eat the bread):* Tell me, Uncle . . . Where's the city of Sultan Nuʻman, father of Princess Sunshine?

(The ghost—an old man—points with his hand beyond the hill without speaking. He is engrossed in eating.)

SUNSHINE: What did he say?

PRINCE: He pointed beyond the hill . . . toward the other side . . . I'll look. *(He turns and shouts.)* It's true. Here's a city . . . a large city, with golden domes. It's near here, and we didn't know. The hill hides it from us.

SUNSHINE: Come then. Let's discuss what has to be done.

PRINCE *(coming down the hill):* The enchanted village! . . . Truly, I've learned something.

SUNSHINE: Rest a bit now. Climbing up the hill on foot no doubt tired you.

PRINCE: So be it . . . but it was fruitful.

SUNSHINE: You realized that?

PRINCE: Yes . . . a person who travels on foot sees things one on horseback doesn't.

SUNSHINE: Listen, Hamdan! The destination is at hand. The city, as you saw, is behind the hill, within sight. My opinion is that you should go alone.

PRINCE: Alone?

SUNSHINE: Yes. You must face Sunshine by yourself.

PRINCE: And you, Moonbeam?

SUNSHINE: I will remain here with our companion Moonlight and await your return.

PRINCE: My return?

SUNSHINE: Or a sign from you telling us of the result. Our every hope is that the result will be happy, that your effort will be crowned by success, and that we will see you victorious.

PRINCE: Yes, the time for departure has come . . . but . . .

SUNSHINE: Don't hesitate. Have confidence in yourself.

PRINCE: Yes, I'll act according to your counsel.

SUNSHINE: So hurry off.

PRINCE: Let me embrace you, Moonbeam.

SUNSHINE: Not now . . . when you return to us triumphant.

PRINCE: Till we meet again, then.

(The prince departs towards the city. Sunshine remains with Moonlight.)

MOONLIGHT: Humph! Now I can breathe. He was a nightmare which has now passed away.

SUNSHINE: I didn't find him tiresome in any case.

MOONLIGHT: He wanted to embrace you! Had he done that he would not have escaped my hand.

SUNSHINE: What business do you have to interfere?

MOONLIGHT: You ask what business it is of mine?

SUNSHINE: You hate him without cause.

MOONLIGHT: I'm sure he sensed a feminine scent in you.

SUNSHINE: What's the harm? At least he has a nose that works.

MOONLIGHT: Tell me what happened that night . . . when you went off with this man to his room . . . and left me struggling in the arms of his attendants.

SUNSHINE: What do you think happened?

MOONLIGHT: He didn't try . . .

SUNSHINE: How can such base thoughts occur to you?

MOONLIGHT: Base?

SUNSHINE: It seems you have forgotten who I am.

MOONLIGHT: You're a woman.

SUNSHINE: It's only now that you learn that?

MOONLIGHT: A woman who allowed herself to be alone with a man.

SUNSHINE: Does this seem strange to you? Why don't you speak of my being alone with you?

MOONLIGHT: I'm something else.

SUNSHINE: I don't see any difference. You're just a man like the others.

MOONLIGHT: I don't know the others. I know myself. I know my moral standards. I don't know the morals of the others.

SUNSHINE: What protects me is not your morality or that of the others. It is my morality.

MOONLIGHT: You're right. This is what reassures me.

SUNSHINE: Reassures you? What is your tie to me?

MOONLIGHT: Amazing! Isn't there a tie between us?

SUNSHINE: Of what type?

MOONLIGHT: Aren't you my fiancée at least?

SUNSHINE: At least?

MOONLIGHT: For example.

SUNSHINE: No, Sir. Not at least and not at most.

MOONLIGHT: Didn't we leave your father's castle on this basis?

SUNSHINE: Yes . . . on this flimsy or imaginary basis. For you resorted to it only to protect us from what people would say. But in reality, you weren't adhering to it.

MOONLIGHT: Who said that?

SUNSHINE: Your long hesitation over being linked to me.

MOONLIGHT: Women! . . . Have you forgotten the reason for that? My hesitation over the bond was not for my sake but for yours . . . in order to leave you your freedom. For the sake of your right to a free choice . . .

when I became worthy of that . . . after you made a man of me. Have you forgotten all this?

SUNSHINE *(laughing):* I—make a man of you?

MOONLIGHT: Why do you laugh? Wasn't it for this reason we set out together . . . to travel over the wide earth . . .

SUNSHINE: For me to form you!

MOONLIGHT: Yes.

SUNSHINE *(sternly):* You cunning deceiver! Which of us has formed the other? . . . Speak!

MOONLIGHT: What do you mean?

SUNSHINE: You're the one who has shaped me. You knew that, but you pretended and feigned . . . I will never forgive you for this.

MOONLIGHT: You will never forgive me . . .

SUNSHINE: This deception.

MOONLIGHT: Be confident I never thought to deceive you. Everything proceeded naturally. We went out together to life . . . and you are an intelligent woman . . .

SUNSHINE: But you set out to teach me . . . and you taught me. Why? What was your goal? Perhaps you came to the castle with this plot in mind. Why? So you've achieved your goal . . . or part of it. What do you want from me now?

MOONLIGHT: I have no wish . . . It's up to you.

SUNSHINE: You have no wish?

MOONLIGHT: I don't dare . . .

SUNSHINE *(looking at him for a time):* I don't know you.

MOONLIGHT: You don't know me?

SUNSHINE: I know you as the one who shaped me, but I don't know your real nature. I don't know what's inside you. I don't see your heart.

MOONLIGHT: My heart . . .

SUNSHINE: Yes. There's another man . . . whom I have shaped. For that reason, I know him. I know what's inside him. I can see his heart.

MOONLIGHT: Who is he? Prince Hamdan?

SUNSHINE: Yes . . . Hamdan.

MOONLIGHT: Do you love him?

SUNSHINE: I won't speak of love yet . . .

MOONLIGHT: You see! I was right to leave you free to choose. Here the hour has come to choose. Your heart has in fact turned to the person who . . .

SUNSHINE: It has not turned to anyone.

MOONLIGHT: But in any case it has begun to feel who is closer to it.

SUNSHINE: Perhaps.

MOONLIGHT: Yes. The princess and the prince . . . Things have returned to normal.

SUNSHINE: Don't be silly!

MOONLIGHT: Don't think I object. To the contrary . . . I welcome it.

SUNSHINE: There's no need for your opposition or acceptance. I haven't decided anything yet.

MOONLIGHT: You mean there's still some hope for me?

SUNSHINE: Who advised you to despair?

(She takes her knapsack to depart.)

MOONLIGHT: Where to?

SUNSHINE: Here, just a few steps from you.

MOONLIGHT: What are you going to do?

SUNSHINE: You will know shortly. *(She disappears.)*

MOONLIGHT: Oh, my Lord! Why did this man come my way? If you really love him . . . what's my fate? Would I be able to leave you? Can you hear? . . . It would be better if you were at a slight distance, so you wouldn't hear what I say. Then my emotions wouldn't influence your choice. Is this true? . . . or is it that my pride refuses to let you see my torment? *(He calls out.)* Sunshine. Sunshine . . . She's far away now and doesn't hear. Yes, this is better, but who knows? Perhaps you are listening and pretending not to . . . So be it. So long as I am not addressing you directly . . . Tell me now frankly why you favor this Hamdan? You will answer you shaped him and put in him a part of yourself . . . and here's the disaster! We indeed do love our creations, while for our creator we feel only respect . . . So there's no hope of your love? . . . And I'm the one who has waited so long for this moment. I'm not the one who will take this . . . and sense your arms around his neck.

(Moonlight is silent and bows his head. Sunshine appears. She has changed from her military uniform and put on a woman's gown.)

SUNSHINE: What do you think?

MOONLIGHT *(looking at her in surprise):* What's this?

SUNSHINE: I requested this gown from one of the women in Hamdan's castle. Isn't it splendid? Here I've become a woman again.

MOONLIGHT *(having lowered his eyes again):* Yes.

SUNSHINE: Why do you say it sadly?

MOONLIGHT *(without looking at her):* Because you're beautiful.

SUNSHINE: This is the first time I hear you describe me like that.

MOONLIGHT: Did you put this on for his return?

SUNSHINE: Whose?

MOONLIGHT: Hamdan . . . No doubt he will return shortly.

SUNSHINE: Of course, he must return . . . after he learns in the city what has become of Sunshine.

MOONLIGHT: Yes.

SUNSHINE: He will be astonished when he learns that Sunshine was with him all the time without his knowing it.

MOONLIGHT *(downcast):* Yes.

SUNSHINE: You might ask me why I sent him to the city and didn't tell him what happened . . .

MOONLIGHT: I won't ask.

SUNSHINE *(continuing):* There are many reasons . . . Perhaps the one that concerns us now among them is my desire to clear up the situation in his absence . . . in a calm atmosphere . . . so that no quarrel would arise between you.

MOONLIGHT *(rising):* The situation does not require clearing up . . . I will shorten the procedure.

SUNSHINE: Sit down, Moonlight! I need your advice.

MOONLIGHT: You no longer need anyone.

SUNSHINE: You will learn now . . .

MOONLIGHT: I don't want . . . This is all a waste of time.

SUNSHINE: Where's your composure, Moonlight? A little composure, I beg you. Listen to me a moment . . . before he returns.

MOONLIGHT: Speak!

SUNSHINE: I'm perplexed, severely perplexed.

MOONLIGHT: I know.

SUNSHINE: Yes . . . you perceived that and said it clearly when you were addressing me from afar . . .

MOONLIGHT: You heard then?

SUNSHINE: Of course.

MOONLIGHT: The treatment for all this is simple . . . Marry Prince Hamdan. Please your heart and please your father.

SUNSHINE: Would I please my heart? No . . . not completely. I would lie to you if I told you that you occupy no part of it.

MOONLIGHT: A part!

SUNSHINE: I would lie to you also if I told you I wouldn't think of Hamdan if I married you.

MOONLIGHT: You would think of Hamdan?

SUNSHINE: Can you accept that? . . . For me to marry you and then keep thinking of that man I formed with my hand so that he could in turn form his land and reform his people. I attach great hopes to him.

MOONLIGHT: Be by his side then . . . Strive together.

SUNSHINE: And you?

MOONLIGHT: I'll return where I came from.

SUNSHINE: Where? Can you imagine that I haven't asked you yet who you are . . . nor where you came from? Your personality alone concerned me.

MOONLIGHT: The question is out of place now. *(He rises and takes his knapsack to depart.)*

SUNSHINE: Wait, Moonlight.

MOONLIGHT *(turning on her violently)*: First of all, my name isn't Moon or Moonlight! I'm not a prince . . . or anything at all. I don't know who my father was or my mother. I grew up among the people in a humble quarter. I have worked as a herdsman, a woodgatherer, a carpenter, a muezzin in a mosque, a Qur'an reciter, and a teacher for children. I have roamed about doing anything or everything. I have assisted those in need of help to the limit of my knowledge and ability. People have called me by a name the origin of which none of us knows. But it is my name in any case . . . my true name. Would you like to know what this name is—it's Dindan!

SUNSHINE: Dindan? *(She laughs.)*

MOONLIGHT: Yes . . . a laughable name as you see . . . What else do you want to know about me?

SUNSHINE: Listen . . . Dindan! *(She breaks into laughter.)*

MOONLIGHT: Laugh as much as you want . . . I'm nothing but Dindan. This is the person who dared to present himself to you.

SUNSHINE: And who hesitated to marry me . . . and consented only under pressure to be my fiancé! Do you still cling to the engagement bond . . . Dindan?

MOONLIGHT: Of course not . . . especially now . . .

SUNSHINE: What would you say if I insist on this bond now?

MOONLIGHT: Is this the time for comedy?

SUNSHINE: I'm totally serious.

MOONLIGHT: And Prince Hamdan?

SUNSHINE: Hamdan? No . . . I like the name Dindan. *(She laughs.)*

MOONLIGHT: Because it will make you laugh all the time.

SUNSHINE: What harm is there in that?

MOONLIGHT: I believe you have other tasks before you more important than laughing at me. *(He picks up his gear to depart.)*

SUNSHINE *(serious and stern)*: Wait! Do you think . . . ? Are you able to go off alone? Wherever you go, you will find me with you. Stay where you are and don't be stupid. I thought you were more intelligent than this. How is it you have been unaware of what I feel toward you and of what binds me to you.

MOONLIGHT *(sarcastic):* Since when?

SUNSHINE: Since the first day . . . you in the depths of your soul must have felt . . .

MOONLIGHT: Perhaps . . . until we met that prince.

SUNSHINE: Hamdan? You'll make me laugh again. How dull-witted men are! Even the simplest methods suffice to arouse the jealousy of a man of your cleverness.

MOONLIGHT: Doesn't he occupy a portion of your heart?

SUNSHINE: I'm proud of him . . . I believe he actually has changed . . . that he truly will reform his land . . . But love is something else. You should have understood that, Stupid . . . Dindan.

MOONLIGHT: I can then . . .

SUNSHINE: Kiss me if you wish. It's the first kiss I give a man . . . and this man is my fiancé and my husband.

MOONLIGHT: Your husband?

SUNSHINE: I will never love anyone but you. I won't marry anyone but you!

MOONLIGHT: I . . .

SUNSHINE: Here he is—hesitating again!

MOONLIGHT: Listen, Sunshine!

SUNSHINE: No . . . I entreat you. We have wasted a lot of time. Let's go.

MOONLIGHT: Go where?

SUNSHINE: To get married.

MOONLIGHT: Get married? . . . Now?

SUNSHINE: Of course now. Do you think I changed from my soldier's uniform to the gown merely for sport?

MOONLIGHT: Did you put it on now for this purpose?

SUNSHINE: Certainly! Would it have been possible for you to marry a soldier?

MOONLIGHT: This was all thought out in advance then?

SUNSHINE: Precisely and carefully.

MOONLIGHT: I marry you? Am I in a dream . . . I should take you in my arms?

SUNSHINE: Yes . . . if you would stop talking and speed your steps. Let's go. Off with us . . . to marriage.

MOONLIGHT: Where will the marriage be?

SUNSHINE: In the city of course . . . It couldn't be in the desert.

MOONLIGHT: In your father's city?

SUNSHINE: It is the closest.

MOONLIGHT: And after the wedding?

SUNSHINE: Are you thinking of what will happen after the marriage?

MOONLIGHT: Where will we live? . . . In the castle?

SUNSHINE: If you want . . .

MOONLIGHT: Of course I don't want to . . . I'm not capable of living in castles.

SUNSHINE: If you prefer a hut, be confident I prefer it.

MOONLIGHT: The two of us together?

SUNSHINE: Haven't we lived together out of doors?

MOONLIGHT: Yes . . . but I don't have the right to force you to roam homeless all your life. It wasn't for this that such care went into your formation. It was so that you could do something useful. You expect Hamdan to reform his land . . . I believe your land is no better than his .

SUNSHINE: That means . . .

MOONLIGHT: Yes . . . that means you should follow the same path as Hamdan . . . to return to your country and work to reform it.

SUNSHINE: Alone?

MOONLIGHT: Yes . . . alone. Your people need you. They won't accept change and reform from anyone but you who grew up and developed among them.

SUNSHINE: And you?

MOONLIGHT: I'll return to my life . . . the life I must lead with those among whom I grew up.

SUNSHINE: And our happiness?

MOONLIGHT: Let's think of the happiness of others.

SUNSHINE: What an oppressive life that is which awaits us!

MOONLIGHT: People with a mission have no rest.

SUNSHINE: Isn't there another solution?

MOONLIGHT: There are many solutions . . . but I have chosen the most difficult.

SUNSHINE: Yes . . . and the harshest.

MOONLIGHT: But is is the worthiest one for your personality.

SUNSHINE: Do you think, Darling, that I can stand resolute . . .

MOONLIGHT: You can more than I . . . It's not appropriate now for me to disclose to you the burden that I bear . . . but we must be brave.

SUNSHINE: If that's what you wish . . . then it's the best . . .

MOONLIGHT: Farewell, Sunshine!

SUNSHINE: Farewell, Moonlight!

MOONLIGHT: Dindan!

SUNSHINE *(hesitating, with sorrow):* Dindan . . .

MOONLIGHT: Say it with a smile, so that we can part with a smile.

SUNSHINE *(with a sad smile):* Yes . . . a smile!

> *(Each of them picks up his belongings and starts to depart, each in a different direction . . . but before they disappear they stop. They turn around suddenly. They look at each other. Then they dash spontaneously towards each other and embrace heartily.)*

SUNSHINE: I can't . . . I can't . . . The sacrifice is more than I can bear.

MOONLIGHT: Yes . . . more than we can bear.

SUNSHINE: I think we aren't capable of separating.

MOONLIGHT: Our spirits will never separate.

SUNSHINE: Our love is stronger than anything else.

MOONLIGHT: Yes, but . . . but your mission is stronger.

SUNSHINE: My mission? . . . yes.

MOONLIGHT: Yes, Sunshine, don't forget that.

SUNSHINE: Yes . . . yes . . . nor will I ever forget you.

MOONLIGHT: Nor I.

SUNSHINE: We'll meet, Darling . . . We'll meet, and you'll be proud of me and my work. I'm confident.

> *(Sunshine leaves him in silence without looking at him. He stands watching her depart until she disappears.)*

Note

[1] A fabulous island said by Arabic geographers to be off the coast of Africa or Asia.

Angels' Prayer

For the Friends of Humanity

Characters

FIRST ANGEL
SECOND ANGEL
GIRL
MONK
SCIENTIST
FIRST TYRANT
SECOND TYRANT
CHIEF AIDE
PRESIDING JUDGE
AN OFFICER
TYRANTS' AIDES
MILITARY JUDGES
SOLDIERS

Scene One

Two angels in heaven.

FIRST ANGEL: Look. What's this smoke rising to us from Earth?

SECOND ANGEL: It's human beings burning each other.

FIRST ANGEL: Do you suppose they've forgotten what our God said to Cain: "What have you done? The voice of your brother's blood cries to me from the Earth. Now you are cursed from the Earth which opened its mouth to receive from your hand your brother's blood."[1]

SECOND ANGEL: What do you suppose the Earth is saying when it opens its mouth today to receive clashing seas of blood from a million Abels.

FIRST ANGEL: Woe! Shall we remain in our lofty heights quietly looking down on them?

SECOND ANGEL: What can we do for them?

FIRST ANGEL: Descend to them to restore order to their minds and open their eyes to the light of the truth.

SECOND ANGEL: They are drunken, not seeing, hearing, or giving heed.

(The sound of voices praying reaches heaven.)

FIRST ANGEL: Do you hear . . . What are these beautiful voices ascending to us from the Earth?

SECOND ANGEL: That is a communal prayer which a few wise people address to heaven.

FIRST ANGEL: Listen. It's rising from three directions: from the East, the West and the center of the Earth. After that, don't you wish us, heaven's inhabitants, to make an effort?

SECOND ANGEL: I tell you that you can't do anything for these people.

FIRST ANGEL: And these pleas issuing from noble hearts? Are the gates closed to them? Shouldn't they find a path to our ears and a seat in our spirits? How merciless heaven's inhabitants would be if they reject these pleas, turn away these prayers, and let them fall back on the heads of their kneeling authors as cold, hollow echoes. I'm going by myself.

SECOND ANGEL: Descending to them?

FIRST ANGEL: Yes, answering the call. Even if I can't do anything for them, let me live among them at least, bearing a portion of the agony like one of them . . . one of the simple people possessing nothing but a heart.

SECOND ANGEL: I'm afraid of what they may do to you.

FIRST ANGEL: There's no need to say that. Farewell.

SECOND ANGEL: Until we meet again.

Scene Two

A forest in Europe . . . The first angel in the attire of a simple villager is sitting on the bank of a brook, tired and perplexed.

ANGEL: Oh . . . here at least is a place where the sounds of destruction, devastation, and explosion don't reach me. My companion was right. Merely descending to this Earth is like plunging to the lowest levels of hell. *(A sound is heard from the brook. He cries out.)* Who's there?

(An impoverished girl appears from among the trees carrying her belongings with a vessel in her hand which she has filled from the brook.)

GIRL *(fearfully):* Who are you?

ANGEL: I . . . I'm from the city.

GIRL: I too come from the city. I can see you are tired. Can I give you a little water from the brook?

ANGEL: No, thank you. I'm thirsty for a little calm.

GIRL: This is a calm place here.

ANGEL: Yes.

GIRL: I'll go so I won't disturb you.

ANGEL: No, stay. Sit down and talk to me, Girl. Why are you roaming alone in this wild forest?

GIRL *(with tears in her eyes):* I don't have any family left.

ANGEL: Don't weep.

GIRL: My mother died of a disease. We didn't have the price of the remedy. My father followed her. The war took my brothers. I don't know whether they are living or dead.

ANGEL: Why are they fighting?

GIRL: I don't know.

ANGEL: What will you do?

GIRL: I want to find a job. Can't you give me work, Mister?

ANGEL: I?

GIRL: I'm sorry. Perhaps you too are looking for sustenance. There are many like us who can't find food, medicine, or shelter.

ANGEL: Alas.

GIRL: What's wrong, Mister.

ANGEL: Nothing.

GIRL: Your voice is weak and your face pale. No doubt you're hungry.

ANGEL: Don't worry about me.

GIRL *(taking an apple from her bag):* Eat this apple. I picked it at dawn this morning from a tree growing wild at the edge of the forest. It's still green, but its juice is sweet and tasty. *(The angel looks at her for a long time.)* Why are you looking at me like this?

ANGEL *(taking the apple and holding it in his right hand):* Thank you, Girl.

GIRL: Why don't you eat it?

ANGEL: I have eaten and quenched my thirst.

GIRL: When?

ANGEL: Now, from the compassion of your heart.

GIRL: Rather you should eat it. Compassion is not sufficient food for us.

ANGEL: It's all I eat or drink.

GIRL: O my good-hearted friend . . . will you permit me to call you a friend?

ANGEL: You will light my spirit with joy.

GIRL: Let's travel together through this forest. Perhaps we will be guided to our goal . . . Sorry, how selfish I am. I didn't ask you about your status.

ANGEL: I . . . my goal is to see you are all right. Let's go. How beautiful the Earth would be if man here were able to see, to love, to let compassion flow from his soul like the water of this brook.

GIRL: Look, Friend . . . this green bird taking water from the brook. Beside him there's a wild hare. Do you see it? Behind the grass. He too is drinking, just as though they were friends.

ANGEL: Yes, yes.

GIRL: Listen . . . now that the bird has drunk from the stream's cup, he's opening his bill and singing.

ANGEL: This hare does not jump or flee. It seems he's accustomed to listening to his friend. Look: his ears have opened like two lilies, and his eyes are sparkling like turquoise.

GIRL: Do you know what this bird is saying?

ANGEL: He can only be talking about goodness, peace, and hope.

GIRL: You're right. He's addressing this wild flower from which the dew is still trickling. *(She sings.)*

> *O smile of morning to the creatures,*
> *This dew is not a drop of water;*
> *O flower of hope to the creatures,*
> *Your tear is heaven's daughter.*

ANGEL: Sing it again.

GIRL: What's the matter? I see a tear glittering in your eyes, Friend.

ANGEL: Sing once more: "Your tear is heaven's daughter." You're right. You're right, Charming Friend.

GIRL *(looking at him for a while):* O Lord!

ANGEL: Why are you looking at me so long?

GIRL: I don't know.

ANGEL: Don't be afraid. Let's go. Give me your hand.

GIRL: I haven't asked you your name.

ANGEL: I too have not asked you yours. What's the use of names? I already know all I need to about you.

GIRL: Me too.

(They hear the sound of someone approaching.)

ANGEL: Who's coming?

GIRL *(looking):* He looks like a monk to me.

(A monk appears carrying his belongings on his shoulders.)

MONK: Who are you?

ANGEL: Where do you come from, Monk?

MONK: From the greatest disaster, the darkest night, and the supreme affliction to encompass mankind . . . there where man rains down the flames of fire on his brother, beyond the fire of hell.

GIRL: Sit down, Father. You're tired.

MONK: Give me a drink of water.

GIRL *(giving him water to drink from the vessel and an apple to eat from her bag):* Drink and eat. Rest.

ANGEL: Why are they fighting?

MONK *(while eating):* Because today they worship a new god which makes genocide licit and proclaims the law of the fittest . . . a god with talons and fangs, plated with iron and steel.

GIRL: Yes. What a trial!

ANGEL: And you, Monk. What are you waiting for to defend the true God who proclaims the law of justice, love, and human brotherhood?

MONK: Defend with what?

ANGEL: With your holy weapon: the truth.

MONK: The truth! I'm waiting till the truth grows fangs.

ANGEL: Truth won't grow fangs, nor does it need to, because truth is a light which penetrates the heart.

MONK: Haven't you heard that the reign of might today extinguishes all light, no matter whether it shines in cities, alleyways, or hearts?

ANGEL: Is this what a man of religion says?

MONK: Where did you fall from, Man? Religions themselves have today fallen into the hand of tyrant might. They invoke its patronage and lend it their banners, as though they were districts of the Earth.

ANGEL: Don't let doubt seize you concerning the purity of your mission,

Monk. Hope would be lost if that happened. All this murder, arson, and destruction which have afflicted the Earth would be less dangerous for it than destruction of faith in the sovereignty of truth.

MONK *(looking for a long time at the angel):* Naive Man, who are you?

GIRL: Please don't argue. The best thing is for the three of us to direct ourselves to heaven and ask assistance for quelling the fire of evil and for establishing goodness among mankind.

MONK: You too, Simple Girl, think heaven hears our three weak voices when it hasn't heard the reverberation of artillery and the bombs exploding?

GIRL: Father, has heaven truly forsaken us, leaving us face to face with our cruelty, bestiality, and sins? Is there no hope? Is there no solace? Speak, Monk. O Father, when will we be able to shout from our hearts: "Sing heavens and Earth rejoice. Let the hills resound with song, for the Lord has consoled His people. He is compassionate with His wretched ones."[2]

MONK: Don't weep, Little Girl.

ANGEL: Yes, smile, Charming Friend.

GIRL: There's a tear in your eyes, too.

ANGEL: Smile and sing.

GIRL *(smiling):* The wild flower song?

ANGEL: Yes.

GIRL *(singing):*   *O smile of morning to the creatures,*
This dew is not a drop of water.

ANGEL *(completing):*   *O flower of hope to the creatures,*
Your tear is heaven's daughter.

MONK *(listening attentively):* Listen. Don't you hear a rustling among the trees?

GIRL: Yes.

ANGEL *(looking):* It's a man wandering aimlessly.

MONK: He's another outcast.

(A man appears carrying his belongings and his stick. He sways slightly.)

MAN *(standing and gazing at the three of them):* A youth, a girl, and a monk! When these three gather together, it means a wedding is in progress. Am I wrong, Gentlemen? You've been lacking one person: the witness. *(He points to himself.)* He has arrived with wine and glasses. *(He brings out a bottle and a glass from among his belongings.)* Here I am!

MONK: Creature, who are you?

MAN: A chemist.

MONK: Can every drunk with a bottle claim a knowledge of chemistry?

SCIENTIST: And can every person who carries a bottle be called drunk, Monk?

MONK: Do you want me to call him a saint?

SCIENTIST: If you call me that you won't be too far wrong, but I'll be satisfied with less than that from you. Call me simply a man of conscience.

MONK: You, by the practice of heaven, are a man guilty of rebellion against the faith.

SCIENTIST: Oh, spare us the dictionary of your profession and your memorized words, Monk . . . Be satisfied with the youth and the girl: two customers. Pour out some of what you have over their heads. Leave me and my affairs alone. I have come to this forest simply because I am a man of conscience. Don't you believe it? Don't you all believe it?

ANGEL: I see the purity of your conscience.

SCIENTIST: Here's a good-hearted man with a generous soul. To you alone will I address my words, for I'm confident you understand me. As for the others . . .

ANGEL: Yes, I understand you.

SCIENTIST: Rest assured first of all that I am a scientist, a chemist.

ANGEL: I believe that.

SCIENTIST: Now give me your hand and take a glass.

ANGEL: No. No thanks. I'm not thirsty.

SCIENTIST *(drinks):* As for me, I wish to fill my head with wine to drown knowledge. Don't think that I have abandoned the sobriety of scientists. Neither science nor scientists retain any sobriety.

ANGEL: Why?

SCIENTIST: That's a long story which I don't care to recount now. Don't remind me of what has passed, Man.

ANGEL: Perhaps I could do something for you.

SCIENTIST: You?

ANGEL: I'm a simple man, but I can understand you, because I sense what is in your soul. Your pain touches me.

SCIENTIST *(turning towards him and looking for a while):* Who are you? You seem to be a poor man, wretched, a fugitive. Yes, I thought about you once, you and the other wretched millions like you. That's the reason they sacked me and persecuted me. For that reason I'm with you in this place.

GIRL: Because of the poor and wretched.

SCIENTIST: All of them, you included, and this monk too. I spent twenty years thinking about you, twenty years making a plan to make you poor creatures happy. Science was going to be able to end your misery, to stop your hunger, sickness, nakedness, to turn your hell into an expansive paradise. Chemistry had led me to great results at reasonable expense. But here's the joke: the day came when the tyrant leader summoned me and told me: "Get this superstitious research out of your head and use your science in the way of glory." I asked him: what's the way of glory? He shouted his answer: "We want bombs. Bombs! We want artillery. Artillery! We want your chemistry to change milk into bombs and butter into artillery while you want to transfer the milk and butter to the mouths of stupid fools like yourself, Crazy Scientist."

ANGEL: God have mercy on me.

SCIENTIST: Do you see, Brothers, how my dream was dissipated? Now here I am having lost my faith in the loftiness of science's mission. Oh! God's curse on a science which is content to take food from the mouths of human beings to put it in the mouths of cannons. *(He drains his glass.)*

ANGEL: You shouldn't despair.

MONK: Naive man, if this is not the time for despair, what is?

ANGEL: Not so fast. Don't be so alarmed by the power of evil.

SCIENTIST: Young man, you don't understand the extent of the power of evil. A single match can burn a city. A single tyrant has inflamed his nation with the fever of destruction. He threw all its wealth into preparing the instruments of destruction. He was able at the same time to infect his neighbors, then his neighbors' neighbors, and finally the whole world. Thus each of the Earth's nations is throwing its treasures and its children's nourishment into this oven. Billions of billions flow from all over the Earth in this infernal course. Humanity as a whole no longer thinks of anything except the weapons of destruction and of spending billions of billions on them. I used to dream of a single billion to aid all of mankind. All the streams of gold which spring from the heart of the Earth are now melted and cast to wreck the Earth. This vile fever which has afflicted all human beings is like any fever. It started from a germ, a single germ in the form of a tyrant. He penetrated the body of the tranquil, content world. He set off in it those poisonous secretions and hysterical convulsions which may bring it to dissolution, collapse, and death. *(The sound of an explosion is heard.)*

GIRL *(frightened):* What's that? Did you hear?

SCIENTIST: It's a bomb which has fallen in the forest.

MONK: Hush, I hear the drone of airplanes.

GIRL: My God, won't they spare even the tranquil, smiling forests.

MONK *(looking to the sky and calling out the words of the Sacred Book):* "Awake, awake, put on strength, O Arm of the Lord. Awake as in the days of old . . . Are you not the dragon slayer? Did you not dry up the sea and the waters of the great flood, making its depths a path for the redeemed to cross?"[3]

ANGEL *(reciting):* I . . . "I am your consoler. Who are you to fear a man who shall die and the son of man is made like grass."⁴ *(An explosion resounds loudly.)*

SCIENTIST: Here's a bomb which has exploded near us.

MONK: Let's seek shelter before we're hit by fragments.

SCIENTIST: I won't hide. They want my life, so let them take it. They have already taken the best of it, my scientific freedom.

GIRL: I shan't hide either, for they've taken my family.

MONK: And you, Young Man?

ANGEL: I'm here only to serve you.

MONK: Then I won't be the one to weep for my body. Let's all stay put. Let them take this decaying flesh, if they wish.

SCIENTIST: You're right. It's nothing but decay and flesh after it has been stripped of freedom, thought, creed, belief, and happiness. Indeed they've even stripped us of humanity. They've taken everything to use as fuel for those fires they've lit, so that their undistinguished names may appear bright to the eye of history.

MONK: History! . . . History! This jug you scientists created with your hands and filled with the wine of bloody victories to intoxicate those bloodshedders and tyrants. They in turn emptied it from their mouths into the souls of the subjects and peoples.

SCIENTIST: You men of religion . . . have you not been content at times to confer the cloak of sanctity on the massacres of those bloodshedders and tyrants?

ANGEL: Enough quarrelling. Why don't you reach an understanding? Each of you is a believer, and each of you is a monk. For what is religion save the belief of the heart, and what is science but the belief of the intellect?

SCIENTIST: You're right. We've had enough quarrelling between science and religion for hundreds of years.

ANGEL: Oh, if the heart and the intellect had united long ago against the animal instincts, man today would be quite different.

MONK: These scientists have mocked us for a long time. They said they were superhuman, because they search for reality.

SCIENTIST: No science is superior to humanity. That's always been my creed. I told my colleagues that the day they interrogated me and stripped me of my scientific insignia and titles. They did not object to serving tyranny. I shouted at them: science must be humane, otherwise it becomes bestial. For what slips from the hand of one falls to the other's claw. There is nothing, and never will be, anything other than that on this Earth. Oh, you don't see the extent of the power of evil. Do you know how great the expenses of the last great war were? Listen to what my colleague, the American Dr. Butler⁵, who spent years collecting statistics, said. He mentioned in his report which he presented to the Rockefeller Foundation that the amount spent on that war during its four years—had it been put to constructive rather than destructive purposes—would have been sufficient to give every family in the world a small house with a pretty garden and to establish in every city of over twenty thousand inhabitants a library costing a million pounds and a university for another million pounds. There would remain after that a sum great enough for founding hospitals in all corners of the Earth. But . . . but people have not yet dared assume some of these financial burdens for the sake of their own good and happiness.

ANGEL: Give me your hand, Monk.

MONK: What are you doing?

ANGEL: I'll put it in this scientist's hand.

MONK: Yes, put it in his hand. My God in the heavens, I feel my complete faith returning to my heart like the wandering ewe to the fold.

ANGEL: You can be confident, my brother monk, that the heart and the intellect which are the two lofty and luminous principles in man cannot long remain in the captivity of the talons and fangs.

MONK: Who are you, Young Man? You must tell us who you are.

ANGEL: I . . . am leaving. I must now depart to do something else.

SCIENTIST: And leave the girl?

ANGEL: She is safe and secure with the two of you.

MONK: Won't you wait for us to wed her to you as our brother the scientist said?

GIRL (with tears in her eyes): I'm not worthy of him.

ANGEL (tears in his eyes): O Flower of Hope, don't cry, for your tear is heaven's daughter.

GIRL: Farewell.

ANGEL (waving the apple at her with his right hand): Tree of love for the creatures, I will never part with your apple or with your memory, Most Gracious Mortal. (He disappears.)

Scene Three

A conference room . . . The two tyrants are standing alone, contemplating a world map on a table. They have closed the doors.

FIRST TYRANT *(pointing with his finger to part of the map):* I want to rule these nations and peoples.

SECOND TYRANT *(pointing to another part):* I want to rule these nations and peoples.

(The angel appears from behind one of the drapes.)

ANGEL: The nations and peoples were created by their Lord to be free. Don't divide and plunder them as though you were dividing up booty and livestock.

TYRANTS *(alarmed):* Who's this?

ANGEL: How could you have forgotten God's words in the Torah: "I raise my hand to the nations, and to the peoples I lift up my banner . . . Will any booty be plundered from the mighty? Will any captive escape the victor? Thus says God: even the captive of the mighty will be plundered and the booty of the tyrant rescued. I will contend with your adversary and free your children. I will feed those who oppress you, their own flesh, and they will become drunk with their blood, as though with wine."[6]

FIRST TYRANT: How did this man get in?

SECOND TYRANT *(whispering):* Hush . . . Don't move. He has a small hand grenade shaped like an apple in his right hand.

FIRST TYRANT: I understand.

SECOND TYRANT *(to the angel):* So then? We are at your service.

ANGEL: I am rather at your service. If you would be so kind, open your hearts a little to heaven's mercy.

FIRST TYRANT: No doubt you have mistaken the place where this language is understood today.

ANGEL: I have not despaired of making you understand it.

FIRST TYRANT: But you should despair quickly, for we have another language now and new sacred books dictated by the new spirit of our people and its ambitions.

ANGEL: What are the ambitions of your new people?

FIRST TYRANT: To rule over the other peoples and races.

ANGEL: So that it itself may be ruled by suffering, hunger, and oppression.

FIRST TYRANT: It is prepared for the sacrifice.

ANGEL: Sacrifice . . . to whom? To you, Tyrant, for those are your ambitions not the people's. No people can truly seek those goals from the depths of its soul. The conscience of the people is simpler and purer than that. Leadership, might, and tyranny are deceptive ambitions which arise in the head of a single man. Then he subjects his poor people as a whole to bearing the burdens and sacrifice. He gives in return these words which intoxicate without satiating. Who are the people in fact but that woodsman in the forest, the farmer in the field, the worker in the factory, the merchant in the shop, and the spouse at home. Do these aspire to rule nations and races? Why? All they ask from life is to find good food, peace of mind and conscience, soundness of body and belief, freedom of speech, work, and thought. Their true ambition in life is to master human suffering, not to master their human brothers. What would be simpler than to fulfill their noble hopes if you, Tyrants, truly wished to make them happy. But you wish only to make yourselves happy by seizing what you believe to be crowns of glory to decorate your iniquitous brows.

FIRST TYRANT *(whispering to his comrade):* This is a dangerous man.

SECOND TYRANT *(whispering):* What if he addressed these words to the people? But how have your men left him free until now?

FIRST TYRANT *(to the angel):* This is a brilliant speech. Man, who are you?

ANGEL: I'm a stranger come from afar.

FIRST TYRANT *(whispering):* Luckily!

SECOND TYRANT *(whispering):* In spite of that, there's a reassuring naiveté about him. You can press the buzzer near your finger, but . . . cautiously.

(He does that. The door opens and some of their aides enter.)

FIRST TYRANT *(pointing to the angel):* This noble gentleman visited us unexpectedly, uninvited.

CHIEF AIDE: How did he get in?

FIRST TYRANT: This is something that must be investigated.

CHIEF AIDE *(surrounding the angel with his men):* Follow us!

SECOND TYRANT: Amazing! He didn't resist.

ANGEL: What are they doing with me?

FIRST TYRANT *(sarcastically):* What they did with the Messiah before you.

SECOND TYRANT *(sarcastically):* To glorify your worth and the worth of your mission which you revealed to us.

ANGEL: Oh . . . "But this is your hour and the reign of darkness."[7]

FIRST TYRANT *(to his aide):* This man must not mingle with the people for a moment. Interrogate him quickly and execute him.

SECOND TYRANT: Beware of what he has in his right hand.

AIDE *(seizing the right hand of the angel):* This is an apple.

FIRST TYRANT: Really?

AIDE: Yes, the morning dew is still on it.

ANGEL *(entreating):* Don't take it from me. Don't take it from me!

Scene Four

A Military Tribunal

PRESIDING JUDGE *(to the angel impatiently):* And then? Don't you wish to answer.

ANGEL: I've answered.

PRESIDING JUDGE: Listen to me. It's my duty to warn you once again of the evil destiny awaiting you if you insist on hiding the facts.

ANGEL: Am I hiding the facts? Why? . . . I wouldn't know how to hide a fact.

PRESIDING JUDGE: I asked you your name. What is your name?

ANGEL: My name? The truth is I haven't thought about that. I didn't have time to pick a name. What I was busy with was greater and more exalted than that, but all the same . . . What's the difference between one name and another? All names are alike. Choose whatever name for me you like.

PRESIDING JUDGE *(turning to the other members of the tribunal around him in despair):* And your country . . . your nationality?

ANGEL: Amazing! This too is something I didn't think about. I'm simply on this beautiful Earth. That's enough. What's the difference between one spot and another, one race and another? All places and races are equal. Choose whichever one for me you wish.

PRESIDING JUDGE *(turning to those around him, shaking his head):* Your family?

ANGEL: My family? Amazing. Why do you ask me these strange questions. My family? Everyone is my family, because all the sons of man are my brothers, even you who are judging me. You too are my people. I love all of you. I love mankind.

PRESIDING JUDGE: How did you enter the leaders' chamber?

ANGEL: In just the same way I entered this chamber . . . in the same way this light enters. *(He points to the rays of sunshine entering through the window.)*

PRESIDING JUDGE: There were guards around the place.

ANGEL: I did not see the guards, and no one prevented me from entering.

PRESIDING JUDGE: Why did you enter?

ANGEL: To open the tyrants' hearts.

PRESIDING JUDGE *(whispering to the tribunal):* He has finally confessed. *(He turns to the angel.)* Open their hearts? With what weapon?

ANGEL: With the weapon of radiant truth.

(The presiding judge shakes his head in disappointment.)

PRESIDING JUDGE: Didn't you have another weapon with you?

ANGEL: I can't carry anything else.

PRESIDING JUDGE: Bearing this weapon, in any case, is enough by itself to convict you. Do you have accomplices?

ANGEL: Yes.

PRESIDING JUDGE *(takes up his pen hopefully):* Dictate their names.

ANGEL: Put your name at the top.

PRESIDING JUDGE *(taken by surprise):* What are you saying?

ANGEL: And put the names of these members of the tribunal who are around you, and those of the guards and soldiers, and of the remaining individuals of this nation and of all peoples. You won't find paper sufficient for all the names. Everyone who has a heart is my accomplice, because every heart recites the same words in its depths and sings the same songs. But the ears hear nothing of this, because there are moments when the sound of evil drowns out all other sounds.

(The presiding judge consults in a whisper with the tribunal members.)

PRESIDING JUDGE *(turning to the angel):* Do you have any other defense to express?

ANGEL: Defense of whom?

PRESIDING JUDGE: Of yourself, of course.

ANGEL: Myself? O heavens, how amazing! Have I come to defend myself?

PRESIDING JUDGE: Then your trial is terminated. The military tribunal has decided that the defendant constitutes a danger to the safety and security of the state and has sentenced him to death by firing squad before sunset today.

ANGEL *(as though speaking to himself in astonishment):* A danger to the safety and security of the state—someone who tells people to love each other.

PRESIDING JUDGE *(somewhat sarcastically while rising):* The tribunal regrets it is unable to have the honor of placing you on the cross, for crucifixion is not a punishment set in the law for military tribunals.

(The tribunal session is dissolved.)

ANGEL *(in despair among his guards):* O my God, what are these humans who count incitement to brotherhood an unpardonable crime?

Scene Five

The angel before the firing squad.

OFFICER *(to the angel):* Do you want anything?

ANGEL: No, thank you.

OFFICER *(to one of the soldiers):* Cover his head.

(The soldier comes forward with a black cloth to cover the head of the angel.)

ANGEL *(pushing him away gently):* Why would you hide the sight of the beautiful Earth from me at the last moment?

OFFICER: It's another sight we wish to hide from you.

ANGEL: The sight of you shedding my blood . . . even this sight must not be hidden from me. For I know how to love you in spite of that and to pity you. It's you soldiers they always describe as courageous, misrepresenting and misguiding, to deceive you about the essence of human life. They tempt you to a life like predatory animals in the jungle. Fighting and being fought . . . that's the entirety of your glorious work. That's all the life they wish for you on this Earth. You don't see its beauty. You don't hear its song. Because they cover your heads and your eyes with these heavy helmets.

OFFICER *(shouting):* Enough! Enough! Are you ready?

ANGEL: Ready. God, I testify that I have done what I could for their sake.

OFFICER *(observing the angel's hand):* What are you holding in your right hand?

ANGEL *(raising his hand with the apple cautiously and fearfully):* Don't take it away from me!

OFFICER: An apple? What will you do with it now?

ANGEL *(pleading):* It's the best remembrance I carry from Earth.

OFFICER *(looking at his watch):* The time has come.

(He calls to the firing squad. The soldiers raise their rifles and aim them at the angel's chest.)

ANGEL: God, I testify that I don't wish to leave them or be free of them. It's only that they . . .

(Bullets are fired into his heart. His words are cut short.)

Scene Six

In heaven . . . chanting of angels and the sound of prayer from different parts of the sky.

SECOND ANGEL *(to the first angel):* You returned to us quickly.

FIRST ANGEL: Woe to the inhabitants of Earth. Satan has settled among them in great anger, for he knows his time is short.

SECOND ANGEL: Didn't I tell you they wouldn't listen to you? You suffered from them what I suffered.

FIRST ANGEL *(looking at the apple in his hand):* Oh, but in spite of that . . .

SECOND ANGEL: What is this apple? Were you too expelled from Earth with an apple as Adam was expelled from heaven?

FIRST ANGEL *(singing softly):*   *O tree of love for the creatures,*
                                       Your tear is heaven's daughter.

SECOND ANGEL: What's the matter? You've returned to us with a different expression from when you left.

FIRST ANGEL *(listening):* What are these voices and chants?

SECOND ANGEL: This is the prayer your angel comrades are conducting for your sake—since they learned you were on the Earth in danger.

FIRST ANGEL: They are praying for my sake? Let the prayer of all the angels be for the sake of the poor inhabitants of the Earth!

Notes

[1] Genesis 4:10-11
[2] Isaiah 49:13
[3] Isaiah, 51:9-10
[4] Isaiah, 51:12
[5] Nicholas Murray Butler (1862-1947), president of Columbia University and winner of the 1931 Nobel Peace Prize with Jane Addams.
[6] Isaiah, 49:22, 24-26
[7] Luke, 22:53; the words of Jesus on his arrest, to the priests and elders.

Preface to *The Wisdom of Solomon*

This story is based on three books: the Qur'an, the Bible, and *A Thousand and One Nights.* I have followed the same procedure I used in "The Sleepers of Ephesus," "Shahrazad," and "Pygmalion," and have made use of the old texts and ancient legends to create a picture in my mind . . . nothing more, nothing less.

Postscript to *The Wisdom of Solomon*

When "The Wisdom of Solomon" was first published in 1943, that great event in human history—the release of the terrifying power from the atom resembling the release of the jinni from the jug—had not yet occurred. The capacity to do something had not yet appeared in its frightening form to threaten wisdom. The war raging constantly in man's depths had not yet disclosed its true visage . . . the war between the instinct for domination and reckless ambition on the steed of unruly action on the one hand and reasoned wisdom which wishes to grasp the reins of the dangerous mount on the other.

Today, at the end of 1948, when the second edition is about to appear, it seems to me that the play "The Wisdom of Solomon" presaged the ongoing conflict which is being played out on the stage of the world. The jinni released from the jug overwhelms the soul. Power is blind. As soon as someone obtains it, he hastens to trample others with it. The ability to act is a temptation. As soon as one is able, he rushes to do both what is proper and improper.

The human crisis now, as always, is that mankind advances more quickly in technology than in wisdom. The nails of the first man developed into stone weapons, into a sword, then into the gun and the atomic bomb. But his means of governing his instincts have not developed equally at all times to check unleashed ability. Because of this, there is the inevitability that disaster will occur or failure ensue . . . until the world finally realizes the necessity for wisdom.

We do not desire, having been granted this human existence with its good and evil, to kill the jinni within us with his cleverness, genius, and high aspirations. But we hope always that we will create a barrier from the goodness of our souls to stand in the face of his temptations whenever he rages.

T. A.

Introduction to *King Oedipus*

In the name of God, the Compassionate, the Merciful.

Dramatic literature is a door which was not opened in the Arabic language until the modern age. Arabic literature has hesitated to accept this genre which was foreign to it. For some time it left it outside its walls. It heard about it from spectators without thinking of turning to it or wading into it.

There first appeared about a century ago in some of the Arab lands like Syria, Lebanon, and Egypt a type of theater in which the serious was mixed with the comic, and acting with singing. Some Western stories were translated for it either literally or freely. They were presented either in their original garb or in that appropriate for the East. Sometimes they were in literary language and at other times in a language form more readily understood by the common people.

At that time, the theater drew from French and English literature. We saw Molière's "L'Avare" presented in verse. We saw Shakespeare's "Romeo and Juliet" presented as a musical.

The originator of the Arab theater in the East was, as is well known, Marun an-Naqqash. He was followed by his disciples, al-Qardahi and Abu Khalil al-Qabbani, among others. Then its banner was carried by ash-Shaykh Salama Hijazi followed in turn by the 'Ukasha family who inherited his stories and his songs. They followed his track, but the Egyptian revolution and the outpouring of national spirit impelled them to turn to Egyptianizing their stories. The writer of these lines began his theatrical life at that time. He wrote some plays for that troupe in the manner in which work was carried out in those days.

All this was happening without any one of those who wrote for the theater desiring to call his work literature. Arabic literature gave no thought to considering this form of writing to be literature of any kind. Shawqi afterwards submitted some of his stories to the theater. They were a success with the audience, but he as well did not think of printing them before they were acted. He did not think they would have an illustrious existence at a distance from the lights of the theater. In his opinion, only the ode he submitted to the daily papers or to a publisher within a collection of poetry was ready for a victorious entry into the castle of literature with the heads of the *literati* bowing before them. The barrier, then, between the world of the theater and the world of literature, was a perplexing matter requiring explanation.

This writer travelled to Europe at that time where a puzzling secret was revealed to him. It was not difficult to come upon the key to the reason . . . the theater world and the literary world in Europe are intertwined. There is no separation or barrier between them. The cause for that is obvious. Drama is a branch of literature studied in the institutes and universities as literature before being submitted to the stage. Europe inherited this literature from the Greeks. It examined and studied it. It built and wove on its foundation. Drama was part of its national artistic tradition and grew and developed with the passing centuries, whether performed or not. It had a separate existence. It was similar to the sciences of logic, mathematics, and philosophy with their inheritance from the Greeks. For that reason, the writer found it necessary to begin at the beginning and return to the source when he desired to study dramatic literature.

He thought the affair would be simple and the way easy. He would begin wherever he wished. He would devote his attention to this modern dramatic literature which would not require effort to study nor be difficult to understand. He was told if he were serious, he should go back to the Greeks. He returned to Aeschylus, Sophocles, Euripides, and Aristophanes. Here he realized why Arabic literature pays attention to the ode and does not recognize the play even if it is poetry. The ode is a form inherited from the distant past, just as dramatic poetry is inherited by Western literature from its past.

Nothing is stronger than inheritance. If immortality has a hand, it is this inheritance by which beings are transferred from one age to another. The characteristics of individuals, the peculiarities of peoples, and the distinguishing marks of nations are nothing but an inheritance of attributes and characteristics which are handed down from generation to generation. What is said to be deep-rooted in a people is nothing but its qualities inherited from remote times. The characteristic originality of things and creatures is in that continual retention of inherited excellences from one who becomes adult to the next, link after link. This can be said of a people, a man, or a horse. It can likewise be said of art, science, or literature. The deep-rooted part of literature is its character preserved and handed down from the past.

America desired to find a shortcut for the art of music. It originated that variety of Black music called jazz. But it failed to persuade the cultured world to venerate that music with no venerable origin or revered lineage. Had America's language not been English, its literature would also have had this fate. But American literature could be a literature only because it rested on its recognized inheritance from English literature. The truth of the matter is that it is only a recent bough of the many branched tree of Saxon literatures.

Arabic literature, then, is like other deep-rooted literatures. It does not lightly accept change to its substance or character without research, examination, caution, and circumspection. When in the last century it took this cautious attitude towards the theater, it was not to be censured or blamed for that. For the way the theater was introduced in the Arab East it had no foundation which could justify it in the eyes of that deep-rooted literature.

If only a literary figure had risen among us during the last century or two to cry out questioningly: "O Arabic literature, from ancient times there have been between you and Greek thought close ties and bonds. You have reflected on it and taken the sciences and philosophy from it. You have, however, turned your face away from the poetry it has. How far will this rupture go? When will a truce be concluded between you and Greek poetry? Consider it a bit. Allow it to be translated and researched. Perhaps you will find in it something to reinforce your inheritance and to augment your bequest to future generations."

This voice was not raised during the past centuries. Therefore, the rupture continued to exist between Arabic literature and Greek literature. The persistence of this rupture has made it difficult for the theater to stand on a solid foundation and to find a place among us within the colonnades of literature, thought, and culture.

There must be a truce then between the two literatures, if we wish to have established within the deep-rooted history of Arabic literature this dramatic genre, whether in poetry or prose, in a valuable and lasting way. But how is the truce to come about? We must first of all learn the reasons for the estrangement so that we can work successfully afterwards and take the measures necessary for a covenant.

Before anything else, we must ask ourselves whose responsibility it was that Greek poetry was not translated into Arabic. This question leads us to study the way the Greek legacy was translated and the causes and reasons for that.

It is known that following Alexander's conquests the Greek spirit penetrated Asia. Syria and the area of Mesopotamia, between the Tigris and Euphrates rivers, were among the most important regions which were subject to the influence of Greek civilization. There, in the cells of the Syrian ascetics throughout those areas, for a period of centuries an extensive movement of translation was energetically carried out for scientific and philosophic works from Greek to Syriac. It was from these Syriac translations that the Arabs later drew inspiration and made translations.

If this account is correct, the Arabs can say that they translated what they found. Poetry was not something those monks cared about . . . but what happened was that many Arabs afterwards learned Greek and were able to translate from it directly.

Among the works translated into Arabic was the book of poetry or *Poetics* of Aristotle, containing his definitions of tragedy and comedy and their characteristics as parts of dramatic poetry. Ibn Rushd came and showed us with his famous commentary on the *Poetics* that the Arabs did not intentionally close their minds to knowledge of the art of poetry among the Greeks. How was it then that curiosity did not impel them thereafter to translate some of the representative tragedies or comedies into Arabic?

It is understandable that they would refrain from translating lyric poetry like that of Pindar or Anacreon, for in pre-Islamic or 'Abbasid Arabic poetry there are comparable works of that type. But why did they—since they were, as we know, eager to learn—fail to translate the tragedies of the Greek poets?

For us to answer that we must know first what tragedy is? How did it arise in Greece? There is no longer any doubt today that tragedy originated from the worship of Bacchus, the wine god known to the Greeks under the name of Dionysus. Every spring, religious celebrations were held for this god. There was boisterous drunkenness with an outpouring of gaiety. People danced and sang at these times around a statue of the wine god. They were decked out in goat skins and leaves. This dancing and singing was at first improvised. After that, with the passing of time, the performance was refined. The people prepared them according to patterns with set elements. That singing was soon mixed with a type of praise for the deeds of that god in the form of a narrative recital of praise for his triumphs, his adventures, and his amazing journeys. Then the matter of the troupe of dancers developed till they began to vary their costumes and portray different characters—not just goats and animals. The narrative also developed and began to take on different ideas unrelated to the life of the god whose festivals they were celebrating. This led reactionary and conservative elders to make a row about this innovation. They said, "There is nothing about Bacchus in this." This phrase later became proverbial in the Greek language.

But from this innovation which aroused criticism and anger came the dramatic art. It was not long before a man appeared, called Thespis, whose reflection led him to compose what the chorus would have to recite and the words of a dialogue for one actor to hold with the chorus. He gave this actor different masks and costumes. He was able in that way to take on a number of characters by himself.

In this fashion, the matter passed from the stage of narrative recital to that of dialogue and action. Drama was born and tragedy came into existence. After Thespis there came a poet named Phrynichos who took this art another step. It was said that he was the first to introduce women characters into the performance. He divided the chorus into two sections. One of them could address the actor in a tone of approval of his actions. Meanwhile the other addressed him in a tone of displeasure and criticism. It was as though the chorus with its two parts were the people in society, including those who support the deeds they see and those who oppose them. History also mentions to us that two of the poet's contemporaries, Choirlos and Pratinas, each played a part in improving this form of art. All of these prepared the way for the appearance of the great masters of tragedy: Aeschylus, Sophocles, and Euripides.

That is a quick look at the genesis of dramatic poetry in Greece. From it we see that worship of Bacchus was the mother of tragedy. This art then poured out to us like wine . . . from the jug of religion. In this way, the great poets of tragedy proceeded to weave their immortal works from their religious legends, from mythology. They imbued them with a spirit of the struggle between man and divine powers. Do you suppose it was this religious character which discouraged the Arabs from embracing this art?

This is the opinion of a group of scholars. They assert that Islam stood in the way of the acceptance of this pagan art. I do not share this opinion. Islam has never been an obstacle for an art form. It permitted the translation of many works produced by heathens. There was *Kalila and Dimna* which Ibn al-Muqaffa' translated from Pahlavi. There was Ferdowsi's *Shahnameh* which al-Bundari translated from the Persian. It is about their pagan age. Similarly, Islam did not prevent the circulation of the wine poetry of Abu Nuwas, the carving of statues for the palaces of the caliphs, or the expert portraiture of Persian miniatures. Likewise, it did not prevent the translation of many Greek works which mentioned pagan customs. No, it was not the pagan quality as such which turned the Arabs away from dramatic poetry. What did hold them back then? Do you suppose it was the difficulty of understanding a story in poetry which revolves entirely around legends which could only be understood after a long explanation spoiling the pleasure of the person trying to understand them and ending the enjoyment of someone desiring to sample them? Perhaps there is some truth to this explanation, for I was astonished by the comment of the critic Francisque Sarcey counselling the spectators when "Oedipus Tyrannus" was presented on the stage of the Comédie-Française in 1881 A.D. I consider it, of the Greek tragedies, the one least immersed in religious mythology, the clearest and purest of them, and the one closest to the soul's naked humanity.

The critic said: "I advise the audience—in particular the ladies among them—to open a book or dictionary of Greek mythology and to read in it before seeing the play performed, a summary of the Oedipus legend. This will spare them the boredom of losing the thread and wandering through the obscurities of the first act."[1]

To whom was this advice directed? To the public of a nation whose culture was based on the Greek legacy . . . a public most of whom had been to school where they were taught—and there is no doubt about what they were taught—Greek literature with its tragedies and comedies. If a public like that, in that modern age, still needed a summary or dictionary to follow the tragedy of Oedipus, what are we to think of the Arab reader in the 'Abbasid or Fatimid eras?

But, despite the validity of this explanation, I do not believe that it, either, would have prevented translation of some examples of this art. For Plato's *Republic* was translated into Arabic, and I have no doubt that it contains ideas concerning that ideal city which would be difficult for the Islamic mentality to digest. Yet that did not prevent its translation. Indeed it was precisely this difficulty that moved al-Farabi to take Plato's *Republic,* wrap it in a gown of his thoughts, and pour it into the mold of his philosophic and Islamic mentality.

Something similar could have happened for Greek tragedy. It would have been possible for a tragedy like "Oedipus" to have been translated and then afterwards taken up by a poet or prose author. He would have removed from it the hard-to-understand mythological references and stripped it of the obscure pagan beliefs. He would have presented it, clear and unambiguous, in its bare human structure. Or, he might have thrown over it a diaphanous gown of Islamic belief or Arab thought.

Why did not that take place? Because there was another reason, no doubt, which turned the Arabs away from adopting Greek theater. Perhaps the reason was that the Greek tragedies were not considered at that time to be literature meant to be read. At that time, they may have been something that would not be independently read the way Plato's *Republic* was. They were written not to be read but to be performed. The author knew that his work would be presented to the people in performance on a stage. He would therefore leave his texts and his dialogue free of explanations, observations, or information necessary to grasp the story's atmosphere. He could rely on the spectator's perceiving it visually, realized and portrayed, when it was produced. In truth, the Greek theater reached a precision and complexity in its machines and instruments that excites astonishment. It had machines that moved and rotated as well as theatrical tricks and devices sufficient to allow those people to produce "Prometheus Bound" by the poet Aeschylus which contains sea nymphs which appear out of the clouds and the sea. Prometheus comes in mounted on the back of that fabulous animal with the head of an eagle and the body of a stallion.

Perhaps this is what made the Arab translator stop perplexed before tragedy. He would cast his eyes over the silent texts trying to see them in his mind throbbing and moving with their characters, atmosphere, locations, and times. But that mind would not comply with his wishes. For he had never seen this art acted in his land. The chorus among the Greeks created acting. It was the actor Thespis who created the play. The play did not create the theater. The theater was the creator of the play. So long as the Arab translator was certain that he had before him a work not made to be read, for what purpose would he translate it then?

Perhaps this is the reason that Greek dramatic poetry was not translated into Arabic. The activity of translation of Greek works was designed to be useful. It was not merely for the love of discovery or just from curiosity. In this case, the benefit from the ideas and thoughts of the tragedies was lost, because they could not be grasped or attained solely by reading. In order to make them clear, there had to be a means for presenting them. That was not something that was available or known. The question, however, which must then be posed is why there was no acting in Arab culture. Why wasn't it known?

The Arabs too had their pagan age. Among their poets of that age were those said to have travelled to "Caesar's land," like Imru' al-Qays. There he no doubt saw the Roman theaters looming tall. They had inherited this art from the Greeks. Could not the sight of the theater have inspired the pagan Arab poet with the idea of importing, transmitting, or adapting it?

Where would he have taken it? Here is the problem. The homeland to which the pagan Arab poet would have transmitted this art, had he wanted to, was nothing other than a desert vast as the sea. Through it hastened camels like ships, roaming from island to island. These were scattered oases which would gush with water one day and be green with plants. On the morrow the water supply would dwindle away and the green growth would wither. It was a homeland moving on the backs of caravans, running here and there in pursuit of a drop from the clouds. It was a homeland continuously rocked atop camels in a rhythmic, harmonic way encouraging the riders to sing. From this, Arabic poetry was born. It originated with the camel chant, as the person holding the reins of the first camel raised his voice to chant to the beat of that faint, hidden music coming from the camels' hoof beats on the sand.

Everything, then, in the moving homeland separated it from the theater. The first thing the theater requires is stability. The Arabs lacked a settled feeling. That is, in my opinion, the true reason for their neglect of dramatic poetry which requires a theater. The theater of Bacchus, the ruins of which have been uncovered by archaeological work in modern times, was a solid building with a massive foundation. It was an establishment belonging to the state. Anyone who becomes acquainted, from the ruins or from drawings, with that enormous structure and its capacity for thousands of spectators will judge at once that this is something which must have been the product of a settled community and of a concentrated and united social life. A researcher would have the right to object that the Arabs under the Umayyad and 'Abbasid dynasties and thereafter experienced that sedentary community and united and concentrated society. Why did the Arabs in those eras refrain from erecting a theater when they were capable of it? We see that they surveyed different cultures and adopted from their architecture elements they used to establish a stunning architecture bearing their new stamp.

There is a simple answer to that. The Arabs under the Umayyad dynasty and later continued to consider the Bedouin and desert poetry the finest example to be imitated. They looked to pre-Islamic poetry as the most perfect model to be followed. They sensed their lack of architecture, but they never felt a shortcoming in poetry. When they wished to borrow and sample from others, they went in every direction and looked at every art—except the art of poetry. They believed that they had reached the ultimate in it long before. Thus we find ourselves turning round a complex group of reasons each of which could have discouraged the Arabs from becoming interested in drama.

However, was it necessary for Arab literature to produce tragedies? Is tragedy a genre necessary for the development of Arabic literature to complete its personality? Anyone who reads the famous preface to *Cromwell* by Victor Hugo finds a partial answer. He divides the history of mankind into three ages. The primitive age in his opinion is the age of lyric poetry. Of it he says that in the primitive age man chants as though breathing. He is in the age of chivalrous youth, of breaking into song, etc. Then comes the antique age, the age of the epic. The tribe has developed and become a nation. The societal urge has replaced the urge to travel. Nations have been formed and become important. One of them rubs against another. They clash and engage in battle. Here poetry arises to narrate the events that have taken place, to tell the story of what happened to the peoples and what befell the empires. Finally comes the modern age which is the age of drama. In his opinion, it is the complete poetry, because it includes within it all the varieties. It contains some of the lyric and some of the epic.

Let us listen to him summarize his thought: "Human society progresses and matures while singing of its dreams. Afterwards it begins to narrate its deeds. Then it finally undertakes to portray its thoughts."[2]

Hugo invites us to test his doctrine on each literature individually. He assures us that we will find that each bears out this division. According to him, the lyric poets always precede the epic poets, and the epic poets precede the dramatic poets.

Do you suppose this doctrine can be applied to Arabic literature? In my opinion it can be, if we disregard the genres and confine our investigation to the objectives. There is no doubt that Arabic poetry did sing of dreams, describe wars, and portray ideas. It did not change its method, leave its genre, or deviate from its principles. On its way, it followed the same order that Hugo set forth. In the 'Abbasid era alone we find al-Buhturi [d. 897 AD] is before al-Mutanabbi [d. 965 AD] and al-Mutanabbi before Abu al-'Ala' [d. 1057 AD]. Had these poets been planted in the Greek soil, al-Buhturi, the Arab cymbal player, would have been Pindar. Al-Mutanabbi who makes our ears resound across the generations with the ring of swords would have been Homer. Abu al-'Ala' who portrayed for us thought about man and his destiny and the heavenly hosts would have been Aeschylus. The development, then, in terms of content was completed. But the development with respect to form was hindered by those circumstances which attended the growth of the Arab state. The circumstances, which as we have seen did not limit the Arabs' mentality or restrain their artistic nature, were able in any case, against their will, to keep them away from this one of the literary arts at that stage of their history.

There is then no inherent animosity between the Arabic language and dramatic literature. It is a question rather of a temporary estrangement, resulting from a lack of the instrument. The matter for the Arabs here is like that when they knew no riding animals other than the camel. Had circumstances conspired to deny them the horse, they would have continued to the present day without knowing how to ride it. But no sooner had the horse entered the desert than the Arabs became horsemen. They mastered the arts of rearing it and of describing it. What is there to say today anywhere in the world about the original horse before the Arabian? If a splendid description of the traits of the horse is sought, where is it but in Arabic poetry?

The whole question then is one of instrument. It is as though the Arabs in the age of camels were saying: "Give us the horse; we will ride it." They might similarly have said: "Give us the theater and we will write for it."

There is no doubt that the world has changed today. Theater in the broad sense of the word has become one of the necessities of contemporary life. It is not restricted to

any one class. It is the daily nourishment for the minds of the people. Its richness
varies according to their cultural level. In the final analysis it is the instrument of art
which spreads through the Eastern and Western lands of the earth. By 'theater' I
mean here every art which sets out to portray things, persons, and thoughts on a stage,
screen, page or over the air in such manner that they appear alive, conversing and
debating, displaying their secrets and thought before a viewer, hearer, or reader.

There is no longer any way to ignore this worldwide style of presenting ideas in a
living way in dramatic form. Wherever we go today in the Arab world we find high,
lofty, ornamented buildings, the most luxurious in our cities. These are the theaters!

Thus we have the theater, that is, the instrument. For our Arab way of life, it has
become one of the necessities like bread and water. Every day the field of operation
for this instrument called acting has expanded until it has become—with the spread of
broadcasting—daily nourishment entering every home. All of this ought to have
reached the ears of the deep-rooted Arabic literature and prompted it to pay attention
to this art and lay foundations for it within its own procedures and categories. It is my
guess that Arabic literature yearns to do that, for it is not a dead literature nor ossified.

But how can this be done? It cannot be expected to open a door into its noble
frame and set within it an art with no foundations. For it is not a frivolous or spurious
literature. These are the people who have preserved the lineages of human beings and
horses. We must not give them cause for distress over their long-established literature
at this late date. We must then create the missing link of the lineage and return to it so
that it can firmly bond Arabic literature with dramatic art. This link can only be Greek
literature.

For all these reasons, there must a truce between the two long-established
literatures. Here we approach the great question: how can this reconciliation be
achieved? Is it sufficient to be, with care and concern, devoted to Greek dramatic
literature, transmitting all of it to our Arabic language? This matter is obviously
necessary, and most of that has been accomplished. Indeed, *Oedipus the King* by
Sophocles was presented for all to see on the Arab stage more than a third of a century
ago.

But the mere transmission of Greek dramatic literature to the Arabic language
does not achieve for us the establishment of a dramatic literature in Arabic. Similarly,
the mere transmission of Greek philosophy did not create an Arab or Islamic
philosophy. Translation is only a tool which must carry us to a farther goal.

This goal is to ladle water from the spring, then to swallow it, digest it, and
assimilate it, so that we can bring it forth to the people once again dyed with the color
of our thought and imprinted with the stamp of our beliefs. This was the way the Arab
philosophers proceeded when they took the works of Plato and Aristotle. We must
proceed in that same way with Greek tragedy. We must dedicate ourselves to its study
with patience and endurance and then look at it afterwards with Arab eyes.

Before us, an analogous course was followed in the history of French literature.
Its tragedians returned to the ancient Greek works, to the works of Aeschylus,
Sophocles, and Euripedes. They ladled from them and transmitted them without
changing the subject, characters, or action. Yet they bestowed on those works all of
their French spirit.

That is the way to the truce, indeed the marriage between the two spirits and the
two literatures. There must occur a marriage between Greek literature and Arabic

literature with respect to tragedy comparable to the marriages that took place between Greek philosophy and Arab thought and between French literature and Greek literature. If that is completed in any fashion, whether in poetry or prose, I have no doubt that Arabic literature will recognize this new-old form without regard to the age in which that marriage took place. For time is of no significance in the long history of literature, so long as the links for it are strongly connected, logically fastened, with a progression that makes sense.

It has always been my opinion that modern Arabic literature is nothing but a continuation of the innovative movement which al-Jahiz undertook in the third century of Islam. This is so despite an occasional relapse as well as reliance on tradition during intervening periods over this long time. It is so despite what has been said of its blind imitation of Western literature in the recent past. This [Western] influence, which some of the superficial Orientalists have noticed, does not go beyond the form, appearance and dress. It is a natural matter in the history of the literatures of all nations. The outer cloak is a property owned in common by the prevalent culture in any age. The difference is in the substance, the character, the sensitivity. Arabic literature never lost its spirit, thought, or sensitivity over the years, whether it stood still or advanced, froze or developed.

Thus I was moved to study the dramatic literature of Greece. I did not look at it as a French or European scholar but as an Arab scholar, an Easterner. The two viewpoints are very different. This became clear to me later. Despite the European clothing I wore to the Comédie-Française to see "Oedipus" by Sophocles with [Raphaël] Albert Lambert and despite that French spirit [of the production] derived from the tragedies of Corneille and Racine, something in the depths of my soul brought me close to the spirit of tragedy as the Greeks felt it.

What is the Greek spirit of tragedy? It is that tragedy springs from a religious feeling. The entire substance of tragedy is that it is a struggle, manifest or hidden, between man and the divine forces dominating existence. It is the struggle of man with something greater than man and above man. The foundation of true tragedy in my opinion is man's sense that he is not alone in existence. This is what I mean by the expression "religious feeling." No matter what the play's form, frame, style, or the effect it produces in the soul, it is not permissible in my opinion to describe it as tragedy so long as it does not rest on that religious feeling. This divine element in the spirit of tragedy has not retained its heat and radiance over the course of the centuries. Since the age of Latin, you find poets who precisely imitate the Greek tragedies in all their external aspects and yet preserve little of the substance. When the Renaissance came, they went farther down this road. Poets no longer distinguished between tragedy and atrocity. Whenever they piled on terror and heaped up horror, they thought they were making a tragedy resembling the Greek tragedies. In the seventeenth century we are confronted by tragedy which has become a struggle between a man and his soul. With Corneille it is based on incidents of history. Let us listen to the scholar Brunetière as he says approvingly: "But is not history the spectacle of the struggle between one will and another? . . . It is natural therefore that history should become an inspiration for theater which . . . rests totally on the belief in the sovereignty of the will."[3]

With Racine, tragedy became a struggle between one emotion and another. Love with the jealousy, envy, malice, and hatred which accompany it became the domain in which his feeling and thought moved. Both of them, in addition to that, wrapped their tragedies in the French spirit. The poet Corneille "Frenchified" history to some extent. Napoleon, in a later time, preferred him to all other poets. He used to say of him: "This man discerned the meaning of politics. Had he had practical experience, he would have been a statesman . . . A decree of the state has taken the place with the modern poets of a decree of fate among the ancients. Corneille is the only one of the French poets to have sensed this truth."[4]

Napoleon's admiration for this attitude of Corneille's is apparent in his frequent praise for it and in his expression of regret that Corneille did not live in his era. Otherwise, as he said, "I would have made him a prince. Indeed, I would have appointed him prime minister." Napoleon found nothing to do for this Corneille except to search for his descendants. Of them he found only two women. He ordered that they be provided with pensions of three hundred francs a year.[5]

At precisely this time, it seems it was not easy for the people to experience the Greek tragedies in their true form nor even for the elite among them to penetrate to their spirit. Napoleon desired to see Sophocles' "Oedipus" performed on stage. He encountered stiff opposition from France's leading actor at that time, the great [François-Joseph] Talma. Napoleon explained his point of view as follows:

> I did not desire with this request to rectify our contemporary theatrical situation. I did not wish to introduce any innovation into it. I wished rather to witness the effect the antique art might produce on our modern notions and circumstances. I am convinced that that undertaking would bring the soul pleasure. I would like to know what impression the sight of the Greek style troupe and chorus would have on our tastes.[6]

That was with respect to Corneille. Racine did not go beyond portrayal of the psychological condition of his epoch, presenting it on the stage in that framework to which he gave the name 'tragedy.'

With the passing years then that religious feeling which made the first tragedies a conflict between man and what is greater than man has been dispersed and has evaporated in the winds of time. Perhaps this was a harbinger of the scientific renaissance of that century.

Whatever the reason may have been, the poets and people had changed in their belief. They had come to believe that there is nothing but man in this existence—his state, his government, his leaders and his authority.

Once this religious feeling is extinguished, in my opinion, there is no hope of producing tragedy. Perhaps this is the reason for the death of tragedy in our present age. There is not a single poet in the world today who can write a single tragedy of lasting value, comparable to the tragedies which came before. The reason for that is that no thinker in the Western world today truly believes in the existence of a god other than himself.

The last of the ages for tragedy, properly understood, was the seventeenth century. In spite of what we mentioned about Corneille and Racine, they at least had a remnant of the religious feeling which provided their works an ember from the heavenly heat. Racine's relationship with the Jansenist religious sect and the explanations critics expounded for some of his tragedies, especially "Phèdre," according to the light of the teachings of that sect, are matters the history of literature has explained in detail.

I think there is no need to speak of the tragedies of Voltaire! This sarcastic doubter had in his heart belief only for his intellect. He looked at Shakespeare more than back to the Greeks. Voltaire is the person who prepared the way for the modern artistic mentality and a first model for the Western thinker and the European author of the present day.

In this atmosphere of the present century from the sky of which that religious feeling in its former sense has disappeared, I was reading and watching tragedy. I perceived its true substance with a hidden sensitivity. What is the secret?

It is not a strange secret at all. All there is to the matter is that I am an Easterner, an Arab. I still retain some part of my original religious sense. I have not traversed those previously mentioned stages that the European mentality has. My position before Greek tragedy is that of an Arab thinker of the third century of Islam.

With this feeling I returned to Egypt. Not much time passed before I wrote the play, "The Sleepers of Ephesus." That was in the year 1928. The 'Ukasha troupe had finally gone out of existence. So I had in mind no vision of a special theater or of a particular actor. I found no one to confide my work to but paper. When the writer lacks a theater and his thoughts take control of him, he sets up his theater at once between the covers of a book. My aim in composing "The Sleepers of Ephesus" was to introduce the element of tragedy in an Arab and Islamic subject. This was tragedy in its ancient Greek meaning which I have retained: the conflict between man and the unseen forces beyond man. I desired my source to be not the legends of Greece but the Qur'an. My aim was not simply to take a story from the Holy Book and put it in the dramatic mold. The goal was rather to look at our Islamic legends with the eye of Greek tragedy. It was to effect this intermarriage between the two mentalities and literatures. I did not wish to provide that work with an introduction when it was published to avoid directing the reader's thought and pointing him to someone else's opinion. What concerned me was to see the effect of the work on the souls of its readers removed from any guidance or suggestion. No matter what interpretations that book received, what was firmly established in the minds of the literary people of that day was that there was something which had been composed on some foundation. The literary figures without exception considered this work a form of Arabic literature, whether acted or not.

In this way, that goal I referred to at the opening of this introduction was realized. It was for Arabic literature to accept this dramatic literature without reference to the theater. It is an amazing result. For Shawqi, as I have said, had plays which were known first to the theater before they were known to literature as a book to be read. Moreover, it is easy for a scholar to notice that Shawqi in his plays has absolutely no connection to the Greeks. He proceeds in them in the manner of the French tragedians. He too wove the subjects for his plays from history and love as in "The Death of Cleopatra" and "Layla's Majnun." There is no question that the conflict between one emotion and another or between one will and another is the easiest type of conflict to present to an audience.

For that reason, the difficulty of presenting plays centered on a conflict between one idea and another on a stage other than that of the mind is evident. Yet this mental theater is necessary, so long as there are subjects which must be presented which are based on bare thought and immaterial characters. The struggle between man and the unseen forces which are greater than man, like time, reality, space, etc., cannot be given a bodily form appropriate for the material theater, unless we have recourse to the pagan method of personification. Aeschylus, for example, did this when he made power and the sea actual characters who speak. This is an affair I think the Islamic, Arab mentality would not swallow. It has purified 'Allah' of any personification and compelled the mind to accept the concept as it appears solely in thought, bare and unblemished by any coarse outer cover.

Aeschylus, moreover, himself, despite his personification of the hidden forces, was tucked by critics into the group of authors who are better read in a chair than presented on stage. That question has also been raised in relation to Shakespeare, although it is an obstinate exaggeration in my opinion. I have read of a study by a critic called Boulenger about what he terms, "theater in an armchair." In it, he expressed his astonishment that Shakespeare's plays have more the spirit of the book in them than of the theater. Remy de Gourmont was also of this strange opinion. He said, "There is none of Shakespeare's plays which has not disappointed me on the stage."[7]

Confronted by these views, the critic Thibaudet undertook to divide dramatists into two groups: one group which takes human life in itself as the subject of its action and endeavor and a second which makes of that life an intellectual melody. One group portrays the movement of human beings in life. The other portrays the thought of human beings in life. In his opinion, the first group can be easily presented in the material theater. He includes Shakespeare among them despite the intellectual melodies in some of his plays. Of the Greeks he includes Sophocles and Euripides. In the second group he puts Aeschylus.[8]

Our conclusion based on all this is that it is the play's subject which determines the type of theater. If the play is based on the motion of human beings, its place is the material theater. If it is based on the motion of thought, its place is the mental theater.

Here a question appears: is it not possible to present to the audience in the material theater some Greek tragedy covered with a veil of the Arab mentality in which there appears the conflict between man and the sublime, unseen forces, without so baring the thought in it that it falls into the mental type of plays? To answer this question, I devoted no small amount of time to studying Sophocles. I ended up selecting "Oedipus" as the subject for my experiment.

Why did I choose "Oedipus" in particular? For a reason that may appear strange. It is that I considered it a long time and saw in it something that never occurred to the mind of Sophocles. I saw in it a struggle not between man and fate, the way the Greeks and those following them to the present day have thought of it. I saw in it rather the same hidden conflict that arose in [my] play, "The Sleepers of Ephesus."

This struggle was not just between man and time as its readers were wont to think. There was rather another concealed war that few have paid attention to, a war between fact and truth. There is the fact of a man like Mishilinia who returned from the cave to find Prisca. He loved her and she loved him. Everything was ready for them to lead a life of ease and happiness. Only one obstacle stood between them and this beautiful fact. That was the truth. The truth of this man Mishilinia which became clear to Prisca was that he was the fiancé of her great-aunt. The two lovers strove to forget this truth which rose to destroy their fact. But they were unable with their tangible fact to repel this mysterious, intangible thing called truth.

Oedipus and Jocasta, themselves, are none other than Mishilinia and Prisca. They too loved each other, but when they learn the truth of their relationship to each other it destroys what they had in common. Man's strongest adversary is always a ghost. It is a ghost given the name 'truth.' This was my motive for choosing "Oedipus" in particular. I had my view and idea of it, but there remained the execution. In what manner should I treat this tragedy?

At this point I succumbed to anxiety for a time. I knew the pains which had tormented those poets and authors who had dealt with it before me over the course of the centuries. When I recollected Seneca's shortcoming in "Oedipus," Corneille's failure in "Oedipus," and Voltaire's puniness compared to Sophocles in "Oedipus," I was afflicted by vertigo. Then if I left those poetic geniuses and turned to those of the contemporary rebels who have treated Oedipus and to the failure and defeat to which they have exposed themselves, I was overcome by anguish. I remained for a time despairing and indolent, postponing the execution of this work. At last I began to take heart. I said: Let me work. It is better for me to err than to be anxious and paralysed. Let me take those who have failed as my model. Let me fail like them, for they in any case did their duty. They still deserve praise, because they courageously advanced and made mistakes. I can benefit from that and avoid their errors. I can turn my face in another direction where perhaps there is another type of error. So be it. The mistakes of artists and authors are sometimes beneficial and preferable to what is correct.

I knew that among the living poets who had treated Oedipus were the English language poet Yeats and the German poet [Hugo von] Hofmannstahl. The two did not add anything to Sophocles' tragedy.

Then I knew of three contemporary French prose writers who each adapted "Oedipus" from Sophocles. The first of them was Saint-Georges de Bouhélier. The second was Jean Cocteau and the third André Gide. De Bouhélier cut up the story of Oedipus. He divided it into numerous scenes, following the practice of Shakespeare in his plays. No sooner was it performed on the stage than the critic Lucien Dubech said of it:

> While in Sophocles Oedipus is preoccupied with the action he is directing and living through without time for him to ponder his destiny, de Bouhélier leaves him alone for long periods. He confides his doubts, regret, and the wakefulness of his conscience like Hamlet or Lady Macbeth . . . It is futile for us to remind de Bouhélier that nothing surpasses [in Sophocles' immortal tragedy] that great dramatic force which issues from that massing of action and the accumulation of events, in that strong unity and narrow focus . . .[9]

I truly have benefitted from this error, for it had occurred to me as well to put the story of Oedipus in numerous scenes as I did in "Shahrazad" and "The Wisdom of Solomon." God protected me from the evil of this action, for I saw the experiment fail at the hand of de Bouhélier. Jean Cocteau also composed an "Oedipus" with numerous scenes which he named "La Machine Infernale." He presented it on the stage, but I have never seen it acted nor read the critics on it. I perceived from reading it printed in a book, however, that Cocteau was superficially influenced by the Greek theory about "Oedipus." But he too was artistically influenced by Shakespeare. He had the spirit of the father of Oedipus appear on the walls like the spirit of Hamlet's father. It is amazing that there should be so much influence on "Oedipus" from Shakespeare instead of from Sophocles who is indisputably the peak of the tradition of the art of tragedy.

After that comes André Gide with his story "Oedipus." In it he moved towards Sophocles, but he made us feel a loftiness in Oedipus that does not originate from man's link to what is greater than man so much as from man's link to himself.

André Gide was able to derive from his faith in man the substance of a humility taking the place in the soul of that submission to the sublime, hidden forces. He summarizes for us with truth and sincerity the whole European credo today: there is nothing in existence but man; there is no value in existence but man's. André Gide is not the only one responsible for this belief. It had existed for about a century before him, since Blanche saw in Aeschylus' character Prometheus, "Man forming himself by himself." Indeed, Edouard Schuré saw in "Oedipus" what André Gide did. Schuré, in his book, *L'Evolution divine du Sphinx au Christ,* published in 1912, said the following:

> Oedipus is not an initiate, or even an aspirant; he is the strong, proud man who plunges into life with all the energy of his unbounded desires, and dashes himself against obstacles like a bull against his adversaries. The will for pleasure and power ruled in him. By a sure instinct he guesses the riddle that the Sphinx—Nature asks of all humanity on the threshold of life, and gives the answer as 'Man.'[10]

This is the gist of Schuré's idea. This is what Gide as well saw in "Oedipus." I believe he summarized in it the current European mentality. We can trace that mentality back to the days of Voltaire. He was the one who began to level the fortress of belief in hearts with the varieties of sarcasm with which he pelted the Supreme Being. He was, however, indulgent on occasion. He allowed the concept of God to live on without frankly rejecting it. It was Renan in the nineteenth century who began to raise doubts for people about what he called the antique ideas about God. He said, "People are living on whiffs of perfume which emanate from an empty container."

Afterwards, Nietzsche devastated intellects and souls with his views which frankly denied the existence of any unseen world or of any divine sovereignty. He declared it certain that nothing above man existed! The will for power in him is his excellence and his paradise. He announced: "The super man has today taken the place of God. God has died."[11] Under the influence of that, religious belief was shaken. No one believed any longer in anything besides man. That is Europe's belief today which Gide summarized excellently in the story of Oedipus. It has resulted in man's victory, even in his tribulation, over the manifest and hidden forces. Thus contemporary European thought sees nothing but man, alone in this existence. It is something that my intellect can apprehend as it follows the developments of the human intellect, but my religious, Eastern heart does not believe it. I too have seen in the story of Oedipus a challenge of man to God or the unseen forces. I have made this challenge stand out, but I have also emphasized at the same time the consequences of this presumption. For I have never felt that man is alone in this existence.

This feeling is the basis of all my work. Anyone who reads at one time the thirty books I have published may sense this feeling pervading all of them just as Gide's idea of man alone in existence pervades his works. The dedicated reader or specialist critic may see this idea or feeling in cloaks, recesses, and tendencies which have escaped me.

Our modern Arabic literature does not yet know the reader or critic who pursues an idea or tendency through the works of an author. Literary criticism here is still at the stage of newspaper criticism which reviews the book divorced from the author's body of works. There is no doubt that this stage will be followed by a higher level, that of constructive criticism in which the critic concentrates on the totality of a particular author's works in order to extract an idea from them and to formulate a doctrine.

My feeling is that the Easterner always lives in two worlds in the way I mentioned in *Bird of the East*. That is the last fortress left for us to shelter from Western thought which lives in a single one, the world of man alone. This feeling of mine is nothing other than an extension of the feeling of Islamic philosophy.

The substance of the renewal which Islamic philosophy brought and which influenced Europe in the thirteenth century AD was not that it transmitted the works of Plato and Aristotle nor that it alone wrote commentaries and explanations for them. It was that it had also studied the thought of the School of Alexandria, Neoplatonism, and the thought colored by the religious spirit of the first period of Christianity. It had then taken all of that and combined it, although it was difficult to combine. It combined the logic of Aristotle with the religious spirit, not the way it was received from the School of Alexandria but stamped with an Islamic character. Thus Europe learned what it called Arab or Islamic philosophy, that is, the amazing doctrine which rests on two pillars one would not have thought would stand side by side: the intellect and religious dogma.

It is not strange then if someone like me preserves some trace of that philosophy and finds it pacing through his blood in spite of himself. Our contact with European civilization is responsible for providing us with imported styles and modern clothing, but it is not capable of plucking out the spirit or erasing the character.

I always move in two worlds and base my thought on two pillars. I think that man is not alone in this existence. I believe in man's human nature. I think his greatness is that he is a human being, a human being with his weakness and defects, his limitations and errors. But he is a human being inspired from on high.

This is the nature of the difference between me and André Gide or those preceding him who deified man. They put him in a single world to be master of himself and of existence, ruling by his command with no master over him other than his will and intellect.

Gide was sincere in his admiration for man. He put Oedipus in a framework of veneration for man's pride. He went to the limit of belief in this boasting and of praise for this arrogance. It is a noble framework which shook my soul and delighted my mind. There is no way for me to deny that.

The splendor with which André Gide has surrounded his story, however, does not prevent me from rejecting his method of proceeding. It is a purely intellectual splendor which delights those like myself who love abstract thought. Those with a taste for works of the theater of the mind will have no objection to it. Had I done an "Oedipus" ten years ago, I too would have stripped it of everything except the opinions I wished to pour into it. I acted in this manner in 1939 with the play "Praxa: The Problem of Ruling" which I adapted from Aristophanes and then in my play "Pygmalion."

But today, I wish to pay attention to the elements of plays with respect to their being something presented to an audience. I have asked myself with respect to André Gide's story why he did not preserve the theatrical splendor of the tragedy of Oedipus. He seems to have deliberately removed everything in it of dramatic value, sometimes without cause. Consider this inquiry that Oedipus carries out to discover the truth. As a former investigative prosecutor, I think he shows great skill in its direction and in his debate with the witnesses. Spectators over the centuries have thought it a breathtaking theatrical experience with great impact on the soul. Why did Gide abbreviate it this way? Why did he contract and disguise it as though it were irrelevant? He took his idea and rose with it to the intellect without support from the situations which inspire it.

It would be an error then to call Gide's story a tragedy. He had no intention of presenting tragedy to us in its artistic beauty and emotional splendor. What can we call this work of his then?

I rather think it is an intellectual commentary on "Oedipus" by Sophocles or a mental tragedy from which all the theatrical elements of tragedy have been removed.

For that reason, I was most desirous to preserve all the dramatic power and the theatrical situations of the tragedy "Oedipus." My whole concern was to prevent any trace of reasoning from appearing in the dialogue so that it would not overwhelm a scene or weaken the action. I strove to conceal the thought within the action and to fold the idea into the scene. I have encountered difficulties, however, which I believe I have not surmounted. I remembered Sarcey's advice to the audience at the Comédie-Française to turn to a dictionary of Greek mythology before the performance. I would have to summarize, then, what happened to Oedipus before the beginning of the play. I had to strip the story of some of the superstitious beliefs that the Arab or Islamic mentality would scorn. I had to violate the principle of unity of time and place which Greek tragedy observes. I was compelled to violate this principle. I would have wished to retain it, but I thought the family atmosphere in the life of Oedipus was something which ought not to be neglected. For it is the pivot around which revolves the idea for the sake of which I chose this tragedy in particular. The family atmosphere in "Oedipus" cannot be set outside the house. It is true that the events in Greek tragedy always occur in a public square or out of doors. This was a result of the spirit of ancient Greek life. Otto Müller[?] says:

> The action of plays was moved from inside homes to the outside. In Greece, all important events and great matters transpired only in a public place. The social relationships between people did not arise in houses but in the markets and on the roads. The Greek poets were forced to observe these traditions of Greek life when they wrote their dramatic works.

I thought, however, despite that, of the possibility of retaining this principle in this story if a theatrical director were to insist on it. I have provided him with a stratagem whereby he can show the house and the square at the same time without the need to change scenes or violate the principle of unity of time and place.

In conclusion, I do not know what I have made of this tragedy. Have I been right to proceed with this or wrong? Will Arabic literature accept it in this form?

I have tried. This is all I have been able to do.

T. A.

Notes

[1]Francisque Sarcey, *Quarante ans de théâtre* (Paris: Bibliothèque des Annales, 1900-1902), III, 312.

[2]Victor Hugo, *Oeuvres complètes: Cromwell* ([n. pl.]: Editions Rencontre, 1967), p. 26.

[3]Ferdinand Brunetière, *Les Epoques du théâtre français (1636-1850)* (Paris: Calmann Lévy, 1892), p. 65.

[4]cf. L.-Henry Lecomte, *Napoléon et le monde dramatique* (Paris: H. Daragon, 1912), p. 401.

[5]*Ibid.*

[6]*Ibid.,* pp. 421-422.

[7]cf. Albert Thibaudet, "Les Spectacles dans un Fauteuil," *Réflexions sur la littérature* (Paris: Gallimard, 1938), I, 83.

[8]*Ibid.,* p. 86.

[9]Lucien Dubech, *Le Théâtre 1918-1923* (Paris: Librairie Plon, 1925), pp. 210-212.

[10]Edouard Schuré, *From Sphinx to Christ.* Trans. Eva Martin (Philadelphia: David McKay Company, n. d.), p. 217.

[11]cf. Friedrich Nietzsche, *Thus Spoke Zarathustra* (Los Angeles: Gateway Editions, Inc., 1957), pp. 342-343.

Reply to the Comments of A. de Marignac on the French Translation of *King Oedipus*

[Aloys de Marignac's comments for the French translation of "King Oedipus" which were translated and printed in Arabic in later editions of the play included the following points.

Between 1614 and 1939, twenty-nine French dramatists have attempted to adapt Sophocles' "Oedipus Tyrannus." None of these authors equalled Sophocles. A principal reason for the failure was the subject matter of the play. The Christian, Catholic world, cannot accept the idea of a predetermined fate planned by malicious gods. Since Tawfiq al-Hakim is a Muslim, he has the advantage of being more comfortable with the idea of blind predestination. He strips his hero of the legendary grandeur to lend him a greatness based on his human merit. The legend may have been stronger than the Egyptian author, but the play is an exciting attempt. It poses the great problem of the imitation of the antique.]

My dear Monsieur de Marignac!

The failure of thirty authors in different ages, some pagan or Christian and then finally a Muslim, with the tragedy of "Oedipus" is itself a tragedy. The reason for this failure requires study too. Despite the care I took not to damage the dramatic force of Sophocles' tragedy, something no doubt has escaped beyond our grasp. That goes back, as you said, to the subject of "Oedipus" itself. It is the subject of harsh, predetermined fate not subject to choice or rejection. It hits a man with its full force before he is born. This is the secret of the power of Sophocles' tragedy.

Whoever is satisfied with this thought and proceeds with it without turning it in any other direction is safe to some extent, on condition that he believes in it in the same way as the ancient Greeks. The predicament of the author who occupies himself with "Oedipus" is that he does not wish to accept this idea or to make it the basis of his work. The observant Christian will not accept it in its severe form. The free-thinking Christian will accept only a man who rules his own destiny. Each of them must, nevertheless, confront the superstition in the story of Oedipus, for without this superstition there is no story at all. It is that superstition which decreed before the birth of Oedipus that he would be subject to the predestined blow of fate. Thus the authors also have met a kind of sphinx waylaying them. It is the internal contradiction into which they fall. It is as you say: They cannot accept the superstition the way it is. At the same time, they cannot treat the story of Oedipus without the superstition.

With reference to what concerns me as a Muslim, my religious belief refuses the idea of God planning injuries for man in advance for no purpose or offense. Indeed, the idea of predestination for the events to befall a man has not found acceptance with the most important Muslim philosophers.

Ibn Rushd says of God: "He wills the existence of a thing at the time it comes into existence. He does not will its existence at times other than that in which it comes to exist. If it is said that He wills matters which are recent with an old willing, that is a heretical innovation."

If we turn to the scholars of religious law, we find that Abu Hanifa refuses to join the Jahmi school or the followers of the determinist sect. He likewise does not accept man's absolute free will. He takes for this difficult problem the stance which I wished to follow when I dealt with "Oedipus." Abu Hanifa said: "My statement is the middle way. There is no determinism, no delegation, and no handing over of power . . . God the Exalted does not impose on people what they cannot bear. He did not wish of them what they do not do. He did not punish them for what they did not do. He did not ask them about what they have not done. He is not pleased for them to plunge into something they do not have knowledge of. God knows our condition."

These truths about Islam appear to be unknown in the West. Westerners still believe that Muslims accept the idea of fate in the way it was known to the ancient, pagan Greeks. I have turned to the Flammarion dictionary and then the Larousse to investigate the word for fate. I was amazed, for I saw these two dictionaries specify that absolute, predestined fate was the belief of Greece and Muslims. I perceived from the inclusion of the [Arabic] word *maktub* in the Flammarion dictionary that this mistaken idea had entered Europe by means of popular circulation not through scientific examination.

I dismiss this widespread and mistaken idea and quote the words of Abu Hanifa: "He does not punish them for what they do not do . . . He is not pleased that they should plunge into what they lack knowledge of . . . " etc. Now it is easy for you to understand the conduct of Oedipus in my play. He has left Corinth in search of the truth, plunging into something he lacks knowledge of. His desire to know the truth brought down on him what modern science has brought down on modern man. Take Freud for example. When he started to dig in man's depths, he found that man secretly is his mother's lover.

For me the cause of Oedipus' calamity cannot be the malice of the gods which would contain deceit and evil. Similarly, it is not possible for me to have wished to eliminate the question because of its conflict with my belief. As you see, I have made the cause of the disaster Oedipus' nature itself, his nature which loves investigation into the origins of things and devotes itself to running after truth.

Oedipus' calamity, however, has another cause with me. It is the activity of Teiresias and his interference in affairs which are proceeding on their own.

Many of the revolutions of history and human ordeals have more often than not resulted from the volition of a swelled head and the rebellion of blind insight. There are divine snares there, no doubt. God, however, did not set them for a particular man but for any person who breaks the laws. They are like the traps which the owner of a field puts out to catch foxes which ruin the grapes. He is not after any particular fox. Yes . . . God is cunning and mocks the cunning troublemakers . . . When does He do that? When is the divine mockery? Has it always existed, ever since God formulated the law and set beside it a snare, expecting it to have a victim from time to time, without concern for his name or identity? Or does the violation happen first and God then cast the net over the perpetrator at that time? . . . This is a subject we should not plunge into.

All I wished to say is that for me the conflict in "Oedipus" is not with arrogant gods who deal brutally with an innocent person they have selected to pursue. It is a conflict between the will of God and that of man.

All of that, however, does not free us from the difficulty of the problem. You have seen one side of this difficulty. This is my attempt to use the ancient legend (which in its unambiguousness does not permit abstruseness or obscurity) for purposes which conflict with the core of the legend.

But there are other sides to this difficulty. One of them was my need to present the question of predestination and free will within the confines of tragedy which cannot expand enough for it without loss of its artistic splendor. It is a question on which the brains of philosophers and scholars of religious law of different faiths have come to grief. In modern times it has moved from the field of religion and philosophy to that of science. The case of predestination or free will has today become a question for scientists in biology, physics and chemistry.

They ask themselves to what extent there is concealed in the sperm a hereditary, predetermined transmission of characteristics. To what degree can the human body be considered a delicate instrument in which everything runs according to a set plan on a predetermined course?

The difference over that is fierce among scientists just as it was among the philosophers. It is, however, recognized today that there is an element of predestination there and an element of freedom. Together they govern the behavior of living things and inanimate ones. For even in the world of gasses there exists some freedom and liberty outside the range of their strict laws. The existence of the law necessitates the existence of some departure from the law. This necessitates as well a type of penalty which is not only a disturbance of the results but a return of the imbalance to order and the rebel back to its place.

Every atom or cell has its law with the law's mocking snares into which falls anything trying to violate it. It then returns to its place in the general order. All of this is within the ever-existing canon according to which existence runs.

The spirit of Islam is harmonious with this view. For that reason, I had to subject the story of Oedipus to this reasoning. You have remarked that I have stripped Oedipus of his legendary greatness in order to award him another greatness arising from his humanity. That too goes back to the spirit of the Islamic religion which boasts that its great prophet was a human being.

None of these goals will get us anything so long as we are conscious that they have extracted the heart of the ancient legend on which the tragedy of "Oedipus" is based. I don't know how the extent of my particular failure relates to that of the previous twenty-nine. My task was harder than theirs.

They by virtue of their Greco-Latin culture found nothing in the work alien to them or their literature which is based on the Greek and Latin. I, however, am attempting today to fasten this new art to our Arabic literature and to put it on its Greek foundations. It is a piece of work which we ought to have done centuries ago.

I have spent four years in this attempt. I have studied, unhurriedly, each scene, each character, and each issue. I have been concerned with the details and minutiae requiring a new justification to satisfy our Arab, Islamic intellects.

This oracle for which Creon went to the temple at Delphi . . . how could it know about the murder of Laius? The blinding blow struck by Oedipus . . . was it from an excess of pride, as Gide had it, or out of a desire that Oedipus should attain the peak of suffering just as he had attained the peak of glory, as Cocteau had it?

In my opinion, those are just rationalist, literary explanations. I think, however, that Oedipus was intensely devoted to his family and deeply in love with Jocasta. His grief for her when he saw her dead this hideous way was more than he could bear.

It was no doubt a moment of temporary insanity which stormed through his head. He was unconscious of it as he struck his eyes shouting at the queen: "I will weep for you only with tears of blood."

This is the only interpretation I can accept. Sophocles does not make that clear to us. The legend he based his work on, for all its power and force, prevented him from explaining. It was the feeling of Oedipus that he received this blow from the arrogant gods, in particular from Apollo who hated him. It made him think of the accident as a true curse. He had no way to resist it except by committing that atrocity on himself which might gain him heaven's sympathy.

But I think that Oedipus could not concede for a moment that anything that happened was stronger than his love for Jocasta. For him, nothing was more powerful than his love for her. So what he did to himself was only because of her.

Apart from that, there are many fine points and numerous details from which the persistent scholar can glimpse the obstacles and difficulties which stand in the way of anyone who attempts to occupy himself with Sophocles' tragedy.

I do not believe that there occurred to the mind of any of these writers for a single moment the thought of soaring to the level of the Greek original. Its artistic perfection is based not only on the genius of Sophocles but on the power of the legend in its original pagan essence and the poet's belief in it and the fact that he derived the whole tragedy from it alone.

No one disputes at all that in "Oedipus" Sophocles reached a peak of artistic perfection. It is a source of pride for the human mind. Perhaps Shakespeare perceived that by his artistic instinct. He did not touch it despite the allure of the subject. He borrowed the subjects for his works from stories from Denmark, Italy, Rome and Greece.

Do you suppose he feared to take on Sophocles in his lair? Had he done that, the history of European literature today would preserve countless discussions describing this fearsome encounter.

Adaptation of the ancient is a truly difficult problem. Indeed, it is almost impossible in some cases. It is as if we wished to make at once an aged wine from new grapes. There is no doubt a hidden secret about the formation of that old wine which gives it an incomparable taste.

In conclusion, it is enough for us that we have tried something difficult. We have known full well that failure was awaiting us at the end of the road. Sometimes the greatest reward is the work itself, not the result. What a great reward I have received, what a fruit has fallen to me, from merely passing a few years in the shadow of this ancient tree, which is always green and fruitful: the tragedies of Sophocles.

T.A.

Man's Fate

(Thoughts on *Shahrazad*)

[From *Taht al-Misbah al-Akhdar* ("By the Light of the Green Lamp," 1941)]

I read yesterday, by the light of my green lamp, in a new book by Maurice Maeterlinck which appeared this month this thought: "Man will reach a moment when he will reject life, unless he can return to carnality." I was at once reminded of King Shahriyar in my play "Shahrazad." He was a person who tried in vain to savor life in his final days. He had reached such a degree of mental abstraction at that time that he was separated from humanity. This man had passed through each of the stages known for man's life. He had lived the life of an animal at the time he had a virgin brought him each night to be slain in the morning. He lived the life of the heart when he met Shahrazad. He loved being with her and forgot about killing and slaughter. He sat with her looking into her eyes and listening to her stories. Then he lived the life of the intellect when Shahrazad's conversation had awakened his thought and he had gained a vision of the wide horizons of the limitless worlds. He rose to his feet and set off to roam through thought's stratosphere. He was entranced by love of the unknown and discovery of the hidden. When science did not help him, he had recourse to magic. Magic did not slake his thirst, and so he returned to discursive reasoning. The earth proved too constricted for him, and so he examined the sky. But mankind does not reach the sky, and Shahriyar did not wish to return to earth—that earth which he loathed. Its material and spiritual fruit disgusted him. He had exhausted both its lower and higher delights. He had finished with everything and been satiated with everything. There was nothing left on this earth to tempt him to stay except knowledge. He wanted to know. To know what? To know what a human being is not allowed to comprehend—that was the single pleasure left him. That was the thread of hope binding him to life. At that point he was afflicted by a near insanity. He spent the night gazing at the stars in the sky as though asking them to answer the questions of his disturbed reason. His mind grew tired and agitated in the edifice of his weary body. He became convinced that his body was the peg securing his spirit and joining his thought to the earth. He rebelled against the body and wished to free himself from its prison. The prison of the body is place, just as water's prison is the container. He thought he might flee from its walls with travel, by journeying. He roamed populated and desert regions until he found himself at last returning to his point of departure. He realized that travel is simply a change of one receptacle for another. When was water freed by a change of container? He cast himself after that into the saloon of Abu Maysur in search of escape from body and place in the forgetfulness of smoking hashish.

Throughout all of this Shahrazad was watching over him with affection and dismay. She knew he was a dying man. He had left the earth but not reached the sky. He was suspended between earth and sky and sapped by anxiety. She began to plot a treatment for his malady. Since it is insane for a person to think of attaining the sky while yet a man, she had to bring Shahriyar back to earth if he was to live. She used the serf to help revive the animal perishing in the depths of Shahriyar. The attempt, treatment for his malady. Since it is insane for a person to think of attaining the sky while yet a man, she had to bring Shahriyar back to earth if he was to live. She used the serf to help revive the animal perishing in the depths of Shahriyar. The attempt, however, was not successful. Shahriyar had to disappear from the theater of existence.

It is strange that since I wrote this play (about fifteen years have passed since its composition) I have been thinking of bringing back this unhappy king in a story I have wanted to call "Return of Shahriyar." But I have found his return a difficult if not impossible matter. He would of course not return the way he was when he departed. Otherwise there would be no need for a new story. So he must return as a different person. Here the difficulty is: what will cause this man to return? He left at that moment at which it is necessary for each human life to cease. Shahrazad herself could do nothing. What can I do? She had seen his state and realized that he was a white hair to be plucked out. He, like everything in this existence, had in the end gone full circle. If he returns it will be in a new round as a newborn person passing through the animal stage again.

Preface to *Princess Sunshine*

This is a didactic play . . . Didactic works of literature or art from *Kalila and Dimna* to the fables of La Fontaine, the plays of Brecht and other monuments of this variety have as their goal provision of guidance for the conduct of the individual or of society. Frequently they do not conceal their intentions and select expressions that will reach the souls directly and sink deep into the minds. They select the clearest and simplest means of expression. At times they make a weapon of the formulation of wisdom and the moral in an immediate way. They, unlike the other art which conceals its true face and leaves you to discover what it hides, remove their veils and say: "Yes, I want to preach to you. Will you listen to me?"

Confronted by their frankness we listen to them willingly. Thus we have listened and continue to listen to the maxims in *Kalila and Dimna,* the lessons of La Fontaine, and Brecht's "Badener Lehrstück" without being irritated by what we hear. The reason is that a sermon presented to us in a beautiful form is itself art.

My hope is that this play's content has been presented in a form not tedious to the soul and that it may realize, even to a trivial degree, the goals it aims at.

Alternate Ending For *Princess Sunshine*

[*When the play was performed at the National Theater it was thought that the end should be changed to unite the two resolute lovers . . . So the author composed another ending which follows.*]

SUNSHINE: Yes . . . if you stop talking and speed your steps . . . Let's go . . . Come on . . . to marriage.

MOONLIGHT: Let's go . . . Come on . . . Wait. *(He stops and looks into the distance.)* What's this . . . It's the sound of a horse galloping.

SUNSHINE *(looking in the direction of the sound to identify the person coming):* It's Hamdan.

MOONLIGHT: Hamdan . . . God's curse on him!

(Hamdan enters carrying an extra sword in his hand in addition to the one hanging from his belt.)

SUNSHINE: You've returned quickly, Hamdan.

PRINCE: You could have spared me the errand.

SUNSHINE: I wanted you to learn the truth by yourself.

PRINCE: My heart sensed it the first moment I saw you, but today I learned why I have always hated this man.

MOONLIGHT: A feeling that has always been reciprocated.

PRINCE *(throwing him a sword):* Catch. Defend yourself.

SUNSHINE *(shouting):* What are you doing?

PRINCE: One of us must die.

SUNSHINE: Have you gone mad?

PRINCE: I can't live to see this man win you.

SUNSHINE: He won me before you saw me.

PRINCE: This is all the more reason for me to kill him.

SUNSHINE: Suppose you kill him. What will be the reult?

PRINCE: My heart at least will be at rest . . . Defend yourself. I must kill you honorably, although you don't deserve this honor. For you're a tramp!

SUNSHINE: Alas! I thought you had learned something.

MOONLIGHT: This is your pupil . . . your creation. But you're not responsible. The dough was spoiled.

PRINCE: Shut up! I'll kill you like a dog. *(He attacks him, and they exchange blows.)*

SUNSHINE *(shouting and intervening):* Enough, Hamdan! . . . Enough! . . . Enough! . . . Enough! You must have lost your mind!

PRINCE *(on the verge of collapse):* How could I help but lose my mind? . . . Lose my mind, Sunshine? How could I help but lose my mind, when without you I've lost everything.

SUNSHINE *(softening towards him):* Come here, Hamdan. Come here and calm yourself a little . . . Calm . . . calm . . . calm. *(She takes him aside.)*

PRINCE *(repeating as he puts his head between his hands and almost weeps):* Oh . . . oh . . . Everything is lost! Everything!

SUNSHINE: Don't cry like an infant!

PRINCE: What is my fate now without you . . . when I've grown accustomed to being near you, to your conversation and voice when you were in a soldier's uniform. I am now part of you . . . part of your spirit.

SUNSHINE: If you are truly part of me and my spirit, then be brave. Endure your destiny bravely.

PRINCE: My destiny! . . . Far from you!

SUNSHINE: Yes.

(A moment of silence.)

PRINCE: Do you love this man so much?

SUNSHINE: He's my fiancé whom I chose for myself. Didn't they tell you that in in the city . . .

PRINCE *(head bowed):* Yes.

SUNSHINE: Didn't we come to you from the desert together? Hadn't I lived together with him? Didn't you ask yourself how a woman could go off alone with a man if he was not her fiancé before God and the people?

PRINCE: Yes . . . but . . . I imagined in spite of that you were leaning to me.

SUNSHINE: I truly uncovered a good nature in you. I'm proud of that. I believe you will make something of your land and people. I have said all this to my fiancé, Moonlight. You can ask him.

(The prince does not look at Moonlight.)

SUNSHINE: Why don't you look at him? . . . Look at him and ask him what we used to say about you, about our regard for you and our hopes for you.

MOONLIGHT: It's no use . . . He won't look at me. I'm a tramp.

PRINCE: But you won! *(He rises.)* Farewell!

SUNSHINE: Don't forget, Hamdan, that you, as you say, bear a part of my spirit. This requires you to be, always, a revolutionary reformer.

PRINCE: I know very well what I bear, *(suddenly with force)* but this man—what does he carry of you?

SUNSHINE: He's the one who formed me.

MOONLIGHT: And she's the one who has formed my heart with love.

SUNSHINE: Yes, each of us has formed the other. Each of us is shaper and shaped, creator and created, at the same time. For that reason, our union is complete. Do you understand now, Hamdan?

PRINCE: Yes . . . Congratulations to you . . . Farewell!

SUNSHINE: May success be yours, Hamdan! Perhaps we will visit you one day, my husband and I . . . to congratulate you on carrying out your mission.

PRINCE: Before I go, fairness and conscience require me to tell you something . . . The people in your country, Sunshine, revere you for leaving your castle and choosing a man of the people, of humble origins. You will see with your own eyes how the populace rallies round you when you enter the city together.

(He goes out sadly leaving Sunshine and Moonlight who have come together. They follow his departure with their eyes until he disappears. The curtain falls as they cling together.)